The Making of
Working-Class Religion

published to print with a grant
Figure Foundation
that meaning may soon find us

The Making of
Working-Class Religion

MATTHEW PEHL

UNIVERSITY OF ILLINOIS PRESS

Urbana, Chicago, and Springfield

1 2 3 4 5 C P 5 4 3 2 1
∞ This book is printed on acid-free paper.

Library of Congress Cataloging-in-Publication Data
Names: Pehl, Matthew, author.
Title: The making of working-class religion / Matthew Pehl.
Description: Urbana : University of Illinois Press, 2016. |
    Series: The working class in American history | Includes
    bibliographical references and index. | Description
    based on print version record and CIP data provided by
    publisher; resource not viewed.
Identifiers: LCCN 2016022066 (print) | LCCN 2016000556
    (ebook) | ISBN 9780252098840 (ebook) |
    ISBN 9780252040429 (cloth : alk. paper) |
    ISBN 9780252081897 (pbk. : alk. paper)
Subjects: LCSH: Working class—Religious life—Michigan—
    Detroit. | Detroit (Mich.)—Church history—20th
    century. | Race—Religious aspects—Christianity.
Classification: LCC BV4593 (print) | LCC BV4593 .P44 2016
    (ebook) | DDC 277.74/34—dc23
LC record available at https://lccn.loc.gov/2016022066

Contents

Introduction

In 1961, the Detroit Industrial Mission (DIM) published a provocative essay titled "Work: Curse or Joy?" For four years, the middle-class Protestant ministers of DIM had toiled on assembly lines at Detroit-area factories, hoping to understand the religious mentality of workers. They had reached an unsettling conclusion. "[I]n general," DIM asserted, "[workers] hate their jobs" and find industrial labor "a distasteful necessity." Managers seemed oblivious or defensive, insisting that "workers in industry are happy," or that, if they were unhappy, they could find another job. The union, meanwhile, appeared to have resigned itself to the philosophy that: "(1) Work in most of modern industry is Hell, particularly on the production line;" and, "(2) this essential hellishness cannot be changed." Work, according to union leaders, might be made bearable and remunerative—but not enjoyable. The entire dilemma, according to DIM, alienated people from each other and from God: it stood opposed to the "Biblical tradition," which insisted that work was meant to be "a source of joy." Joyful work necessarily offers people a chance to become richer, deeper, fuller human beings. Was not something wrong with the very soul of modern society, DIM asked, if so many people were dehumanized by their work?[1]

The biblical reading of DIM ministers offered a creative and thought-provoking analysis of the human (indeed, the spiritual) costs of industrial capitalism. Yet, their insistence that the biblical tradition unambiguously promoted work as an inherently ennobling human experience reflected their specific theological, historical, and class position. For centuries, laborers within the Western religious tradition learned a very different lesson: work was proof of the curse of human sinfulness. In the mythical fall from paradise, work entered the world as a human mandate. People must "earn their bread by the sweat of their brow," not because labor was innately rewarding, but because God demanded it.[2] This exegetical debate over the religious meaning of labor was not limited to the learned ministers of DIM, but was wrestled with by working people themselves. Bill Goode, a skilled worker and later a union activist, witnessed this tension play out before his eyes. At lunch one day, Goode overheard two Finnish coworkers discuss whether there would be work in heaven:

> Their answers were instantaneous and diametrically opposed. One maintained that work was punishment for the sin of Adam and Eve and that, of course, there would be no work in heaven. The other asserted with equal vehemence that work was fulfillment, that there would certainly be work in heaven. The argument raged all lunch hour, and it was probably one of the most interesting debates I have heard on the nature of work.[3]

As these sources suggest, religion matters in working-class history. However, recognizing the *importance* of religion to working-class history doesn't necessarily get us any closer to understanding its *meaning* or *significance*. What, exactly, is a scholar to make of these two conflicting sources? Does an assessment of religious culture add any unique insight for understanding the power relations and social experiences of industrial work, or does it obscure deeper historical, economic, or political structures? Did religion entice workers into silently enduring suffering and injustice, or did it offer one of the few sources of dignity, autonomy, and resistance that workers possessed? How did working people interpret the role of religion in their own lives, and how do these readings compare with those of contemporary observers or subsequent scholars? Because human labor is embedded in socially constructed webs of culture and ideas, the experiences of work inevitably raise profound moral and philosophical questions, as well as difficult puzzles for historical interpretation.[4]

Scholars' struggles to understand the relationship between religion and class, and the role of religion within working-class culture, was present virtually from the creation of the modern intellectual debate about class formation and capitalism. As early as 1844, Karl Marx had staked out a damning critique of religion when he described it as "the sigh of the oppressed creature, the sentiment of a heartless world, and the soul of soulless conditions. It is the opium of the people."[5] Religion, in Marx's understanding, offered a compensation for life's sorrows but no political or historical solution to the class exploitation that produced such misery. Marx's interpretive shadow fell far and broad, not only among his direct European social-science descendants like Max Weber or R. H. Tawney, but over historians as well. When the influential British "Group" historians of the 1950s and 1960s began to reinvent the field of labor history, they largely preserved Marx's understanding of religion. For E. P. Thompson, the Methodist insurgency of the early nineteenth century offered thin gruel compared to promise of trade unionism or political reform; meanwhile, Eric Hobsbawm allowed that religion may have inspired "primitive rebels" in rural Sicily to resist exploitation, but only as a way station on the road to "real" political resistance. Students of U.S. religion offered similar readings. When Paul Johnson examined the evangelical revivals of Jacksonian-era Rochester, he concluded that the Second Great Awakening amounted to "a middle-class solution to problems of class, legitimacy, and order generated in the early stages of manufacturing": in other words, religion enabled social control. Scholarship on the rise of the Pentecostal movement, likewise, built on historical and social-science explanations of religion as a cultural "compensation" for working-class folks with no access to quality education, health care, political representation, or economic power. Even Lizabeth Cohen's innovative and far-ranging account of industrial workers in interwar Chicago outlined a narrative in which parochial, fragmented, and apolitical ethno-religious communities were triumphantly undermined by the CIO's politicized "culture of unity" in the 1930s.[6]

But, if scholars have long persisted in viewing religion as a tool for exploitation (at worst) or a compensation prize for history's losers (at best), another scholarly tradition has insisted on religion's radical potential for inspiring social and political movements of lasting significance. Herbert Gutman set the tone for this more appreciative approach in his landmark article from 1966, in which he argued that Gilded Age workers found in Protestantism "a transhistoric framework to challenge the new industrialism and a common set of moral imperatives to measure their rage against and to order their dissatisfactions." Ken Fones-Wolf brilliantly built upon Gutman's call to arms in his study of the relationship between the American Federation of Labor and Christian reformers in Progressive Era Philadelphia, while scholars of antebellum religion like Jama Lazerow and William Sutton offered correctives to Paul Johnson's analysis of Rochester. More recently, a host of scholarship has linked working-class religion to social activism. Joe Creech and Michael Kazin have shown the deep symbiosis between populism and evangelicalism in the late nineteenth century, while Jarod Roll and Erik Gellman have illustrated the commingling of radicalism and religion across the early-twentieth-century South. Leslie Woodcock Tentler, Evelyn Savidge Sterne, Kenneth Heineman, William Issell, and James Terence Fisher have all documented the important role of Catholicism in politicizing Catholic immigrants and encouraging their participation in the (nonradical) labor movement. And, historians like Nick Salvatore, Kimberly Phillips, Angela Dillard, and David Chappell have all argued for the centrality of religion to the African American freedom movement throughout the twentieth century.[7]

This book cannot resolve the debates between "religion as an opiate" and "religion as a stimulant"—not as a dodge from staking out a "unified theory" of religion and class, but because disagreement, messiness, and ambiguity define the role of religion in working-class culture. Ultimately, the actors in the two narratives that began this introduction debated and disagreed about the meaning and purpose of religion, just as scholars and critics have long disagreed about the nature and effects of religion in working-class life. Indeed, the central theme of this study might be contained by the word *ambivalence*. It is a quality at the heart not only of scholars' explanations of working-class religion, but of workers' experiences as well. Many workers, for instance, sought a religion with deep emotional exuberance, prayed for supernatural patronage and miraculous favors, and prioritized highly personal, individualized religious relationships. Yet, most of these same workers were attuned to the value of social discipline, craved respectability, held fast to traditional standards of morality, and were profoundly attached to a collective sense of religious peoplehood deeply rooted in an actual or imagined history. Religion was a crucial, if sometimes contradictory, mediator between individual spiritual strivings and collectivist values, between the desire to "transcend" into a higher world and the pragmatic demands of the earthly world, between the folk customs of the rural nineteenth century and the commercialized culture of the urban twentieth century. Working-class religions issued paradoxical demands: for submission and discipline, as well as for spiritual (and perhaps social) liberation; for adherence to the status quo but also, at times, for a transformative, purifying rebirth; for acquiescence to the needs of capitalism and nationalism as well as for prophetic critiques of these orders. Ambivalence shot through all currents of working-class religiosity and all forms of its cultural, intellectual, and political expressions.[8]

In addition to a tonal and interpretive emphasis on the ambivalent nature of working-class religions, this book makes three contributions beyond its narrative and analysis. First, this study expands and reconsiders the chronological framework for examining working-class religions. Existing studies of working-class religions are heavily focused on the nineteenth century (usually, either the first or second half of the nineteenth century; a complete examination of working-class religions in the nineteenth century awaits its historian), while studies of the twentieth century tend to focus on the first few decades, usually linking working-class religions to the "new immigration" from Europe and Latin America, to the populist insurgency, or to the development of a Progressive-Era "social gospel." Perhaps historians have tacitly accepted the long-dominant image of the 1920s as a "secularizing" era in which religion fell into disrepute, or agreed with scholar Robert C. Handy that the 1930s marked a period of "religious depression."[9] Regardless, few have examined working-class religion in the 1930s, and fewer still have carried the story past World War II. Indeed, as Jon Butler recently observed, even the best studies of twentieth-century religion "stand outside the interpretive mainstream, which overwhelmingly finds religion in modern America more anomalous than normal and more innocuous than powerful."[10] The present narrative, on the other hand, begins when many studies end: with the merging of two migratory streams of workers, one from Europe and one from the American South, into the urban centers of the North in the years surrounding World War I. The twin experiences of migration and urbanization produced, in cities like Detroit, a fundamentally new "American working class"—and with it, new consciousness of working-class religion. Over the course of two subsequent generations, working-class religions would directly engage with, and be challenged by, the promise of the New Deal, the possibilities of industrial unionism, the existential crisis of the Second World War, the challenges of the postwar metropolis, and the freedom movement for racial equality. Far from eroding after the 1920s, working-class religions were both shaped by, *and a shaper of*, the central social and cultural moments of the twentieth century.

Second, this book offers a much more integrative view of working-class religions than has typically been undertaken. Consider the term *working-class religion*. If class is understood as a material measure of economic status, then the class dimensions of twentieth-century religion appear fairly straightforward. Catholics, Southern Baptists, Pentecostals, Jews (early in the twentieth century), and African American religions remained "lower-class"—below average in income, education, social mobility, and skill level, at least until changes emerged in the late 1950s—while Unitarians, Episcopalians, Congregationalists, Presbyterians, and (later in the century) Jews dominated the upper class.[11] The historical literature on working-class religion, however, remains strongly marked by denominational boundaries, rarely weaving the various threads of working-class religion into a single garment. Such an approach cannot explain much about working-class religion in a polyglot urban center like twentieth-century Detroit, which witnessed a dramatic merging of Euro-Catholics, Afro-American Baptists and Methodists, southern white evangelicals and Pentecostals, and several variations therein. To be clear: these different religious communities did not constitute a single monolithic working-class religion. But combining a narrative of the Euro-Catholics with southern-born black and white Protestant workers provides illumination on themes not clearly visible otherwise. Certainly, middle-class reformers and commentators analyzed these different traditions in much the same way—usually to dismiss them as primitive, overly emotional, demagogic, or antisocial. In this way, the idea of working-class religion came to be both descriptive and evaluative. But workers, too, responded to the major challenges of the twentieth century in remarkably similar fashion, seeking to preserve traditional values while reconciling modern identities rooted in class, race, and gender. While differences matter, they should not blind us to parallel stories that follow strikingly similar patterns.

Class, moreover, is more than an objective material measurement. As E. P. Thompson has argued with great eloquence, class is primarily a subjective, historical identity created over time and expressed in culture. "Class consciousness," Thompson stated, "is the way [class] experiences are handled in cultural terms: embodied in traditions, value systems, ideas, and institutional forms." Religion was one of the central cultural systems for defining, articulating, and performing social class in twentieth-century America; it is best understood, then, not as an inert social category but as a historically evolving and subjectively created worldview that synthesized informal folklore, doctrinal belief systems, and symbolic ritual within the context of the power imbalances inherent in human institutions. In other words, I emphasize the idea of working-class religion as "consciousness": built from the shared experiences, relationships, and value systems that people "made" in the search for meaning. "Americans have been compelled to make and remake their worlds and themselves endlessly, relentlessly, on constantly shifting grounds, in often brutal economic circumstances," historian Robert Orsi observes; "religion," he continues, "has been one of—if not *the*—primary media through which this work of making and unmaking has proceeded." Throughout this book, I emphasize the dynamism of religious consciousness: the contingent moments, the shifting contexts, and the often bitter conflicts through which working people "made," "remade," or "unmade" religious forms and idioms as a means of reconciling ambivalent tensions.[12]

Finally, this study aspires to blend and synthesize various historiographical traditions that have until recently been largely segregated. Obviously, this book is grounded in and indebted to the last four decades of new labor history and, more currently, working-class studies. These works have greatly enriched our understanding of the ideas, politics, social lives, and working experiences of laborers. Religious experience has, for the most part, been minimized in these accounts, although the movement toward *lived religion*—or, the actual practice of religion by ordinary people in particular contexts—has pushed religious studies much closer toward the concerns of the new labor history. Indeed, rapprochement and fruitful integration of working-class studies and religious history are well under way, symbolized perhaps by the dialogue between Joseph and James McCartin, two scholarly brothers openly seeking to reconcile Joseph's pursuit of labor history with James's study of Catholicism. In 2005, the journal *Religion and American Culture* featured a special forum on "Religion and Class," while the journals *Labor* and *Radical History Review* have focused entire special issues on the question of religion. Moreover, a handful of monographs—notably Robert Bruno's examination of life in Chicago's working-class churches and Richard Callahan's careful analysis of the religious worlds of Kentucky coal miners—have laid a solid foundation in creating a new subfield of working-class religious history. The present study seeks to continue and deepen this scholarly interchange.[13]

Detroit offers an exceptionally useful setting for examining these themes. As many scholars have observed, Detroit emerged between the 1910s and the 1960s as perhaps the quintessential American "blue-collar" industrial metropolis of the twentieth century. Nelson Lichtenstein's pioneering studies of the United Automobile Workers (UAW), for instance, have made Detroit's workers and unions central to American labor history, while Thomas Sugrue's celebrated scholarship has illustrated the troubling roots of working-class conservatism, urban decay, and inner-city poverty in Detroit's confrontations over automation and housing. Historians like Lichtenstein and Sugrue have placed Detroit at the center of a national analysis of the American twentieth century that casts tremendous light on issues of race, class, and politics.[14]

Yet, Detroit was also one of the most important, tumultuous, and creative religious centers in the United States during the twentieth century. Consider a brief and truncated overview of Detroit's major religious personalities. Reinhold Niebuhr, the most renowned American theologian of the century, first made his name in Detroit's Social Gospel circles by battling Henry Ford in the 1920s. Charles Coughlin, the famed "radio priest" who captured American airwaves throughout the 1930s, broadcast from his parish church in Royal Oak. Elijah Muhammad founded the Nation of Islam in Detroit in the 1930s. J. Frank Norris and Gerald L. K. Smith, hugely popular fundamentalists, relocated from the South to Detroit in the late 1930s and quickly produced newspapers, radio broadcasts, and political campaigns in their new northern home. Claude Williams, another transplanted southerner, organized one of the country's most radical religious organizations, the Peoples' Institute of Applied Religion, in the mid-1940s. Various Protestant leaders of Detroit—including the nationally regarded theologian Gibson Winter—attempted to reimagine urban religion through their ecumenical agency, the Detroit Industrial Mission, in the 1950s and 1960s. Throughout the twentieth century, numerous African American ministers—including Horace White, Charles Hill, and C. L. Franklin—became nationally celebrated for both preaching and political leadership. And in the 1960s, Albert Cleage emerged as one of the most radical religious voices of the decade in his call for a "black Christian nationalism," while the city's Catholic Archbishop, John Cardinal Dearden, was turning Detroit into an epicenter of experimentation following the Second Vatican Council.[15]

Detroit, then, was not only the quintessential "blue-collar" industrial metropolis of the twentieth century, but, for scholars, it also offers an almost perfect laboratory for examining the intersection of religion and class. In Detroit, as throughout the nation, working-class religion was shaped and molded primarily by three large groups: Catholics (especially immigrant or "ethnic" Catholics), African Americans uprooted by the "Great Migrations" that accompanied the world wars, and white evangelicals (often fundamentalist or Pentecostal), also with origins in the rural South. During the 1910s and 1920s, hundreds of thousands of workers—from Poland and Mexico, Kentucky and Alabama—flooded into Detroit, transplanting and transforming religious culture. These workers had many profound differences, and often disliked or distrusted each other. They certainly did not form a single self-conscious "class" in a political or social sense, and religion often reinforced the insular, even tribal, instincts of migrant workers. Viewed from a historical distance, however, the different religious traditions of Catholic, African American, and white evangelical workers invoked many of the same idioms, served many of the same cultural needs, and deeply shaped both internal and external social identities. All three groups persistently remained in the working classes throughout the rise of the auto industry and well into the 1960s, with comparatively little social mobility. All three were, in various ways, responding to the experiences of migration and urbanization. Without reducing these distinct peoples into a homogenous category, we can nevertheless discern the outlines of a common religious consciousness forged by similar class experiences.

These working-class religions were deeply politicized by the Great Depression and the emergence of the New Deal. Early in the 1930s, workers enthusiastically responded to Mayor Frank Murphy, who drew upon a Progressive-Era legacy of the "social gospel" to link populist religion with a new "age of reform." A pious Catholic with strong links to Detroit's African American community, Murphy helped turn the churches of working-class Detroit into FDR country for more than a generation. At the same time that Murphy was building a new Democratic coalition, the industrial-labor movement was transforming the sociopolitical landscape of Detroit, turning an "open shop" citadel into America's paradigmatic union town. And, like Murphy, union activists often articulated a specifically working-class version of the social gospel. Both the New Deal and the United Auto Workers depended on support from rank-and-file working people, and both found it necessary to communicate in the language of biblical allusions, papal encyclicals, and scriptural passages. The discourse is telling. For many working-class people, religious reimagination was at the root of their political and social reimagination.

As the New Deal era opened new political imaginaries, it also promoted a rethinking of the relationship between faith, work, and politics. Within working-class churches and communities, a vanguard generation of activists responded boldly. For Catholics, African Americans, and southern white evangelicals alike, the experiences of the Depression and the insurgent struggle of the labor movement prompted the exploration of a new set of religious idioms, which I am calling *worker religion*. Catholic clergy established an Archdiocesan Labor Institute to promote worker education, while the laity, emboldened by the call for Catholic Action within the church, formed one of the most important chapters of the Association of Catholic Trade Unionists in the country. A pivotal group of African American preachers—notably Horace White, Malcolm Dade, and Charles Hill—tapped into the "prophetic" biblical tradition, which allowed them to critique paternalism and racism, politicize their congregations, and channel black workers into the UAW. Southern white evangelicals found their leader in Claude Williams, a radical Presbyterian from Arkansas, who formed the Peoples' Institute of Applied Religion (PIAR) in the 1940s and waged cultural trench warfare against conservative southern fundamentalists in Detroit's war-industries plants. While culturally and theologically distinct, advocates of worker religion all sought to deliberately link the newly emerging political and class identities of workers with a much older set of religious stories, images, and rituals. They attempted, in fact, to turn religious identity and class identity into mutually reinforcing pillars of spiritual solace and social strength. Worker religion was highly oriented toward acting in the world; it wanted to bring faith into the union hall and onto the shop floor, just as it sought to bring the values of the labor movement into the daily culture of working-class religious consciousness.

But worker religion immediately proved contentious and divisive. In fact, as the United States entered the Second World War and Detroit emerged as the nation's "arsenal of democracy," the political shape of working-class religion once again emerged as a cultural lightning rod. For proponents of worker religion, World War II was seen as an epic struggle between the forces of fascism and the promise of democracy, one in which the politicization of working-class religion would play a key role. Pluralism, racial tolerance, and labor rights *defined* democracy for the missionaries of worker religion; the "true" faith was thus linked to a particular set of political values. Yet, worker religion did not—could not—monopolize the discourse on religious politics. To the contrary, a number of highly influential rightists and antimodernists—in particular, Fr. Charles Coughlin, J. Frank Norris, and Gerald L. K. Smith—argued that the working class's true struggle must be waged against communism and secularism, which they identified with race-mixing, religious liberalism, and labor rights: in other words, exactly the principles that worker religion represented. This war-era conflict seared working-class religion along lines of political ideology and social identity, shaking denominational unity and undermining the universalistic hope that worker religion might shape the political and spiritual consciousness of all workers.

Worker religion survived the war. By some measures, the idioms of worker religion even seemed to gain strength during the 1950s, as "Labor Sunday" (among Protestants) and the Feast of St. Joseph the Workman (among Catholics) became standard parts of the liturgical calendar. But postwar Detroit was also a rapidly changing city. Automation and plant relocation in the auto industry combined with an emerging housing crisis to redraw the social basis of the city. In addition to demographic changes, worker religion faced another, more persistent challenge: its own inherent cultural ambivalences. Where worker religion had hoped to fuse class identity with religious identity and embolden workers to act for social justice in the public sphere, many workers themselves expressed an entirely distinct, and often apolitical or conservative, cosmology. While worker religion continued to envision faith as a powerful cultural resource that could be affixed to class identity and harnessed to political struggles for social justice, increasingly throughout the 1950s, worker-religion activists also lamented the conservatism and obscurantism of their own institutions.

By the 1960s, the once-promising idioms of worker religion were collapsing. As Detroit confronted a postindustrial future and a deepening urban crisis, religious consciousness was profoundly racialized. Politically, issues of civil rights and inner-city poverty supplanted the language of work and class in the religious imagination. At the same time, the racialization of religious consciousness produced much more explosive consequences than worker religion had ever promised. Because race cut so deeply to the heart of personal, social, and cultural identity, and because the demands for racial justice hit such a raw moral nerve, few communities could escape the implications or consequences of a racialized religious consciousness. Still, even as the culture of worker religion eroded in the 1960s, it provided a valuable legacy of ideas, institutions, and practices for civil-rights and antipoverty advocates.

The Catholics, African Americans, and southern-born whites who dominated Detroit's working class and played such a looming role in the larger national stories of industrial unionism, urban politics, and racial ideology must be granted due consideration as being among the most important actors in the story of twentieth-century American religious history as well. Indeed, these stories cannot be neatly untangled and placed into separate "secular" and "religious" narratives. Religious consciousness remained a crucial part of many workers' lifeworlds, and it was made and remade precisely in relation to the secular forces of the UAW, the voting booth, and the racially diverse urban milieu. To focus *only* on religion (or, even more narrowly, *only* on Catholics, or African Americans, or white evangelicals) is to push religion into a parochial category and implicitly justify its absence in the larger narrative of the twentieth century. Conversely, to focus *only* on matters of class and race is to dismiss, underappreciate, or simply misunderstand one of the most important, resilient, and adaptable cultural forces within working-class life.

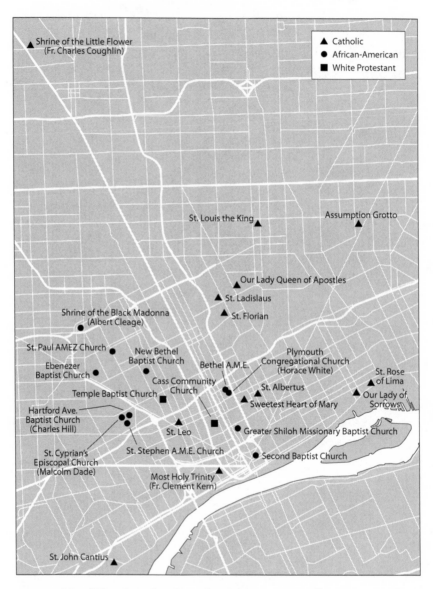

FIGURE 1. Map: "Churches of working-class Detroit, circa 1950."

FIGURE 2. Built with the support of working-class Polish Americans early in the twentieth century, St. Florian's Catholic Church was one of many ethnic parishes in the Diocese of Detroit. Courtesy of Walter P. Reuther Library, Archives of Labor and Urban Affairs, Wayne State University.

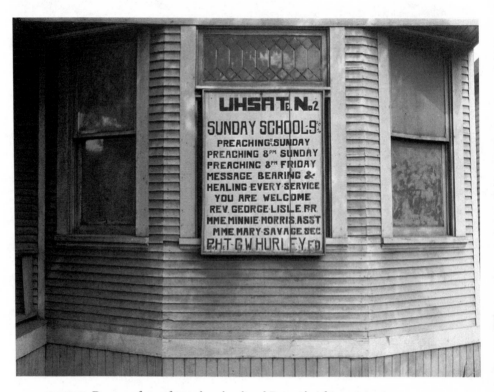

FIGURE 3. Dozens of storefront churches lined Detroit's African American neighborhoods in the 1930s and 1940s. Note the announcements for "Preaching" and "Healing Services." Courtesy Library of Congress.

1. The Contours of Religious Consciousness in Working-Class Detroit, 1910–1935

In the first three decades of the twentieth century, Detroit emerged as America's most dynamic boomtown. All across the city, some of the world's largest, most complex, and most "scientifically" managed factories sprawled across the landscape, pumping smoke out one end and automobiles out the other. Trains chugged into the Michigan Central Depot, spilling out a polyglot cross section of the world's working classes; in 1920, 85 percent of Detroit residents were foreign-born or had at least one foreign-born parent. One awestruck observer described the city as a modern-day "Tower of Babel," transformed from a once moderately sized Midwestern city into America's fourth-largest metropolis. Detroit's wildfire growth in this period swelled the city's population—which topped 1.2 million residents by the mid-1920s—by 157 percent since 1900. Whole swaths of the urban landscape surrendered to the spread of ethnic butchers, barbershops, and honky-tonks—institutions that reflected the cultural heritage of working-class newcomers.[1]

Honeycombed within these neighborhoods of homes and businesses, gathering beneath the shadow of smokestacks and skyscrapers, Detroit's working classes also erected a vast network of religious institutions: churches, schools, recreation centers, soup kitchens. Some were large and ornate structures, their stately brick spires and stained-glass windows starkly illuminating the possibilities of working-class collective action and symbolically laying claim to vast swaths of urban space. Others poked out of dilapidated storefronts or filled the basements of multitenant residences. All reflected the ubiquitous significance of religion in the lives of an ethnically diverse industrial working class.

While the workers of Detroit professed a number of creeds, in pure numbers, Catholics dominated the city's religious landscape. Of 755,572 registered churchgoers in 1926, over half—451,579—belonged to Catholic parishes. Poles were the most ubiquitous Catholic ethnicity, totaling 250,000 on the eve of the Great Depression. But dozens of other groups—67,000 from Italy, 25,000 from Hungary, and tens of thousands more from Belgium, Finland, Lithuania, Croatia, Mexico, and Canada—crowded into the city. The scale of the Catholic imprint on Detroit was neither fleeting, nor limited to a first massive wave of homesick immigrants; even after European immigration nearly ceased in the 1920s, Catholics remained, by far, Detroit's largest religious demographic through the end of the 1960s. Moreover, the Catholic Church in Detroit was, in the words of a 1929 report by the National Council of Catholic Women, "distinctly a Church of the industrial working people." In Detroit—as in cities across industrial America—it is impossible to discuss working-class religion without acknowledging the centrality of Catholicism.[2]

In terms of volume, Detroit's African American population witnessed even more explosive growth than Catholics. In 1910, 5,000 African Americans lived in Detroit, but this number would increase by a stunning 623 percent by 1920. Prior to World War I, only four churches served the city's entire black community, but by the mid-1920s, African American Baptists constituted the third largest religious group in the entire city of Detroit. In 1926, 43 black Baptist congregations were counted; the number was 88 in 1935. Between 1915 and 1935, the number of black Baptists had grown from 900 to 30,000. Other African American denominations were strong as well; nine AME churches claimed 7,663 members, while five Colored Methodist Episcopal churches claimed 1,646 members. By the early 1930s, 146 black churches served over 120,000 people. In fact, one study from 1933 demonstrated that 23 percent of all the churches in Detroit were black churches, even though blacks composed only 7.7 percent of the city's population. Reflecting on the development of black Detroit in 1948, the journalist Ulysses Boykin concluded that religion "has played a far greater part in the community, civic, business and social life than any other social factor." African American Protestantism would stand with Catholicism as the second major strand of working-class religion.[3]

White Protestants from the rural South and Appalachia—often derisively referred to as "hillbillies"—formed the third and final major component of working-class religion in Detroit. Southern whites began migrating into Detroit as early as World War I, mostly originating in the backcountry of Kentucky or Tennessee. A few had experienced industrial working conditions in the cotton mills of Carolina or the coal mines of West Virginia, but most had not and found industrial Detroit an alien environment. Consequently, most southern whites preferred seasonal migration to permanent relocation, at least before World War II. By the mid-1930s, Detroit had evolved into a laboratory for working-class religiosity, in which European Catholicism met evangelistic Protestantism, South invaded North, and black jostled with white.[4]

In addition to Catholics, African American Protestants, and southern whites, two other demographics deserve brief mention: white Protestants from the North and Jews. Socially and politically, northern Protestants were clearly a powerful presence in Detroit. Most of the city's leading industrialists and public figures were Protestants, and mainline Protestant churches towered above Detroit's most prominent downtown intersections. In addition, many of the city's Protestant clergy were nationally regarded and locally influential. However, mainline Protestantism exerted a minimal influence on the religious shape of Detroit's working classes. While some mainline congregations were known for the blue collars of its parishioners, northern working-class Protestants experienced less ghettoization, higher levels of education and training, and a more fluid class structure than Catholics, African Americans, or southern Protestants. Few working-class northern Protestants feared for the class mobility of their children; in general, mainline Protestantism was the province of middle and upper classes, not workers.

Jews provided a somewhat different story from both the largest working-class religious communities as well as mainline Protestants. As with other migrant groups, Detroit proved an attractive destination for Jews; by 1926, the city's Jewish population was 75,000 strong. Like Catholic immigrants from Europe, Jewish immigrants often arrived on the economic margins of Detroit society. Residential segregation characterized the settlement pattern of Jews as much as it did African Americans. Indeed, working-class Jewish neighborhoods swelled the city's central corridor and east side, often pushing right up against—and sometimes fully intermixing with—ethnic Catholic and African American neighborhoods. Jews responded to their situation much as other migrant groups: Jewish charities diligently addressed the necessities of life for poorer Jews, Jewish activists became involved with the labor movement, and some rabbis—notably Leo Franklin—became influential civic voices on social issues. On the one hand, then, Detroit's Jews seem to warrant inclusion as a working-class religion.[5]

However, while many Jews arrived in Detroit poor and often identified with the working class, Jews themselves were infrequent sojourners in the industrial workforce. Instead, Jews preferred to develop their own businesses and often enjoyed success as merchants and shopkeepers. Compared to Catholics and African Americans, Jews enjoyed much higher levels of education and class mobility. And, if Jews quickly learned how to distinguish themselves from industrial workers, Christians often hoped to separate themselves from Jews. Between the 1920s and 1940s, anti-Semitism found fertile ground in Detroit, a prejudice fueled from the top by figures like Henry Ford, but burning strong from the bottom up as well. Indeed, in the religious rhetoric of some blue-collar communities, Jews were imagined as an alien and hostile cabal threatening the "true" American working class, which, according to this mindset, was irreducibly Christian. Thus, although Jews made an important impact on working-class social movements and the overall political life of Detroit, they occupy something of a special case in between the predominant classes, communities, and belief systems.

Finding Work in Detroit

Just as working-class religions came to shape the social fabric of Detroit, so the social forces of the city came to shape the institutions of working-class religion. The new churches rising across early-twentieth-century Detroit were largely planted by people from the global, rural margins of an industrial capitalist heartland. Catholics, African Americans, and southern whites came to Detroit seeking work, and it was the world of modern industrial work that most decisively structured the life options of working-class migrants.

Some immigrant Catholic workers sought to perfect skills or attain a modicum of independence and self-control; a few succeeded. Polish Catholics found work at stoves, ship building, iron and steel work, and a variety of unskilled labor. A handful of ethnic entrepreneurs also thrived. By the 1930s, Poles operated 574 grocery stores, 127 butcher shops, 160 dry goods stores, and 87 clothing stores, almost all within Polish-dominated neighborhoods. Some northern Italians worked their trade as skilled stonecutters and masons, while Italian merchants owned 123 groceries, 13 meat markets, and a handful of other service-related enterprises by the late 1930s. Catholic women, meanwhile, often worked for wages outside the home in addition to maintaining a complex household economy. First-generation Polish women, in the words of an observer from the 1930s, "worked hard at whatever they could find to do": at hotels and restaurants, as domestic servants and laundry workers. By the 1920s, many second-generation women worked in one of the five cigar factories located in Hamtramck (a heavily Polish municipality incorporated in 1922 within Detroit's city limits, on the northeast side). Despite deep cultural prohibitions, Italian women also became wage earners, working as tailors, dressmakers, candy-factory workers, or in laundries. Some educated Hungarian women found work as saleswomen and typists, although most survived in the factories.[6]

Ultimately, however, working life in Detroit between 1900 and 1930 was indelibly impacted by the auto industry. Ever since Henry Ford's first assembly line demonstrated a means of cheaply producing cars for a mass market, Detroit's industrial innovators stampeded into auto manufacturing. Hundreds of smaller shops—parts suppliers, machine shops, rubber- and glassworks—quickly sprang up to support the largest plants (at his River Rouge plant alone, Ford employed an industrial army of 90,000 workers). By 1928 the "Big Three" automakers of Ford, General Motors, and Chrysler employed 200,000 workers, directly or indirectly affecting the lives of nearly two-thirds of the city's workers.[7]

For Polish men, the single most important employer was the Dodge Brothers' auto factory, which opened in the municipality of Hamtramck in 1910. Within a decade, life for the 50,000 residents of Hamtramck revolved around the triad of "Dodge Main," Polish ethnic institutions, and the Catholic Church. Likewise, the majority of Italian immigrants were unskilled workers who ended up in auto factories or on construction sites. Hungarian men worked predominately at the Ford plant in Dearborn, although some also worked at the Briggs Manufacturing Company or the Chrysler plant in Highland Park. Mexicans drifted into Detroit's east side following seasonal work on Michigan sugar beet farms, and more than 10,000 eventually became unskilled laborers at the Ford plant. Catholic women, too, worked in the auto industry; more than 20,000 Polish and Hungarian women became punch-press operators, especially at the large Ternstedt plant on Detroit's west side.[8]

A similar—if starker—working life confronted African American workers. To be sure, a handful of black men were able to avoid menial labor. Amid the severe instability following World War I, John Dancy of the Urban League convinced Detroit's mayor to fill several of the jobs on the municipally operated streetcar lines with black workers. This was a feat with potentially significant social implications, for, as a study from 1921 found, most of Detroit's workers could not locate housing near their work and relied on streetcars for their daily commute; Detroit's working classes thus often came face to face on the journey to work. A few other black men, like Archie Coleman from Birmingham, found skilled work as a railroad fireman. Some of Detroit's black musicians, barbers, carpenters, and brick masons even belonged to unions. Other black migrants became businessmen; in 1929, African Americans in Detroit owned 51 drug stores, 187 restaurants, 91 barbershops, 17 laundries, 3 theaters, 10 dance halls, and 18 cabarets.[9]

But the overwhelming majority of African Americans were unskilled laborers. Elijah Kitchen, for instance, swapped the drudgery of farm labor and cotton-mill work in the South for a job at the Briggs plant in Detroit.

George Newman, originally from Memphis, was lured to Detroit because he had "heard so much about the place" and landed a job at the Cadillac factory. By far the largest employer of black labor was Henry Ford, whose payroll counted 16,500 black workers by the mid-1920s. Dodge Brothers, the next largest employer, claimed only 980 black workers, Packard employed 890, and Briggs and Morgan and Wright, 600 each. Observers at the Urban League were convinced that most blacks were thwarted in their quest to become skilled workers due to the pressure of whites, who made it clear to their employers that they would not work on the "same social scale" as blacks. According to the Urban League's John Dancy, the trouble arose "as soon as they get away from their homes," for "the Pole is bitterly opposed to [the African American] getting a job." This racial animosity between workers (which was at least tacitly permitted, if not openly supported, by industrialists) clearly limited black workers' options: "no matter how capable a worker he is, he can only go so far."[10]

Black women faced even more severe difficulties. For a short while, during the labor crunch surrounding World War I, the Detroit Urban League persuaded the owner of one cigar factory to hire only black women, and a handful of black women worked in department stores or at pool halls. But the overwhelming majority worked as domestics or in laundries, and nearly all found limited opportunities for advancement. But for all African Americans, whether men or women, finding and keeping work could be daunting. In 1926, only 21,000 black men were employed, mostly as unskilled laborers, out of a total black population of 56,000. At the height of the auto industry boom in the mid-1920s, there remained, according to the Urban League, "a large number walking the streets," looking for work.[11]

Building Communities and Congregations

Outside the factory gates, Catholic workers established blue-collar neighborhoods clearly defined by ethnicity and delineated by parish boundaries. Poles claimed much of Hamtramck, as well as large neighborhoods on both the east and west sides. Delray, a river-front community in southwest Detroit, was a mixed but overwhelmingly Hungarian neighborhood. Sicilians and Italians clustered on the near east side, south of Hamtramck. The "typical house" in these ethnic neighborhoods, as a report from the early 1920s documented, consisted of "a small cottage or a two-family house." Many of these residences had been hastily constructed during the massive population influx of war-workers between 1917 and 1919. Built on the fly, they were often cramped, flimsy, or lacking proper sanitation. Frequently, three to four families lived in houses designed for one to two families, with residents sharing "yard toilets" in the back. Added to the burdens and health risks of overcrowding, working-class families often supplemented their income by housing boarders; residents routinely slept in shifts that corresponded with working schedules.[12]

Despite these challenging conditions, working-class Catholics built socially dense neighborhoods that reflected the values of the community and the importance of ethnicity. Home ownership—the ultimate mark of prosperity for formerly landless peasants—was a defining goal of immigrant cultures, an impulse thoroughly encouraged by the Church. Home-ownership associations, in fact, quickly grew within the new parishes. By the early 1920s, Polish immigrants owned parish-based homes collectively valued at $3,888,000 (38 percent of Hamtramck's Poles were home owners). Within these "urban villages," immigrants purchased food in neighborhood stores from ethnic grocers or picked up a newspaper printed in their native language. The Hungarian worker in Delray might drop in to Kovacs Bar to hear the Gypsy orchestra, while the Poles in Hamtramck attended polka dances at Dom Polski.[13]

Catholic churches and schools frequently served as the social and imaginative anchor of immigrant communities, providing symbols of stability, permanence, and peoplehood. Detroit Poles built their first "national" (or ethnic) parish, St. Albertus, in 1871 on Detroit's east side, while a parish for west-side Poles, St. Casimir's, opened in 1882. Hungarians in Delray founded Holy Cross parish with a Hungarian priest in 1906. Northern Italians established San Francesco parish in 1898, while Sicilians and southern Italians erected their own Holy Family parish in 1910; Belgians claimed Our Lady of Sorrows parish. Overall, during the 1920s, Detroit's Bishop Michael Gallagher promoted a construction binge that raised an additional 86 churches across Detroit (the total number of Catholic churches stood at 119 for the 1926 census). By 1933, Catholics throughout Detroit could hear the faith celebrated in 22 different languages.[14]

The congregations of Hamtramck provide a window into the creation of a church-conscious, working-class ethnic community. When the Dodge Brothers' "Main" plant opened in Hamtramck in 1910, it towered over a half-built town of semipaved roads and marshland. But the factory quickly drew thousands of Polish workers, who placed the Catholic parish at the center of the city's social life. Hamtramck's first parish, St. Florian's, had been founded in 1908. While it struggled at first to generate deep support among the people, the expansion of the Dodge factory and the arrival of an ambitious new priest made the difference. Between 1912 and 1914, St. Florian's grew from 250 to 1800 families. When, in 1914, St. Florian's pastor proposed to build a new gothic-style church with two soaring steeples, up to 15,000 people attended the ceremony dedicating the church basement (the new church's proposed cornerstone). Social organizations expanded rapidly: the choir, a Rosary society, benevolent (insurance) societies, Polish Roman Catholic societies, the Holy Name society for Catholic men. Baptisms, marriages, and funerals all more than tripled.[15]

By 1917, St. Florian's basement church was "bursting at the seams," with more than 2,000 people attending each Sunday service. In response, the Diocese of Detroit essentially sliced off the northeastern portion of St. Florian to create a new parish, Our Lady Queen of Apostles. Begun with 23 families who worshipped out of a two-story residential house, Our Lady had erected its own impressive church and claimed several hundred parishioners within ten years. Additionally, in 1920, 300 families living to the south of Our Lady formed yet another new parish, St. Ladislaus. Each of these churches developed its own web of religious and social associations. When St. Ladislaus opened, Detroit was home to 18 Polish parishes and nearly 300 Polish organizations; Polish immigrants had invested an estimated $29,895,000 in church property.[16]

Schools were built almost as fast as parishes were founded. Between 1913 and 1925, the number of Catholic parishes with schools nearly doubled, from 35 to 63. St. Florian's school enrolled 186 students in 1911, a number that soared to 2,120 in 1919 and 2,642 in 1926. At Our Lady Queen of Apostles, 226 students were being taught in two private homes in 1917; the first building the parish built, in 1918, was an eight-room schoolhouse. When the Sisters of St. Francis opened the St. Ladislaus school in 1921, they enrolled 300 students; three years later, enrollment topped 1,500. Across the diocese, enrollment in parochial schools grew by 116 percent, reaching 49,181 students in the mid-1920s. The very existence of these schools speaks to the values and desires of working-class Catholics: the willingness of working parents to sacrifice for the good of family, especially children; the importance of religious identity within the immigrant household; and the confidence of the Church itself in expecting and receiving abundant support from laypeople (the virtually free labor of teaching sisters, who often endured impoverished conditions, was also an obvious requisite).[17]

Where Catholic neighborhoods spread across the city, housing presented a deeper and more enduring challenge for African American migrants because of the overt racial segregation that defined the housing market. John Dancy claimed to see a rough equality in working-class housing, noting that "Negroes, Poles, Italians, Jews; all live together, and live in the same homes. . . . They get along apparently very well together." Dancy's judgment was not entirely misplaced, for working-class groups occasionally overlapped neighborhoods, especially near Detroit's urban center. But in general, clear geographic patterns were visible, and "the housing question," as a report from 1921 put it, was "particularly difficult." Restrictive real estate "covenants" literally trapped most black residents in overpriced, overcrowded, and often deteriorating buildings on the lower east side of Detroit in an area nicknamed the "Black Bottom" (another, more affluent but still decidedly working-class African American neighborhood swelled on the city's west side). In 1924, between one-third and one-half of African Americans were estimated to live in substandard housing.[18]

Most African American migrants, however, who had so recently escaped the abject oppression of the rural South, were enticed and invigorated by the new options of city life. Few would have dismissed their surroundings as a "slum"; instead, they often saw strong, vital, neighborhood-centered communities. Robert Hayden, later a renowned poet, remembered St. Antoine Street in the 1920s as "a lively street with barbershops and pool halls and restaurants and drugstores, and I suppose gambling joints too. In the summer, people used to stand out in front of the various places there and greet their friends." Hastings Street became a cradle of the urban blues. Famous piano players from the South, like "Tupelo Slim," "Fishtail," and "Seminole," flooded into joints like Butch's Club, setting the stage for later Detroit blues greats like John Lee Hooker.[19]

Barbershops, pool halls, and juke joints thrived in intimate physical proximity to the many churches of black Detroit. Of these, perhaps the most important was Second Baptist Church. Founded in 1836, Second Baptist was the oldest black religious organization in Michigan. In the 1840s and 1850s, it served as a waystation on the Underground Railroad; sitting just across the Detroit River from Canada, Second Baptist was often the final American refuge for thousands of slaves seeking freedom. After years of drift, in 1910, the congregation was reenergized by the arrival of its visionary new pastor, Robert Bradby (who led the church until his death in 1946). Bradby's leadership—and, in particular, his outreach to newly arriving southern migrants—proved decisive. Between 1916 and 1918 alone, the church's membership swelled by more than 300 percent, to 3,000 members; it would continue rising, to more than 4,000 members, by the mid-1920s. Twice, in 1916 and again in 1917, the church suffered extensive fires described by one observer as a "calamity"; Bradby responded by raising $53,000 over a single weekend in 1917, while continuing to expand the church rolls—a clear sign of his administrative acumen and the commitment of his congregants. He also vastly extended the social and charitable mission of the church and personally served as the president of the local chapter of the NAACP during the mid-1920s. More controversially, he cultivated close ties to Henry Ford. Second Baptist, in fact, came close to serving as Ford's personal labor clearinghouse. For a newly arrived worker, Bradby's recommendation to the right manager might open the path to a new life in the North; crossing him might mean the difference between factory work in Detroit and farm work in Alabama.[20]

However, while large congregations like Second Baptist and Bethel AME defined the mainstream of African American religion, the most notable and creative adaptation to religious life in the urban North was the rise of the storefront church. By 1926, one observer found "numerous storefronts, basements, front rooms . . . platforms in vacant lots, and other small and insignificant places being used as church buildings." That same year, the Detroit Urban League complained that only 30 of Detroit's 65 black churches were "reputable and under some governing body"; in other words, more than half of all African American church life took place in small, makeshift establishments and operated independently from any denomination. Religious researchers in the early 1930s drew similar conclusions: of 66 churches surveyed, 45 percent were storefronts.[21]

The proliferation of storefront churches, in Detroit as in other northern cities, symbolized the confluence of numerous factors within African American life at the time of the Great Migration. While the established black churches of the city offered useful social services to newly arriving southern migrants, the style of religion practiced in these congregations seemed alien—even hostile—to African Americans from the South. Northern churches had long internalized the importance of "respectability" in the public performance of religion, and many ministers were embarrassed by the exuberant worship style of the southerners. A deacon in one storefront church, for example, explained to a researcher that his "long, loud prayer" seemed displaced in the larger and more affluent congregations, so he left to organize his own storefront. Indeed, the spread of church storefronts was evidence of ruptures *within* the African American community, and the refusal of southern migrants to accommodate a religious style they read as unwelcoming from both a theological and a class perspective. In the words of historian Wallace Best, northern storefronts became "islands of southern religious practice and community," embodiments of a shared identity rooted in the idioms of religious diaspora and symbolizing continuity with the southern past.[22]

If storefront communities sought continuity with the past, they also embraced the innovative changes of urban life. For instance, nearly all African American churches in the South were either Baptist or Methodist, but storefront congregations in the North often embraced Holiness, Pentecostal, and other insurgent evangelical movements that had begun sweeping through the South in the 1890s. Some storefronts freely blended the symbols and motifs of Catholicism, Protestantism, and *spirit conjuring* (traditional African American folklore) into an entirely novel religious vernacular. Often, storefronts represented entrepreneurial ventures, in which self-educated ministers sought congregants hungry for a particular religious experience. Marvin Arnett's family, for instance, lived in a modest, multitenant building on Detroit's west side amid a motley cross section of "factory workers, domestic day workers, welfare families, and just plain hustlers." When a local evangelist converted the building's first floor into a small church, Arnett's mother regularly attended. The urban environment, in other words, produced a dramatically larger religious marketplace and an often-bewildering number of choices for the spiritual seeker. Choice, of course, indicates agency, and storefront churches represented a literal assertion of working-class ownership and authority over their daily urban environment, creating essential social networks within which experience might be interpreted and beliefs expressed.[23]

The Contours of Religious Consciousness

Detroit's working people were subject to powerful historical forces. The external experiences of migration, industrial labor, and urban living starkly etched the parameters of social life and contributed much to defining the particular shape of working-class culture, institutions, and identity. But workers were agents as well as subjects, and purposefully engaged in the making of what I am calling a *religious consciousness*. Working peoples' religious consciousness emerged out of a complex, ambiguous, sometimes paradoxical worldview; anthropologist Michael Jackson termed the resulting reality a *lifeworld*, which he eloquently described as a "social force field, a constellation of both ideas and passions, moral norms and ethical dilemmas, the tried and the true as well as the unprecedented, a field charged with vitality and animated by struggle." Internally, religious consciousness mediated competing tensions; externally, religious performance communicated identity.[24]

Scrutinizing religious consciousness also offers insight into workers' attitudes and beliefs on a wide number of important subjects with both moral and political implications: why people were made to work, what it meant to be a man or a woman, how ethnic peoplehood was defined, what was right and what was wrong, how to live a good life, and what a person could expect from human existence. Working-class religious consciousness did not function as a transparently consistent intellectual system. Formal mastery of doctrines and creeds was less important than the personal satisfaction and sense of social or cultural power that worshippers drew from sacred narratives, rituals, and practices. Rather than representing any systematic theology, working-class religious consciousness might be better described as a network of idioms, the proper use of which permitted believers access to spiritual resources and supernatural patrons. Vital in defining peoplehood and community, working-class religion simultaneously erected sharp (if sometimes malleable) boundaries between "insiders" and "outsiders." Often fueled by raucously emotional worship, working-class religion also enforced strict norms of discipline, sobriety, and respectability. Oriented toward "otherworldly" engagement with the supernatural, working-class religion was also resolutely pragmatic and "this-worldly." Seemingly premodern in some of its habits, working-class religion easily reconciled modern mass culture and industrial life. Within religious consciousness, the often contradictory dynamics of beliefs, experiences, and desires common to working-class life were fused, combined, and reconciled.

Creating a Sense of Peoplehood

One of the major cultural functions of religion is to instruct people about their history, morality, and identity. Religion tells people: this is who you are; this is where your people come from; and this is how our people go about the business of life. In making a religious consciousness, believers were also invariably shaping an identity rooted in a sense of group-based peoplehood. This sense of ethno-religious community was vital to the migrants' adaptations to the industrial metropolis; indeed, as historian Leslie Woodcock Tentler has noted with specific reference to the Catholic working class, "ethnic consciousness was generally a necessary antecedent to class consciousness." The dynamic cut two ways. As Detroit's Progressive-Era Catholic and African American migrants created a consciousness of religious peoplehood, they simultaneously separated "their" people from "others." Because they were shaped by the context of the early twentieth century, religious ideas about peoplehood were awash in—indeed, contributed to—the pervasive beliefs, fears, and fantasies about racial hierarchy that marked the time.[25]

For working-class Catholics—so often, first-generation migrants from rural Europe—religious images, rituals, and narratives created an expressive, symbolic template upon which they could define ethnic identity. For Detroit's Poles, no symbol achieved this effect more powerfully than Poland's patroness, Our Lady of Czestochowa. Although no Detroit parish was named in her honor, this very Polish image of Mary was prominently displayed in the largest Polish parishes. The vestibule of Sweetest Heart of Mary, for instance, contained a large image of Our Lady, and St. Josaphat's placed her icon over the church's altar. The image itself depicts a dark, nearly black-skinned Madonna, with three gashes across her face, holding an infant Christ. One Dearborn woman affirmed to an interviewer, "This is a very holy picture and we all wanted to see it."[26]

What did it mean to working-class immigrants in a racially polarized city like Detroit that their most sacred image was dark-skinned? The explanations offered by Polish laity for the dark skin of Our Lady of Czestochowa suggest a measure of uneasiness about the subject. One woman opined that the saint's skin was not actually black, but "golden." Others denied that the skin was "naturally" dark, and explained the color as a consequence of desecration by invading soldiers, who attempted to burn the picture. These responses mirror the ambiguous racial status for many Catholic new immigrants in the Progressive Era. A spokesperson for St. Paul AMEZ Church in the ethnic suburb of Delray may have claimed that the "two or three Catholic churches in the vicinity" were "for white people of course"; but these "white" churches were probably Holy Cross, a Hungarian parish, and St. John Cantius, a Polish parish. The "whiteness" of these ethnic churches was hardly self-evident, as Marvin Arnett, a black woman who grew up in a mixed neighborhood on Detroit's west side, carefully noted. In her childhood neighborhood of the 1930s, "Polish, Hungarian, and Jewish families . . . were white, but not White." For Arnett, class, status, and education all contributed to whiteness; her working-class ethnic neighbors may have shared a color with "Whites," but they did not share the same racial privileges. At least through the 1950s, Detroit's working-class Catholics tended to stress a religiously defined ethnic peoplehood, rather than a racially based preoccupation with whiteness.[27]

In learning and talking about Our Lady, Polish Catholics also learned to think of themselves as sharing an identity and a relationship with a specific divine patron. This reservoir of knowledge was largely controlled by the community itself, not by the Church. Some Poles knew the official Church history of Our Lady: that the image was painted by St. Luke. But many, when interviewed by a folklorist, expressed no knowledge of the image's origins. Some said it was given as a gift to the Queen of Poland, while others claimed it was painted by a Polish king who became jealous when the people loved Our Lady more than his own rule. Likewise, Poles told different stories about the three gashes. Most tales involved a soldier from an invading army, but specifics differed considerably. One woman claimed a soldier slashed the picture and it began to bleed; another said that a rampaging soldier placed it in a cart, but when the horse refused to pull it, the soldier slashed the picture and left it behind. Others held that a soldier slashed the picture and was immediately struck dead, while some sources claimed the original was physically slashed into three different pieces and tossed into a fire, only later to be discovered intact by foraging peasants. These varying accounts suggest that Our Lady of Czestochowa—a widely shared symbol of ethnicity, piety, and peoplehood—was defined by a combination of "official" Church teaching and more autonomous stories passed among family and friends. But all shared a common underlying premise: the piety of the Polish commoner.[28]

Liturgical performances flowed with the changing seasons in Hamtramck and further reinforced a consciousness of religiously defined peoplehood. Holy Thursday of Easter week always witnessed major expressions of piety, as parishioners made pilgrimages from church to church. On Good Friday, men and women formed Honor Guards, rotating in shifts during a 16-hour vigil before a replica of Christ's tomb. Celebration of Easter Sunday began at 5 or 6 AM. The priest, holding aloft the Eucharist, headed a procession that circled the church three times. Thousands of children carrying lilies followed the priest, and they in turn were followed by all the church organizations, passing a replica of the empty tomb and singing the Polish hymn, "Today for Us a Wondrous Day Has Dawned." Mass commenced after a ringing of the bells. And following Mass, each family retired for a ritualized sharing of sacred food that had been blessed by the priest on Holy Saturday (an egg, ham, and Easter cakes). Several weeks after Easter, the feast of Corpus Christi (which honored the sacrament of the Eucharist) again produced large processions in Polish neighborhoods. Adele Jankowski of Our Lady Queen of Apostles remembered the day as "a very well attended service. Altars were set up outdoors on different front porches in the neighborhood." Clara Swieczkowska, a prominent laywoman at St. Albertus, likewise noted the popularity of Corpus Christi.[29]

Peoplehood served an important role in the religious consciousness of other immigrant Catholics as well. St. Joseph's Day (March 19th) produced "some of the largest and most richly observed" celebrations among Sicilians and southern Italians, according to an eyewitness. Following Mass, a procession emerged from the church, led by a large statue of a "stern-faced" Joseph, holding a staff, standing on a velvet draped platform, and carried by twelve young men. The statue was followed by priests, nuns, children strewing flowers, men and women bearing flags, and "loud-playing brass bands." As the procession made its way down Congress Street, over to Fort, and winding on to Champlain, bystanders tossed money at the saint as he was marched along his route. Evidence exists of similar Mexican-Catholic celebrations in Detroit beginning in the 1920s and 1930s. The Day of the Dead was marked in November, and one woman recalled a festival honoring the Virgin of Guadalupe. "We made a float," she remembered, and "it carried several youngsters dressed like the Virgin of Guadalupe and Juan Diego." While these rituals contained elements of private devotion within families, clearly their most important aspect was the "public" nature of the performances. Whether the occasion was Corpus Christi, St. Joseph's Day, or the Dia de la Muerta, the ceremonies that accompanied these holy days claimed public space, symbolically marked turf, and clearly defined the parameters of what "culture" and "community" meant within specific geographic patches of working-class Detroit.[30]

In creating a consciousness of peoplehood, religion also clarified the bright social lines separating one group from another. The people of St. Albertus parish thought of themselves not just as Poles but as Kushubian Poles (from partitioned Poland under Prussian rule). When large numbers of Poznanian Poles arrived at St. Albertus, they perceived the Kashub as clannish and dismissed their coreligionists as "country bumpkins." Moreover, some prominent parishioners at St. Albertus felt that Fr. Herr, their pastor during the early twentieth century, regarded himself as "German," and acted imperiously toward his Polish flock. And neither the Kashubs at St. Albertus nor the followers of the Galician Rev. Dominic Kolasinski at Sweetest Heart of Mary appreciated the "Varsovian" (or Warsaw-born) Poles a few blocks over at St. Josaphat. For John White's father, it was not sufficient for his son to date mostly fellow Irish Catholics—White's father became upset if the women attended different *parishes*. "That's how provincial they were," White lamented to an interviewer. "That was not uncommon. That was of Italian, Polish, and Hungarian, and all the ethnic cultures."[31]

Detroit's African American churches also developed a consciousness of peoplehood, and of what we might call religion-within-race. Black churches had, after all, been among the most important institutions for defining African American peoplehood since the first independent black congregations were created in the 1810s. By the 1920s, the insurgency of the so-called "New Negroes" had pushed the issues of cultural identity and racial pride to the forefront of African American life. In Detroit, perhaps no prophet of the "New Negroes" was more influential than the New York–based Jamaican immigrant Marcus Garvey, founder of the Universal Negro Improvement Association (UNIA) and powerful exemplar of black autonomy and self-determination. Throughout the decade, Garvey called for all descendants of Africa to separate from the global white power structure, reclaim a proud history, create an independent economy, and, ultimately, return to Africa to build a new society. According to historian Manning Marable, fifteen branches of the UNIA were established in Detroit between 1921 and 1933, drawing nearly 7,000 members (including Earl Little, father of Malcolm X). Garveyism, as Randall Burkett has argued, itself became a kind of religion, with constant invocations of religious language and mimicry of religious practice rooted in the legacy of the black church. For many black Detroiters, Garvey's pan-African appeal to racial identity reflected a shifting and remaking of racial consciousness.[32]

Detroit's black Christian churches seemed touched by Garvey's rhetoric. Augustus Duncan, a New-York–based intellectual, argued to a Detroit AME congregation in 1921 that a racially unified and separate church would allow an African American to become "the best possible black man" rather than "the best possible imitation of a white man." Indeed, Duncan chided his fellow African Americans for lacking "proper ideals of race pride," and argued that only a militant church would unite the race for social action. Joseph Gomez, still a young man when charged with the pastorate at Bethel AME in 1919, was the kind of leader Duncan had in mind. Gomez applauded "a growing consciousness of race power" with the conclusion of World War I and saw his church as a means for utilizing this consciousness. In 1923 and 1924, Gomez faced down the Ku Klux Klan to build a larger church in a previously "white" neighborhood. He aggressively lobbied the Detroit Council of Churches to renounce the Klan, but, to his disgust, the DCC repeatedly declined to offer any public denunciation (even as it invited Bethel to join the council and expressed its "deep interest" in African Americans). In 1925, after his own encounter with the violence that accompanied urban turf wars, Gomez was elected president of the Detroit Sweet Defense Committee to assist the family of Ossian Sweet in their murder trial. Additionally, a number of churches—including Bethel AME, Hartford Baptist, and Shiloh Baptist—hosted race-conscious speakers like A. Philip Randolph and Paul Robeson.[33]

Within this tight cultural and institutional linkage of religion and race, the specific theology and worship style of black churches offered a deeply appealing interpretation of history. In particular, the ambiguity experienced by so many participants of the "great migration" to Detroit was reconciled in a uniquely African American religious vernacular. On the one hand, religion sacralized the migration, encouraging migrants to imagine the urban North as a "promised land." Attorney U. S. Bratton made this line of thinking explicit when he declared to a packed Detroit church in 1921 that African Americans "needed a 'Moses' to lead them out of the South." Since the nineteenth century, the Exodus story had probably been the most widely recited and fervently believed religious narrative in African American Christianity. When St. Peter's AMEZ church—nestled in the Polish Catholic enclave of

Hamtramck—celebrated the anniversary of the Emancipation Proclamation in 1927, it united the biblical story of Exodus with the historical experience of Africans in America. Ubiquitous references to Exodus in the context of the Great Migration thus wove black migrants of the early twentieth century into the same sacred drama as the story of their ancestors, one that continued to unfold over time with the ultimate promise of both spiritual and temporal liberation. On the other hand, religion also allowed migrants to understand their dislocation as a type of "exile" from their southern homeland. The metaphor of the Israelites cut both ways: migrants might be leaving the land of slavery, or they might be the victims of diaspora.[34]

Defining Gender Identity

To be a *worker*, as the discourse of the early twentieth century defined the term, was almost by definition to be a man—not just biologically male, but socially masculine, a concept that exhorted a muscular independence in a world uncomfortably structured by dependent labor relationships. Churches, meanwhile, were conspicuously populated by women. In 1926, ten women filled the pews of Detroit's churches for every eight men. A national study from the early 1930s that included data from Detroit found the gender gap among African Americans was even wider: 73 percent of black women claimed church membership, compared to only 46 percent of black men. Despite the strong limitations placed on women's religious authority, most working-class churches would have been paralyzed without the voluntary labor of devoted laywomen. Workers' religious consciousness thus not only engaged with historical relationships along class and ethnic lines, but raised difficult questions about gender as well. Did religion—or, at least, church attendance—jeopardize the masculinity of the average worker? Could a man who already labored for another man place himself under the spiritual authority of yet another man (the minister), attach himself to a social space so associated with women and domesticity as the church, and still retain his identity as a man? Conversely, could wives or mothers be "true women" if they entered the world of wage labor (as many did)? Might religion offer women avenues to some form of social power and cultural authority, or was the domestic ideology that suffused religious rhetoric an impediment to the dignity and autonomy of working-class women? Most broadly, how would the ideologies of masculinity and femininity shape the contours of working-class religious consciousness?[35]

For many working-class men, religion could seem jarringly out of place amidst the "rough culture" of factory work and male camaraderie. Few men enjoyed being preached at, and at least a few resented the moralizing of well-fed ministers. Drinking and carousing were commonly viewed as male prerogatives in many working-class communities; rates of venereal disease in Detroit, which hovered among the highest in the country throughout the 1920s, testify to this behavior. Even the hardened investigators of the American Social Hygiene Association (ASHA) were shocked by the flagrant prostitution they discovered during their investigations in 1926. Hundreds of saloons, pool halls, and gambling dens lined the streets of Detroit's working-class neighborhoods. It was the allure of these institutions, and the masculine culture they embodied, that pushed many black women toward spiritualist mediums who promised to reveal "where her husband spent his free time" (we might imagine Catholic women kneeling before a patron saint during one of the frequent novenas held in area parishes and asking the same question).[36]

Young men, in particular, were likely to resist or ignore the overtures of religion. The Rev. Louis G. Weitzman, a Jesuit priest who worked with Detroit youth, offered a fascinating portrait of one such rebellious spirit. Weitzman asked this ostensibly Catholic young man to articulate specific matters of creedal importance. "Who is God?" the priest asked. Though he struggled with "just how to say it," the young man had clearly imbibed his catechism well. He knew that "Christ died on the cross. . . . Because it was God's will." When pressed further as to why Christ's death was God's will, he answered, "Because God wanted Him to save us from sin." Fr. Weitzman was impressed by the youth's demonstration of doctrinal knowledge—and yet, "his attitude towards the Church was decidedly antagonistic and when we tried to persuade him to go to Mass and confession he ran away and has not been heard of for more than four months."[37]

Religious leaders who ministered to the working class continually worried about the absence of men and the perceived female domination of their churches. J. K. Robinson, the minister of an African American storefront, recognized that ambitions for his church depended on the support of working men. In a letter to Second Baptist pastor Robert Bradby, Robinson recounted his effort to provide a permanent "church home" for his storefront congregation. While he felt he had established "a very good church . . . the most of them are women, and may be, about 20 men. But the men is just a drag, in fact what has made it so hard, it is a membership that are poor." Robinson knew that, without drawing male support, his church was fated to flounder. The Society of St. Vincent de Paul, a voluntary organization of Catholic laymen, sounded a similar warning in 1914, when it argued that "indifferent fathers must be persuaded to get back to their religious duties": regular attendance at Mass, reception of the sacraments, and raising children within the Church.[38]

But gradually, over the course of the 1920s and into the 1930s, the efforts of concerned clergy began to pay off, as many working-class men adeptly integrated their religious identity and masculinity. Sports proved important in this transition. As early as 1918, the African American intellectual George Haynes had declared that every black church and Sunday school should sponsor its own baseball, basketball, and football team, and all should be joined in a church league. By the 1920s, this had become at least a partial reality, as a growing network of summer camps, YMCAs, and church-based sport leagues kept young black men within the orbit of church life. Catholics responded in kind. In 1933, the Catholic Men's Athletic Association of Detroit was established, and the Catholic Youth Organization—which organized scouts and other recreational activities for young people—followed in 1935. Boxing—a venerable working-class sport—proved especially popular; 98 parishes hosted boxing programs by 1937, with a total of 12,000 participants in all sporting events.[39]

The growing reach of church-sponsored sports programs provided a bridge between "rough culture" and "church culture." An item in the St. Florian parish newsletter is especially revealing of this process. In an effort to introduce young men to the Holy Name Society, Fr. Szczesny drew upon their preexisting knowledge of baseball: "If someone were to ask you, 'Who is the new manager for the Tigers?' immediately you would answer 'Cochrane.' . . . But here is a question you would be pinned by and be kept mum: 'What is the Holy Name Society?'" The priest proceeded to list the opportunities for secular forms of leisure—a gymnasium, swimming pool, and club room—available to Holy Name members. Of course, the larger point of Fr. Szczensy's appeal reflected the church's attempt to incorporate boys and men into parish life, and ultimately integrate them into the pervasive devotional culture that defined 1930s-era Catholicism.[40]

Special appeals were also made to husbands and fathers, whose sense of masculinity was often tethered to a patriarchal conception of respect that flowed from the ability to support a family. Robert Bradby of Second Baptist Church, for instance, attracted "great crowds" to his gender-specific presentations on "Home Problems." For women, he lectured on "Why Men Leave Home," while he challenged men with the question "Is Your Wife a Maid, a Nurse, a Meal-Ticket, or a Companion?" Many black men found their community standing was elevated when they served as deacons, vestrymen, and other positions of authority within their congregations. Meanwhile, Catholic fraternal groups like the Holy Name society grew steadily in numbers and strength throughout the 1920s. Religion did not so much "domesticate" these men; rather, typically "masculine" virtues—physical strength, competitive excellence, and domestic authority—were overlaid with the idioms, rituals, and creeds of religion.[41]

If working-class masculinity blended religion with "rough culture," religion reinforced an emphatically domestic culture for working-class women. Particularly among immigrant Catholics, a "male" world of work often divided from a "female" world of hearth and faith. Southern Italian girls, according to one investigator, were "so strictly guarded that they have little freedom or social life of any kind," while the "Italian married woman of the working class has practically no recreation except what she gets through her church." An investigator of Detroit's immigrant Mexican community concluded that women "remained subordinate, home-centered creatures." One of Mexican women's chief social roles, according to this observer, was to serve as "an inculcator of religious precepts" in their children. Among many Hungarian immigrants, too, women often held to the church more tightly than men. Mariksa Leleszi, raised in the Hungarian community of Delray in the 1920s, remembered, "mother impressed it upon us on her deathbed, 'don't leave your church, do go regularly, do your work there properly.' The church was mother's life." In almost all parishes, sodalities and Christian Mothers' Societies were among the first organizations established, usually far ahead of the male Holy Name societies.[42]

But changes in the sexual practices and family lives of Catholic women were becoming evident. Twenty percent of juvenile "sex delinquents" in the ASHA's Detroit survey were first- or second-generation Poles; among its reports are numerous, in-depth narrative profiles of many other one-time Catholic women driven into prostitution by the exigencies of city life. Most Catholic women, of course, continued to become wives and mothers, but the practice of these roles was changing as well. While marriage across religious lines was very rare, ethnic intermarriage among Catholics grew by 300 percent between 1906 and the mid-1930s, suggesting broad social contact beyond parish lines and the emergence of a more Americanized, pan-Catholic culture. In Hamtramck, a rapidly declining birthrate indicated that birth control and family limitation—both forbidden by the Catholic Church—was surreptitiously practiced by otherwise devout Polish Catholics. Likewise, while divorce remained unusual, one researcher found it was no longer taboo for second- and third-generation Polish American parishioners at Sweetest Heart of Mary; however, despite shifting social norms, almost all of the 111 second-generation members interviewed at Sweetest Heart of Mary "insisted on registering allegiance" to Catholicism. Specific doctrines governing family life and sexuality might have been quietly ignored at times, but defining oneself as "Catholic" continued to carry deep social and cultural meaning.[43]

Additionally, working-class women of many faiths needed to pursue waged work outside the home, and the experiences of industrialism could change the role of religion in these women's lives. A state survey of more than 8,000 working women in Michigan recorded women's own descriptions of the impact:

I'm tired when Sunday comes. . . . I don't have clothes to wear to church. . . . I've forgotten what church looks like inside since I started working. . . . Was forced to go to church when I was a kid/Had all I wanted. . . . I have too much work to do on Sundays. . . . Father had a "spat" with the minister and wouldn't let us go/I don't enjoy going to other churches, . . . I thought once that I couldn't live unless I went once or twice every Sunday/Since I began working I need the rest.

Even for women from traditional backgrounds, the experiences of work could simply change the place of religion in a working person's life.[44]

Catholic women's experiences as workers changed as well. According to the Catholic ideology of the period, women's very engagement with waged work subverted natural law. Mothers were strongly discouraged from working at all, and the young single women whom church leaders recognized as legitimate wage earners were taught to internalize a gender-specific mindset of selfless devotion and quiet suffering for the sake of the extended family. But by 1925, an observer from Detroit's League of Catholic Women noted a major "change which has taken place in the economic status of women." Later in the decade, the Industrial Committee of the National Council of Catholic Women hosted a successful conference in Detroit focused on the theme of "Women in Industry." Its rhetoric drew both from a specifically Catholic theology as well as a broader reform tradition that justified women's involvement in "public" affairs by illustrating the impact of political and economic conditions on the "private" world of the family. When Catholic women took action, the Council claimed "they will be performing spiritual and corporal works of mercy for their own families, the families of their neighbors and friends, families throughout the whole country and families within the Church."[45]

African American women were, like Catholic women, famously devout. Not only did religion serve emotional and ethical needs, but many black women found within their churches a measure of social authority and even autonomy denied them in almost all other spheres of life. Mary Magnum Johnson, for example, became a revered "church mother" in the Pentecostal denomination, the Church of God in Christ. Migrating from Memphis with her husband (a church elder) in 1914, the Johnson couple "dug out" a small storefront church in a neighborhood populated by *bear traps*—low-rent tenements notorious as scenes of prostitution and gambling—and built a stable, successful, and interracial storefront church in Detroit. Likewise, the Rev. Jacqueline Elder became full pastor at the Church of True Believers (a "house church") in the 1930s after the male pastor fled in disgrace. True Grace Baptist Church eventually acquired a full-time male pastor and 150 members, but the congregation began in the home of Beatrice Malone, where three of the four elected officers were women. The Church of God and Saints of Christ, meanwhile, relied on female members (known as "Gleaners") to make public solicitations of charitable funds from the mayor's office in the depths of the Depression. Finally, some women struck out entirely on their own, becoming successful mediums in spiritualist churches, where they interpreted sacred messages or dreams, and sold sacred products like oil, charms, and amulets.[46]

Of course, while black women certainly found fulfillment and a measure of autonomy in their churches, they also operated within a pervasive, traditionalist gender ideology. Mary Magnum Johnson was, after all, a "church *mother*"—a phrase pregnant with the expectations of feminine nurturing. Within all sizable congregations, Mothers' Boards and other maternally themed groups organized the identities of churchwomen around marriage and motherhood. Pastors' wives were always influential and respected figures, but their public role was dependent upon their connection to a prominent husband. Fannie Peck, for instance, was the wife of Bethel AME Pastor William Peck. While Fannie became an outstanding civic leader in Depression-era Detroit, the name of the organization she founded—the Detroit Housewives' League—indicates the limited public roles that black women might legitimately play. In the midst of the Depression, Shiloh Baptist pastor Solomon Ross even went so far as to criticize black working women for losing sight of "her true and shining place" as "wives and home-makers"; despite the devastation that the Depression wrought on black Detroit, and the fact that few black families could survive without the income of women, Ross taught that women should remain "within one's own scope."[47]

The role of gender within working-class religious consciousness was, ultimately, ambiguous and even contradictory. Traditional definitions of masculinity and femininity could be modified by religious norms—masculinity made more domestic, femininity endowed with a measure of agency—but countervailing currents remained powerful, even hegemonic. It was believers' ability to alternate models within a framework of religious idioms and identity that enabled a tenacious religious consciousness.

The Moral Meaning of Work

Religion needed to speak to workers' lives and influence workers' consciousness where the majority of it was formed: at work. The experiences particular to wage labor in an industrial age would have been deeply impressed in workers' psyches and memories. Moreover, the outlines of industrial experience did not bode particularly well for encouraging religious beliefs. From the mechanical magnificence of the plants themselves, to the competitive scramble for jobs, to the rough culture of the floor, industrial life seemed to present a secularized spectacle of rationalized machines and routinized workers. Still, whatever the distasteful aspects of factory toil, most workers respected the importance of work itself, and many felt that labor was an elemental, unavoidable aspect of human existence. Work also bred a certain seriousness and legitimacy. It could nurture a sense of personal self-worth, bind families together in knots of obligation, and grease the wheels of social interaction. Significantly, many workers still looked to religion to provide some greater sense of meaning and purpose for a laboring life. Religious idioms, naturally, offered no single answer to the workers' dilemmas—indeed, given workers' own mixed feelings about their working lives, how could they?—but they did allow workers to fuse ambivalent (sometimes seemingly contradictory) aspects of identity and experience into a comprehensible consciousness.

Within the difficult constraints of industrial life, workers strove for a modicum of control, security, and dignity. This desire was astutely rooted in experiences common to nearly all workers, who frequently endured a pervasive sense of powerlessness in the face of the "shape-up-or-lay-off" ideology. Even during the auto industry's terrific boom of the mid-1920s, insecurity and cycles of unemployment haunted the industrial landscape. In February of 1926, while employers triumphantly reported a new record high of 270,395 men employed in Detroit industries, workers at the City Rescue Mission claimed that they "could not take care of the crowds" of desperate men and had run short of both food and beds. In late 1926 and early 1927, the Ford Motor Company briefly closed to change models and left thousands of workers adrift in an ad hoc welfare system. Moreover, the deprivations of the Depression hit Detroit's economy earlier and harder than most other cities. As early as 1928, John Dancy was advising potential Detroit-bound migrants to reconsider in the face of a menacing wave of unemployment.[48]

Once lucky enough to find steady work, workers faced labor that was unusually hurried, monotonous, tiring, often an assault on the senses, and occasionally quite dangerous. Workers might find their souls quickly deadened by difficult, menial work and a pervasive industrial malaise. Paul Rajewski remembered his grandfather coming home after a workday in the Cadillac foundry and pouring a double shot; "that man didn't speak to anybody until after he killed it." Nestor Dessy started working at the Chevy Gear and Axle plant in 1927, and recalled a similarly mirthless experience. "You went into work, you did your job, you didn't talk to the person working next to you, no smiles on the face, no laughing or cutting up or nothing. You just went in, did your work, stopped and went home." African American autoworkers, meanwhile, were almost always granted the most grueling and grimy jobs available. Typically, this meant a life in the foundry. Charles Denby's first job in the 1920s consisted of shaking out a car's oil pan in Graham Paige's foundry:

> The job was very rugged. I had to work continuously, as fast as I could move. The heat from the cubulos [furnaces which melted the iron] was so hot that in five minutes my clothes would stick with dirt and grease. We'd walk through on our lunch period to talk with a friend. We couldn't recognize him by his clothes or looks. The men working in his section would tell us where he was . . . by his voice.

It should hardly be surprising that such powerful working experiences shaped religious attachments and moral norms. According to Myron Watkins, a sociologist who went undercover on Detroit's shop floors in 1920, the radical individualization of work produced by the assembly line and the rise of scientific management encouraged "a lack of collective morality" among the laborers. Workers responded to their environment with acts of petty rebellion, including "plain thieving and deliberate though unsystematic and uncoordinated sabotage." Although autoworkers were better paid than almost all other industrial workers, Watkins concluded that "their hearts are not in their work" and there was, consequently, "absolutely no loyalty" toward employers. For Watkins, the "work ethic"—that venerable standard of American morality cherished since colonial days—had been overwhelmed by the modern factory.[49]

But Watkins's eulogy for the work ethic was premature. For one thing, work remained revered as a nearly sacred undertaking by Detroit's industrial elite. Cadillac Motors president Henry Leland, affectionately described by the minister William Lovett as a "Puritan of the old type," typified this current. Leland argued that each individual worker should demonstrate the virtues of thrift, honesty, and personal initiative; he opposed labor unions because he felt they undermined these traits. Nobody embodied this ideology more thoroughly than Henry Ford. Ford himself was hardly orthodox in his orientation to organized religion, although he informed Detroit minister Edgar Stidger that he kept "a Bible in every room in his house." As with Leland, the "work ethic" was embedded within a rugged individualism that remained absolutely central not only to Ford, but the broader industrial ideology of Fordism. "Let every American become steeled against coddling," Ford exhorted in one of his memoirs; "let weaklings take charity." For Ford, every industrial problem was essentially a personal problem; with a stronger moral fiber and deeper work ethic, any worker could attain self-sufficiency. A 1908 issue of the *Ford Times* company newsletter, which encouraged workers to "exalt the Gospel of Work. . . . Because idleness is a disgrace . . . and work minus its spiritual quality becomes drudgery" illustrates the religious-cultural underpinnings of Ford's industrial regime.[50]

Workers would become increasingly cynical about such self-satisfied pronouncements during the 1930s; still, they were not insensitive to the appeal of the work ethic. Skilled workers, especially, exhibited tremendous craft pride (one might even say arrogance), and disdained slackers. Most workers wanted to keep their jobs and please their bosses, and hence many no doubt strove to demonstrate their fidelity to prevailing norms about work. Significantly, working-class churches themselves promoted this ethos, often in blunt and didactic fashion. Congregants at the east-side, heavily working-class St. Rose of Lima parish, for example, were sternly alerted in 1928 that the "world is no place for idlers." At Shiloh Baptist Church, worshippers were similarly reminded that "Jesus said to idle men, 'Go ye also into my vineyard and work and whatever is right I will give you.'" Shirking was not accepted in this world.[51]

In fact, religion-based attitudes toward work were complex and ambiguous. Much as workers might have disliked their jobs, the cultural idioms of their religion stressed responsibility, respectability, diligence, and honesty. Within Detroit's laboring classes, work was both a curse *and* a gift. Work could grind a person down; but, on the other hand, it also ensured the survival of the family, long the center of working-class social and economic life and the ultimate font of religious consciousness. Working-class men, in particular, labored not just for wages but also to prove the legitimacy of their authority in the domestic sphere. Working-class women, whether wage earners or not, were also almost uniformly preoccupied with preserving their families. The content of work may have been distasteful, but the *act* of working—of earning a living from the sweat of one's brow—was widely esteemed within working-class communities. With self-discipline came respectability; with paternal rights came responsibility for providing. These currents fed into each other, admonishing destructive behavior and rewarding diligence.[52]

Self-discipline and proper comportment was one major avenue toward respectability, a message thoroughly communicated to parishioners at St. Rose of Lima: "be courteous in church. . . . Do not laugh, talk, or distract others." These stern words did not demean most Catholics. To the contrary, they inculcated a respect for sobriety and stability essential for the maintenance of working-class families. Similar currents animated African American churches. Even in makeshift storefront churches, men and women dressed as well as possible, attesting to the social importance of the church and the respectability of its supporters. Ernst Goodman, a Jewish union organizer, learned this lesson in the 1930s when he appeared one Sunday morning to speak to the congregation. "I had never been in a storefront church," Goodman recalled. "I walked in, in a shirt and trousers, without a jacket and without a tie. As I walked in, I saw all these people dressed up in their Sunday best. . . . Finally, the pastor saw me and called on me to speak. He introduced me by saying that Mr. Goodman doesn't understand the custom about Sunday church and has just come from home. I felt so embarrassed. . . . I wouldn't have gone to a white church the way I was dressed, but I did to a black church because I didn't understand." Many African American men who worked at the Ford factory wore "Ford badges" to church, thus reclaiming their difficult labor in the context of the church and its significance for black communities. African American women, meanwhile, utilized proper dress and disciplined comportment at church services to symbolize that their spiritual lives transcended the material limitations of their class.[53]

Other storefront churches also illustrate the importance of steady habits and disciplined behavior. St. Paul AMEZ church, located in Delray, was one such "basement affair." According to the Urban League, 1,500 African Americans lived in the church's vicinity, and most residents attended either St. Paul, a congregation of the Church of God in Christ, or a large Baptist church (the "great majority" of blacks in the area were Baptist). Employment for St. Paul congregants was "fairly good." Many men worked at area factories or at Ford, and housing in Delray was reported as better than normal. Another Urban League worker visiting a congregation of the Church of God in Christ—often dismissed as one of the poorest and least restrained denominations—came away impressed: "The church here was well-attended and the members were average and above the average in appearance, social bearing and deportment." Although the church buildings were unimpressive and bore the marks of want, these congregations were composed of worshippers who valued work, respectability, and community.[54]

Class, as social scientist Michael Zweig puts it, "is about the power some people have over the lives of others, and the powerlessness most people experience as a result." Religion was one way for workers to mediate economic powerlessness into an overriding cultural narrative of justification and due rewards. At the workplace, grime and denim clothed the working body; at worship, these same bodies were clean and well-coifed, the men were in fine suits, and the women were bedecked in ornate hats. On the job, workers were subject to the often arbitrary authority of the shift boss; in the congregation, worshippers were (at least theoretically) equal to each other, and usually exercised significant control over the careers of pastors (and even Catholic priests). In the market-driven world of work, only money mattered; outside the market-driven world, God raised the talents of drummer-boys above the riches of kings. Working-class religion thus functioned on a dual level: it molded the individual consciousness through the emotional and ethical satisfaction it offered, and it simultaneously tied individuals within the network of an extended community. Perhaps it also contained powerful negative attributes; by reconciling church culture with the norms of industrial discipline, some might argue, religious consciousness limited the social and political imagination of workers who struggled within a system that left them worn-out and frustrated but it robbed them of the tools with which to create a newer, better system. At the heart of this tension was the ambiguity of workers' own efforts to reconcile their working lives with their spiritual selves.[55]

The Clergy, The Laity, and Religious Power

Working people were agents in the shaping of their religious identities. But, as Marx points out, workers were not free to make their lives "just as they please"; rather, they operated "under circumstances directly encountered, given, and transmitted from the past." In other words, workers were constrained by the realities of economic and political power, and, as historian Robert Orsi notes, "power is fundamental" to religious cultures. It is "pointless to study religion without reference to power," Orsi concludes, "pointless and irresponsible." By "power," Orsi means not only the social power that some have over others, but also the ideological power of language, ritual, and belief to shape peoples' "common-sense" notions of right and wrong, civilized and uncivilized, normal and deviant. Church teachings and religious practices erected boundaries between the sacred and the profane, the bodily and the mystical, the exalted and the taboo. In working-class congregations, these everyday lines of power were typically drawn between worshippers in the pews and clergy in the pulpit. Clergy were usually highly respected local figures, and some were unfailingly revered. More than a few Catholic priests, African American ministers, and southern-bred white revivalists were themselves children of the working class; they understood working-class culture and earned their congregants' respect for having risen through brains, talent, and ambition. Nevertheless, working-class congregations could be acutely leery of clergy who accrued too much influence or demanded too many unevenly shared sacrifices. Workers felt a deep sense of ownership in their churches—not least because the churches were built through often-spectacular sacrifice on the workers' part. If autonomy and self-determination was denied them at the workplace and often many other public institutions, they expected otherwise at church.[56]

Working-class Catholics were, famously, highly respectful of clerical prerogatives. The authority of priests and the church hierarchy was widely understood as a nonnegotiable component of Catholic culture. When parishioners at St. Rose of Lima were also encouraged to regularly receive the sacrament of penance, they were also reminded that their priest had absolute authority to judge the sin, could choose whether the penitent deserved mercy, and could demand actions to absolve the sin. The penitent "should abide by the sentence, as all Catholics do." On these clearly *religious* issues, Catholics were indeed willing to revere their priests. In this sense, the local priest wielded tremendous ideological power that shaped and policed the boundaries of religious practice.[57]

When it came to the actual administration of the parish, however, working-class Catholics could prove defiant of authority and stiff-necked in defense of their perceived rights. Especially at ethnic parishes, vociferously contending factions frequently congealed. The most infamous incident occurred at St. Albertus, the city's first Polish parish. When a popular priest, Dominic Kolasinski, was removed in December of 1885 for refusing to show the parish's financial records to the bishop, laity loyal to the departing priest (led by laywomen) barricaded the church and pelted both the new priest and his police escorts with hard clumps of frozen mud. A few months after his removal, Kolasinski dramatically founded his own parish, Sweetest Heart of Mary, just down the street from St. Albertus; 4,000 families joined the renegade priest.[58]

Animosity remained heated between pro- and anti-Kolasinksi factions for years. Indeed, one young man was killed in a fistfight between pro- and anti-Kolasinski parishioners on Christmas Eve, 1891. Even after suffering excommunication from Detroit's bishop, the people of Sweetest Heart staunchly asserted their right to support the pastor of their choice (the parish was later reincorporated into the Catholic diocese in 1894). Well into the twentieth century, Clara Swieczkowska recalled, the feud between St. Albertus and

Sweetest Heart of Mary remained a wedge issue among her east-side neighbors. While friendly on most other issues, people considered the matter of church affiliation too sensitive a topic for open conversation.[59]

The Kolasinski episode was especially acute, but such disturbances were not entirely atypical. In 1919, Fr. Joseph Folta, the third pastor at Sweetest Heart of Mary, was forced to leave after he vaguely reported "negative and untoward happenings." When the priest was reassigned to St. Casimir on the west side, his installation nearly caused a riot. Four carloads of police escorted Folta to his new church and were compelled to patrol the parish grounds until near midnight. Likewise, Fr. Sigmund Dziatkiewicz was "suddenly" removed from Hamtramck's Our Lady of Queen of Apostles parish in 1925, for reasons parishioners found dubious. "This transfer caused one of those controversial episodes which were quite common in Polish parishes, conflict with diocesan hierarchy," the church history candidly admitted. Fr. Albert Mrowka, Dziatkiewicz's replacement, was greeted by a group of parishioners who barred the door. One woman smacked him with an umbrella, and another group of women "formed themselves into a sentry group, taking turns day and night" to prevent his moving into the rectory. The parish itself fell into disagreement, and after Bishop Joseph Plagens made derogatory remarks about the protestors, feeling ran even higher. Eventually, the Rev. Stanislaus Wasilewski was accepted, but half-heartedly.[60]

Polish immigrants were willing to riot and risk official church censure—even excommunication—because for them, as working-class laborers, the building of a parish came at deep personal sacrifice. Consequently, immigrants and their descendants felt deeply invested in their parish and its property—indeed, priests were often unsettled by the sense of ownership in parish affairs that immigrants exhibited. This sense of financial proprietorship was not restricted to Poles. Fr. Ernest Rickert's decision to build a school in the Hungarian-dominated Holy Cross parish produced a $42,000 debt, which was "not looked upon favorably by some parishioners," as the church history gingerly put it. Priests often looked to demonstrate their clerical acumen—and, hence, prove to their bishops that they were worthy of promotion—through administrative achievements and, especially, massive buildings programs. The parishioners of Holy Cross were not insensitive to how their priest planned to advance: through a reckless stewardship of their hard-earned contributions. Fr. Rickert lasted less than one year in the parish.[61]

Money was also a major source of contention within African American churches—silver-tongued singers of the gospel might be prophets, but they might also be after a profit. Even the pious John Dancy recognized that some preachers sought only "money and prestige. You have to watch out for the motives." Ulysses Boykin, too, regretted that many migrants to the North fell prey to "spiritualists, cult leaders, and fortune tellers" who "made large sums from releasing 'tips' to those who played the 'numbers' and policy game." Guardians of Detroit's Community Fund were kept on a constant vigil, seeking to verify the credentials of numerous self-appointed religious leaders who appealed to them for assistance. The United Universal Christian Army, which modeled its quasi-military structure, street-preaching, and tambourine-tapping fund drives on the Salvation Army, was one such organization. When the group sought public monies in 1933, Dancy cautioned against such aid, describing the group's leader, the Rev. C. H. Folmar, as a "boss, straw-boss, and fore-man" of the group—essentially a con artist. Folmar didn't get his grant, but he persisted in Detroit, attempting to administer charity in his own fashion and continuing to run afoul of social service authorities. Even ministers of reputable denominations exposed their parishioners to dangerous financial risks. As Dancy acutely observed, many AME pastors overextended their congregations while trying to "build up [a] reputation as a Churchman with his Bishop." The tensions between ordinary believers and church leaders structured the making of working-class religious practice.[62]

Expressing Emotions

Workers' religious consciousness intertwined powerful sources of personal and social identity within a value system that prized discipline and respectability. But religion also appealed to the imagination with meaningful narratives and powerful symbols. It held out hope—of prayers answered or sin conquered. It provided an ethical interpretation of history, promising rewards for faith and fidelity, with punishment to the haughty and godless. Most importantly, religious expression offered tremendous emotional satisfaction. Through prayer, song, and ritual, religion provided a venue in which the welter of human expression—joy, anxiety, desire, despair—might be channeled, controlled, and expressed in a socially approved manner. Religious consciousness reconciled these competing needs and impulses: on the one hand, the need for discipline and quest for respectability; and, on the other hand, the desire for emotional release and longing for connection with a transcendent power.

For Catholics, this personalized, internalized, and emotional expression of faith was facilitated by the rise of a devotional culture. Devotionalism led to a mass market of material objects: statutes, rosaries, scapulars, even holy water, all of which allowed believers the chance to create sacred space in their own home and tangibly connect with the object of their prayers. It also gave rise to the establishment of numerous "cults" (in a technical, not derogatory sense), in which Catholics pledged special allegiance and offered a set of prayers to one particular saint, usually one believed to confer particularly desirable gifts. This widespread cultural current within American Catholicism certainly found expression in Detroit, as new cults to St. Jude and, especially, St. Theresa, spread across the city. In July of 1930, St. Mary Magdalene Church established a shrine to St. Jude, recognizing that "recent years have witnessed a revival of devotion to [Jude], due to the gratitude and zeal of those who have experienced the power of his intercession." Saints could certainly elicit this "zeal." Folklore collected among Polish American Detroiters that came of age during the 1930s also found that saint stories continued to be orally transmitted within families and were commonly used to describe the natural world. Saints, in short, anchored the emotional center of many lay Catholics' attachment to the church.[63]

"Parish missions" also animated the spiritual lives of the laity. These "missions" were usually conducted by a visiting order of priests over a two-week period, with one week targeting women and another week aiming at men. As the historian James O'Toole has aptly phrased it, "What the altar call was to Protestant evangelism," a return to the sacraments was to Catholic parish missions. Series of intense prayers and masses were intended to culminate in deeper emotional attachment to the church, expressed at the mission's conclusion by a deluge of confessions and reception of the Eucharist. Sometimes, the results of a mission could be long-lasting. For instance, a mission by the Capuchin Fathers in 1921 at St. Alphonsus parish in Dearborn prompted the establishment of the Christian Mothers Society, one of the parish's earliest—and soon numerous—church groups. The interweaving of church-led activities—missions, novenas, devotions, and so forth—with the autonomous practices of the laity combined to produce a rich interior life for many working-class Catholics.[64]

Catholics knew that their faith produced a "strong emotional bond," and that this culture was distinctive. In 1930, a writer in Detroit's Catholic newspaper related a disagreement with one of his non-Catholic friends, who complained that the Church's emphasis on architecture, imagery, and rituals seemed "garish." The writer happily admitted that Catholic churches produced a lush, even sensual environment; in his mind, such an atmosphere more appropriately expressed the "joy of prayer." Two points stand out. First, Detroiters recognized that the style and idioms of religion—not just formal beliefs—mattered, and that Catholic styles and idioms produced a specific lens through which human life was experienced. Second, Catholicism was meant to be felt and lived, not abstracted or sanitized. Juxtaposed against the cool distancing of his overly "intellectual" friend, the writer of the *Michigan Catholic* essay also suggested a class line dividing the world of learned elites from the everyday emotional richness of working-class Catholics.[65]

Emotional expressiveness was even more elemental to African American churches—especially in the storefronts. This drive for emotional fulfillment characterized much of African American church life. However, emotions were rarely uncontrolled, despite the concerns of critics (which are discussed more thoroughly in Chapter 2). An observer from the Urban League offers an important description of worship at a Church of God in Christ congregation: services, he noted, were "well-ordered but quite emotional." We might choose to replace "but"—which worked to temporize or negate approval—with "and." Emotional worship, in other words, was ebullient while simultaneously adhering to standards of discipline almost universally understood by worshippers themselves. But working-class worshippers demanded the right to define these terms on their own. The simple motto of the True Light Baptist Church captured the essence of this sensibility: "Hear the Choir Sing and the Pastor Preach," it promised, "and You Will Come Again." If the music and preaching did not provide an emotionally edifying experience, many working-class African Americans found little reason to attach themselves to a congregation.[66]

Blending "This"-Wordly and "Other"-Worldly

Workers' religious consciousness was constantly attempting to fuse ambivalent threads into a coherent and satisfying whole. One of the more persistent divides that religious culture fused together was the seemingly divergent impulses toward pragmatism and supernaturalism. On the one hand, workers often believed in a powerful world filled with divine agents resting just outside the boundaries of normal human experience. Much of worship and prayer, of course, sought to direct energy out into this distant realm. But on the other hand, workers often thought—and even expected—that supernatural beings visibly acted in the human world. Indeed, they anticipated that devotion to supernatural patrons in the "other" world could, or should, produce pragmatic results in this world.

Working-class people often viewed their relationships with supernatural agents in personal, individualistic terms. This partly explains the ubiquity of home shrines, particularly in Catholic homes. Ida Santini's grandmother, for instance, was "very devout," keeping an altar in her bedroom containing votive candles, a statue of Mary holding the infant Jesus, and a picture of the Holy Family on the wall. But these relationships were often expected to provide some tangible evidence of divine preferment. Santini's grandmother, therefore, also believed that her religious vows would bestow divine favors. Similarly, African American women attended services of the spiritualist leader Father Hurley both for spiritual support and the promise of practical results. While the conviviality of Hurley's spiritual services inspired, he also promised to invoke supernatural powers for any woman who wanted greater control over her marriage.[67]

No other aspect of working-class religion demonstrates its pragmatism with greater clarity than the belief in miraculous healing. Indeed, faith in miraculous cures speaks to the material hardship of working-class life as much as it does the cosmology of the religious imagination. Consider the sobering reality of Polish Detroit. In 1929, the last year before the full onset of the Great Depression, Poles were the second largest group in the city (after "native whites," a category that likely included many second- or third-generation Poles) to present as welfare cases for "alcoholism, death in the family, handicaps, work injury, marital incompatibility, child neglect, non-support, sickness, widow- or widowerhood, and imprisonment." Such conditions caused the Rev. Ralph Cummins, who founded a settlement and a free clinic in Hamtramck, to accuse Poles of "not [caring] very well for the health of their children." It was little wonder that the Bureau of Catholic Welfare lamented "the problems facing the Polish people of our city" that same year. Even as late as 1939–1940, infant mortality rates among Poles were the highest in the city, ranging around 40–60 per 1,000 births.[68]

Given such desperate conditions, folk cures and saint cults held a deep appeal. A perpetual novena to Mary at Our Lady of Lourdes at St. Mary's church in the early 1920s lent credence to these hopes, as reports of miraculous cures emerged and were quickly disseminated in the Catholic press. Folklore, too, often instructed the faithful in the proper method of garnering a saint's healing powers. One woman, raised in a rural Polish community in Michigan before moving to Detroit as a teenager, remembered learning that, "to cure ulcers, kneel in manure and pray to St. Joseph." Poles in Dearborn were instructed to go to a wishing well, close their eyes, and throw something down the well for a sick person; if a petitioner heard the stone drop, the afflicted would be healed. One Polish woman even recalled learning that curing a sore throat required the murder of another person.[69]

If saints possessed the power to heal, supernatural agents might logically be invoked to inflict harm as well. According to Hungarians in Delray, the deaths of twelve neighborhood men were caused by the witchcraft of "Aunt Rose" Veres. A Detroit newspaper reported:

The neighbors tell wild tales of the charms she can conjure and of the havoc she has wrought when she "cast an eye" on some unfortunate. "She has strange powers," they explain naively. "She boasts that she cannot stay in jail, that she knows the magic to get out. We are afraid to catch her eye. She can make our children sick and our husbands lose their jobs. She knows all kinds of magic."

"Aunt Rose" was arrested only after African Americans moved into the neighborhood and agreed to testify against her. Poles in Hamtramck were likewise described as a hard-living people marked by "superstitions and low standards of living which are revealed in fatalism." Similarly, belief in the "evil eye" lingered among some Detroit Sicilians well into the 1950s. The survival of such stories was strongly tied to the creation of ethnic identities, especially for the first-generation migrants.[70]

Attitudes toward health, sickness, and healing also allow another perspective on the folk customs of the African American working class. From the earliest days of the great migration, ministers promoted the benefits of modern, institutionalized medicine from their pulpits. Speakers from the Detroit Department of Health appeared regularly in black churches, instructing worshippers on matters such as hygiene and child welfare. The Detroit Urban League and Second Baptist Church ran their own popular day-care and health clinics. These efforts at medical outreach were, to a large extent, well-meaning and helpful, but they were also undergirded by the broader belief that black workers from the rural South remained in many senses premodern and that their acceptance of progressive medical experts represented a key step in black workers' assimilation to modernity.[71]

While they no doubt appreciated access to modern clinics, many ordinary African Americans simultaneously remained firm believers in, and practitioners of, hoodoo (conjuring), the traditional system of folk medicine that produced both healing cures and enfeebling curses. As with the Catholic belief in saint healing, African American reliance on hoodoo reflected a richly imagined cosmology as well as the often awful reality of life in poor neighborhoods. As late as 1940, nearly 14 percent of all black babies born in Detroit did not survive infancy. Hoodoo, with its strongly pragmatic orientation and emphasis on bodily ailments, offered workers a sense of immediacy and control over important life matters.[72]

Hoodoo also provided a link to the store of memory and culture that African Americans had developed in the South. But, in the process of remaking religious consciousness in the North, practitioners of traditional African American healing often adopted titles—"Doctor," "Reverend," or "Professor," for example—and relied on the black press to publicize their talents. Urged to embrace the medical, educational, and media institutions of modernity, hoodoo workers obliged—in furtherance of traditional practices. Not only did northern hoodoo produce a new class of self-styled "professionals," but the use of roots, herbs, and potions was also melded onto entirely new religious movements. Spiritualism, for instance, combined "communication with the spirit world and deceased . . . magico-religious rituals such as the use of charms and incense, astrology, and an altar" that evoked the iconography of Catholicism. This new church was almost an exclusively northern phenomenon, and nowhere did spiritualism experience the growth it did in Detroit. In 1924, local leaders formed the National Colored Spiritualist Association, and by 1940, Detroit housed somewhere between 200 and 300 spiritualist churches. As these examples demonstrate, working-class religious consciousness was combinative, fusing ambivalent currents and beliefs into a durable, if sometimes paradoxical, whole.[73]

Assimilating Mass Culture

As the mediums and messages of a burgeoning mass culture infiltrated American communities in the 1910s and 1920s, workers and clergy struggled to synthesize the older symbols and rituals of religion with the new, secular paradigm of American popular culture. Within families, neighborhoods, and congregations—at the intimate and particular level of daily life—religious consciousness continued to reinforce a sharply grained identity rooted in the specificity of place and peoplehood. But in the age of radio, movies, and advertising, religion was no longer able to definitively shape the idioms, norms, or narratives of a national culture. Mass culture was, moreover, commercially produced and widely distributed; it operated according to the principle of return on investment, and sought its audience in the aggregate, reaching past the barriers of ethnicity, neighborhood, parish, or fellowship. It attempted not to instruct or censor but to divert, amuse, or titillate. Religious consciousness in the interwar years was therefore shaped by a fusion—awkward and incomplete, but nevertheless important and wide-ranging—between the local world of novenas, prayer meetings, and family altars and the mediums of a national "mass" culture.[74]

The imprint of mass culture on workers was everywhere apparent. As a speaker to Detroit's St. Mark's Brotherhood observed, "[a]ny one who mixes with the immigrant today" knew that working-class newcomers—both African American and European—sought "active" and "primitive" recreation, not the refinements of religion and high culture. Religious leaders agreed with this assessment, and worried that the rise of mass culture presented a threat to morals, social order, and their own cultural authority. "Pleasure is rampant," one minister intoned; "reverence, purity, sobriety, sympathy, fairness," were all threatened as a consequence. William Rutledge, Detroit's police commissioner, cautioned Catholics in 1926 that "recreation has been entirely commercialized" and young people exhibited "little desire to spend the leisure hours in the home." African American leaders especially worried about migrants' recreational habits, claiming frequently that black workers' "recreation and amusement have no less an influence on their personal morals and community life" than disciplined work habits or proper religious comportment. As religious leaders fretted, Detroit's cell of anticlerical socialists prepared to joyously dance on the grave of oppressive superstitions. "Baseball, kelly-pool or the moving picture show are proving stronger attractions for the modern worker than the churches," *The Proletarian* asserted. As long as workers "come into contact with the greasy wheels of industry," the nostrums of the supernatural would begin to seem incredible and unbelievable. Religious consciousness would need to be remade, assimilating elements of the pervasive popular culture.[75]

Movies offered perhaps the most serious competition to the cultures and communities of local congregations. So ubiquitous was the act of moviegoing and the presence of movie theaters that a study of wage-earners' living expenses in Detroit assumed that most families attended the movies at least once per week (and this was in 1921, after two brutal years of postwar recession). Perhaps more importantly, theater owners in Detroit did not build highly concentrated districts but took their products "to the people," as a study from 1923 found. Between 1920 and 1930, the number of movie theater seats in Detroit grew by 69 percent, and the number of theater buildings within 13 miles of the city center grew from 140 to 184. The movie theater, then, became as much a neighborhood institution as the church or parish. Indeed, by the late 1930s, the Detroit Archdiocese counted 30 "Polish" parishes, at a time when 25 movie theaters operated in Polish-dominated neighborhoods; in other words, just less than one theater per church. "Movie theaters," the leader of Detroit's Catholic Youth Organization could say by the late 1930s, "have taken the place of healthful recreation."[76]

Movies posed a twofold threat in the eyes of religious leaders: first, the content of many films seemed to encourage "immoral" behavior, ranging from sexual promiscuity to outright criminality; and second, the physical presence of theaters themselves created an unregulated new social space where young people might amuse themselves in the dark. Catholic leaders seemed especially alarmed by the movies, and moved decisively to discipline moviegoing habits. Scanning the headlines of the diocesan newspaper in the 1930s, one could be forgiven for assuming that the most pressing issue in Catholic Detroit was not the Great Depression, but the corrupting influences of the movies. In 1934, the "Legion of Decency" barreled into Detroit with the full-throated support of Bishop Michael Gallagher. The Legion graded films according to a code drafted by the Jesuit Daniel Lord. Individual Catholics were encouraged to sign pledge cards vowing to abstain from films that fell afoul of Lord's code; at least 300,000 pledges were distributed in Detroit during the Legion's first year. Critically, however, Gallagher realized that, for all the declarative dos and don'ts he might issue, his flock was hardly pliant and docile. Catholics were no longer village peasants who might be commanded into obedience; they were now autonomous consumers in a marketplace of culture. Therefore, Gallagher and his fellow bishops realized that they must tap into the very consumerist logic that the Legion ostensibly opposed. Explaining the Legion's strategy, Gallagher argued that "[T]he only sensitive spot in [moviemakers'] make-up was their pocketbooks." In effect, he presented the Legion as a massive, principled consumer boycott and made participation an act of piety, loyalty, and cultural politics.[77]

The ordinary Catholics who signed Legion pledges and tried to avoid "unacceptable" movies did not reject the new mass media of film; indeed, the Legion knew that such a goal was quixotic. Film remained a powerful purveyor of national culture, and Catholics remained avid consumers. Rather, the idioms and narratives of film were reconciled with religious conscious-ness. One sign of this process can be seen in churches' own private screening of carefully selected films; in some parishes, movies were shown as early as the 1920s, a tacit acknowledgment of the unique narrative power of film. As Hollywood adopted its own "code" (stimulated by the threat of a Catholic boycott), filmmakers began producing movies featuring Catholic characters and themes, from the crime drama *Angels with Dirty Faces* to the inspiring comedy of *Going My Way*. The Catholic reconciliation with movies might be detected in other, subtle ways; when a remodeled St. Aloysius Church opened in downtown Detroit in 1930, the triple-decker architecture bore a pronounced resemblance to the era's movie palaces. For lay Catholics, such strategies likely eroded mental boundaries dividing their church from the broader cultural and economic marketplace.[78]

African Americans expressed an even greater enthusiasm for film. A survey from 1920 found that movies were the primary source of amusement for Af-rican Americans; church socials came second. The experiences of Nathaniel Leach were probably typical for many black youth in the 1920s and 1930s; his "regular Sunday routine" consisted of attending church and Sunday school, followed by a walk down the block to catch a movie. The African American experience, however, stood apart from other working-class groups because of the pervasive racism of the early twentieth century. Black theatergoers were often harassed by hostile whites and sometimes openly barred from attending "whites-only" theaters. Churches thus acquired even more importance to African American social life; as the Detroit Urban League's John Dancy put it in 1926, "Negroes are not made to feel welcome in many of the amusement places so their leisure time is spent in the Church." Lillian Duplessis, a longtime member at St. Matthew's Episcopal Church, agreed with Dancy, noting that, for her family, "all our entertainment, more or less, centered around our church." Jean Ernst Mayfield's parents moved from Virginia to seek the "five dollar day" at the Ford plant, and she too "had lots of fun with all of the surrounding churches. We were surrounded by Tabernacle, Hartford, John Wesley. . . . We would do social things with the church."[79]

But black churches did have strong competition for leisure time: the saloons, pool halls, and gambling clubs that rubbed shoulders with churches along the streets and boulevards. Coleman Young, later a vocal activist and Detroit's first black mayor, remembered that "churches and blind pigs [saloons] shouldered each other tolerantly" in the neighborhoods of his youth, although such equanimity was not always easily balanced. In 1929, for instance, Robert Bradby of Second Baptist Church complained to Detroit's police commissioner of a "gambling house almost wide open next door to our church." The proprietor had tried to disguise it with a "For Rent" sign in the window and a back alley entrance, but the gambling den was clearly an open secret in the neighborhood. Such criminality "right in the face of a church, where there are hundreds of little children who come to Sunday School and to the services, and thousands of people come each week," was difficult for Bradby to swallow. Over time, however, as juke-joint blues became commercialized by record labels and radio broadcasting, it would fuse ever more deeply with the sacred world of the gospel choir and the dynamic preacher (who sometimes found themselves in the same recording studio).[80]

Radio produced an entirely different response among nearly all clergy than had film. Unlike the movies, radio was considered a potentially positive moral force. Throughout the 1920s, radio programming was more easily controlled by local communities than film, providing unique opportunities to ethnic groups and church communities that aimed to saturate the air-waves with their particular values and traditions. Additionally, radio was infused with the ideology of domesticity; buzzing in the heart of working-class living rooms, radio might keep young people nestled within an extended web of family. Clearly, working-class families placed a remarkable emphasis on acquiring radios. When interviewers visited Eva Anderson, they found her living in a small, dilapidated room, with "a radio but no phone." A Wayne University sociologist provided a similarly revealing snapshot when he noted the few material possessions of one working-class Mexican couple: two religious statues, "one of the Blessed Virgin and one of the Sacred Heart," and one luxury item, a radio. For working-class families, radios had become nearly essential items.[81]

Radio blurred the lines between sacred rituals and secular leisure among the working classes. Churches quickly capitalized on the new technology when Detroit's two major radio channels were launched in the 1920s. WWJ, owned by the Detroit News, first broadcast on August 20, 1920, and church services, which began appearing as early as 1921, proved especially popular. William Stidger of St. Mark's Episcopal Church asked listeners to respond to his sermons, and received 25 letters a day for two weeks. Indeed, one young men's Bible class was so moved by a radio sermon that it "went out and stopped people on the street, asking them to join their group." St. Paul's Episcopal Cathedral soon became known as the "Radio Church," with the pulpit open to invited speakers of different faiths. Church choirs became regularly featured on WWJ. In 1923, St. Paul's even donated a van to WWJ, creating a "Radio Church on Wheels." Revealingly, the radio church pastor claimed that he started services by giving "baseball scores, markets, [and] weather forecasts" as a way to "hook" listeners—yet further indication of the growing interrelationship between secular and sacred forms of leisure. The trauma of the Great Depression would make radio religion even more central to working-class religious consciousness: from the Southern Baptist J. Frank Norris to "radio priest" Fr. Charles Coughlin, radio preachers evoked reassuring, even nostalgic, feelings of spiritual inspiration while simultaneously linking religion to a fervent variety of political and economic creeds. Indeed, the road to remaking religious consciousness in the 1930s—forging more explicit links between believers' political, class, and religious identities—often began on the airwaves.[82]

Conclusion

Working-class religions created a complex, sometimes paradoxical set of idioms and practices for mediating the ambivalences of industrial life. Despite the significant differences separating immigrant Catholics and migrant African American workers, Detroit's working classes shared a common historical context, and they internalized and performed religion in remarkably similar ways. Both Catholics and African Americans made a religious consciousness that forged a sense of tradition and peoplehood, while simultaneously providing a source of richness and meaning for individual lives.

But did working-class religion offer anything more than personal meaning? In particular, did it provide a cultural resource for engaging with social problems, for spurring political movements, or for empowering rights at the workplace? As the next chapter illustrates, these would emerge as central questions as Detroiters struggled to resolve the "labor question" in the early twentieth century.

2. Power, Politics, and the Struggle over Working-Class Religion, 1910–1938

Between late 1936 and early 1937, American labor relations were transformed by the legendary sit-down strikes of the nascent United Automobile Workers (UAW) union against General Motors. The success of the UAW sent cultural shockwaves throughout Michigan's working class. Reflecting on the lingering effects of the sit-down strikes in June of 1937, Michigan Governor Frank Murphy admitted to graduating students at the Catholic-affiliated University of Detroit, "the world we live in is a confused and sorely perplexing place because it presents a constant and ever-changing challenge to our social idealism and Christian faith." Murphy was both a stalwart supporter of Franklin Roosevelt's New Deal (indeed, he would soon become a Roosevelt appointee to the Supreme Court) and a devout Catholic. To Murphy, these two identities were complementary sides of an organic whole. As he argued to the students, the ultimate solution to the so-called "labor question" was a combination of "progressive principles of social betterment" and "Christian idealism." Murphy's own role in the sit-down crisis was critical; his refusal to send National Guard units to break the strike largely compelled General Motors to recognize the union. For Murphy, his support of collective bargaining rights was both a political and a moral decision. Working-class voters had sent Murphy to Lansing, and the union itself, in Murphy's view, was a critical tool for building a good and just society. Considered "in the light of Christian principles," Murphy announced, the social movement of workers was "not only desirable but fully in keeping with the philosophy of a democratic people."[1]

Murphy's attempt to combine a religiously based moral vision with a philosophy of democratic politics was deeply rooted in American life. From the founding of the republic, ministers and theologians had argued that, as free citizens, Americans were also "moral free agents." Untethered from state-supported, institutional religious authorities, and thus standing alone to choose either good or evil, Americans surely required some methods and criteria for making the best moral choice. Religion was thus crucial to American democracy, according to this perspective, because it alone could instill the virtue, faith, and self-discipline necessary to maintain social bonds and provide a proper guidance for free individuals engaged in the difficult business of choosing their governors.[2]

If Murphy followed a long line of thinking about the relationship between religion and democracy, however, he was speaking more to his own historical generation when he placed the issues of the working class at the heart of his address. There was no more serious threat to the democratic civic order in the early years of the twentieth century than the massive social changes unleashed by industrial, corporate capitalism and its ungainly twin, rapid urbanization. The growth of a seemingly permanent class of urban wage earners, condemned to toil on the fringes of middle-class security, domesticity, and morality, threatened to undermine the very promises of democratic life. This "labor question," as historian Steve Fraser aptly puts it, was "not merely the supreme economic question but the constitutive moral, political, and social dilemma of the new industrial order."[3]

Influenced by Progressivism in political culture and modernism in religious culture, American religious leaders of the late nineteenth century began to outline a response to the labor question, which they came to call the "social gospel." At its most basic level, the social gospel proposed that Christians could no longer limit their concerns to the salvation of *individual* souls but needed to concern themselves with the *social* "sins" of poverty, child labor, alcoholism, and related problems. Like the Progressivism and modernism from which it emerged, the social gospel was deeply enamored with science, rationalism, and efficiency and confidently predicted that an invigorated democratic state could reform social ills. In order for this to transpire, however, religion needed to meet certain ideological expectations. It should espouse a universalistic doctrine of ethics, promote civic responsibility, and nurture a capacity for critical reflection and intellectual individualism. The religion preached at Detroit's prestigious Central Methodist Church, for instance, contained "a sort of civic aspect," according to religious sociologist H. Paul Douglass. St. John's Episcopal Church, just down the street, boasted "an admirable series of lectures on civic topics" and employed professional social workers with an unusually high "technical competency." The broad-minded and socially engaged religion of Progressive Christianity visible at Central Methodist and St. John's was a necessary precursor for a healthy democracy.[4]

To most social gospellers, the religions of the working classes failed to meet these social criteria. Indeed, working-class religion appeared positively alien and dangerous: alien, because of its "primitive" rituals and beliefs, and dangerous, because of its social disengagement, obscurantism, and presumed susceptibility to authoritarian leaders. Considered from this perspective, working-class religion was less a demographic term than a politicized construct, an invention of language and ideology on the part of culturally powerful observers who ascribed social meanings, intellectual values, and political implications to working-class religious practices. The legacy of the social gospel for the largely Catholic and African American workers of Detroit, then, was ambiguous. On the one hand, proponents of the social gospel were generally hostile toward the religious consciousness that workers made during the Progressive Era. But, on the other hand, the social gospel also offered a potentially powerful discourse for advancing issues of economic justice and for intertwining religious and political identities.

Under the strains of the Great Depression, the relationship between workers' political consciousness and their religious culture shifted decisively. Frank Murphy—a progressive Catholic who attained political success by appealing directly to working-class voters with a religious vernacular—symbolized this transition. At nearly the same time, the rise of the UAW transformed Detroit from an overwhelmingly "open shop" city into America's quintessential "union town." And, just as Murphy heralded a new political imaginary for the working-class faithful, the UAW also initiated a new relationship between working-class religion and the labor movement. Union leaders acutely recognized the deep nature of working-class religiosity, and endeavored to minimize any tensions between religious and class identities. More, the union aggressively claimed the social gospel for the working class, and recast the entire labor movement through the prism of religious consciousness. The remaking of working-class religious consciousness, then, was deeply implicated in the rise of the New Deal Order.

The Social Gospel and the Making of Working-Class Religion

In the winter of 1914–1915, Detroit confronted a sudden epidemic of unemployment. Working-class families across the city entered an economic free fall virtually unbroken by any public safety net. The city's Board of

Poor Commissioners hurriedly requested and received $100,000 for emergency relief—more than double its normal yearly budget. Hordes of "begging men, because of their genuine working-class type, their earnestness and their wretched condition, awoke strong sympathy and stirred the civic conscience. One man, for instance, committed suicide a few moments after appealing in vain for work at the Mayor's office." Detroit's religious institutions responded bravely. The McGregor Institute, a major establishment for the homeless sponsored by the Episcopal Church, accommodated 650. The Social Service Department of the Unitarian Church "procured the use of an abandoned church in a central location at the corner of Woodward Avenue and Sibley Street. It then turned the active management of the place over to a group of working men. . . . This place was commonly known as the 'I.W.W. Flop,' and . . . was run quietly and democratically in spite of the fact that the Police Commissioner 'refused to recognize it, or even to supervise it.'" The United Jewish Charities provided the "most effective sectarian relief society in the city"; meanwhile, the Catholic Saint Vincent de Paul Society located jobs for 510 needy Catholics, and "enlisted the organized aid of neighbor to neighbor more systematically than any other society."[5]

The churches' bracing encounter with the brutal human costs of industrialization during the winter of 1914–1915 epitomized the great moral challenge of the age: how to apply religious ethics to the vagaries of a free-market economy, while preserving a democratic framework. From this context, Detroit's religious leaders joined others around the country and across the Atlantic to promote a social gospel. Key to this new social religion were the core traditional values of charity, empathy, and "witnessing": charity, to supplement the objective material deficits of workers and the poor; empathy, to recognize and dignify the subjective suffering of human persons; and witnessing, to reform morals, promote domesticity, and bring benighted people into a religious community.[6] To this end, churches and charities performed, in an ad hoc fashion, some of the functions of an otherwise paper-thin welfare state, although this aid was always serving the larger mission of remaking working-class religion in accordance with modernist norms.

Detroit's churches and synagogues became enthusiastic sponsors of that most emblematic of Progressive-Era institutions: the settlement house. First Presbyterian Church, for instance, founded the Dodge Community House to deliver essential social services for the immigrants of Hamtramck, while the Congregational Men's Club sponsored the Franklin Street settlement, Detroit's oldest. These and other middle-class, mainline congregations promoted a religion that, its supporters claimed, enriched democratic social functions and hence deserved praise and encouragement. Some of these—such as the

Dodge Community House, the YMCA and YWCA, and the Houses of Hospitality established by the Catholic Worker movement in the 1930s—developed into much more than simply providers of aid; they metastasized into genuine "spearheads of reform," in which heterodox political ideas were discussed, union organizers met with neighborhood residents, and racial boundaries were (at times) purposely rebuked or ignored.[7]

The social gospel promoted specifically *religious* missions, not simply a nebulous set of ethics. The Baptist Christian Center, for instance, recruited African American Ford workers for English lessons and other vocational activities, always laced with opportunities for Bible classes. Other Protestant institutions like the Episcopal City Rescue Mission and the McGregor Institute spread a mixture of charity and religious culture among working-class men, and there are some intriguing indications that at least some men responded to the evangelizing efforts. In 1924, the McGregor Institute not only placed thousands of men in jobs but also ran fifteen religious services including preaching and Bible classes each week. Three hundred men typically gathered for Sunday fellowship, and mission workers were convinced that material aid "leads many of them into religious services." Between January and October of 1926, the City Rescue Mission reported that 89,696 men had attended religious services, 3,258 offered prayer requests, and 1,341 "[c]onfessed Christ." Meanwhile, many unmarried workingwomen found the YWCA a center of both social and religious life. At the Industrial Women's Service Center on East Grand Boulevard, thousands of working women grabbed dinner in the café, socialized in the Recreation Room, and utilized the halls "for patriotic and other parties." In addition, Bible classes were held daily, and Vesper services were held every Sunday afternoon. In 1919, these Bible classes enrolled 225 women, while Vespers attracted 5,179 women over the course of the year. Occasionally, social workers excitedly reported evidence of spiritual energy among working-class women. In 1926, the Esther House settlement boasted of its "beautiful Friday services . . . in the nature of a real old fashioned revival. Seven girls testified to their conversion."[8]

Social gospellers always viewed the family as the ultimate source of both religiosity and healthy communities (indeed, they could not really imagine healthy communities without pious families). Catholic charity workers at the St. Rita Community House exemplified this line of thinking. While investigating conditions east of the Ford factory, they found many erstwhile Catholics "living in a district far from spiritual influence and known because of its moral and sanitary defects as 'Hell's Half Acre.'" In establishing a settlement, the goal was not just the provision of needed services, but also the rehabilitation of Catholic families, a goal that seemed to enjoy some success.

"From a little class of thirty children collected for religious instruction," an early report detailed, "the Sunday School grew to approximately 300, and the first year over 160 children made their First Holy Communion. Indeed in some cases the parents who had not approached the Sacraments for years returned once more to their duties." Another Catholic case worker described the concerns of church leaders and the mission of Catholic charity: "The worker in visiting the home finds father and mother not attending to their religious duties, perhaps even affiliated with another church on account of a friendly neighbor or a visit from a minister. Then begins the missionary work and the center becomes the guiding influence in the family."[9]

But some Progressives found that simple charity and witnessing failed to indict the deeper, socially systemic moral injustice intrinsic to the ascendant Fordist ideology; these mostly Protestant ministers edged toward a more radical, prophetic social gospel of industrial justice. I. Paul Taylor, a congregational minister in Highland Park, worked undercover for several weeks at the Lincoln car company in 1917, and emerged from the experience to write a scalding exposé of auto-work. Arguing for the necessity of higher wages, Taylor argued that "the prophets without exception . . . sided with the people and their rights as over against the rights of property." Critiquing the inadequacy of Detroit's welfare provisions during the economic downturn that followed the First World War, Taylor found his justification in scripture: "I believe it is James who included the care of widows and orphans as one of the qualifications of 'pure religion, undefined.' If we are going to make this a Christian community and country," Taylor insisted, it would be accomplished through establishing decent wages and pensions. Ultimately, in 1920, Taylor left the church and organized the Detroit Labor Forum, an educational program for labor leaders. Taylor was joined in his concern by Detroit's renowned Episcopal bishop Charles Williams (a stalwart supporter of Henry George's "single tax" campaign), who launched the Church League for Industrial Democracy with a daylong series of meetings and speeches intended to unite Christianity with the labor movement. Five thousand copies of the proceedings were mailed to notable Detroiters. Unfortunately, Williams died shortly after launching the organization, and it shriveled on the vine.[10]

Nobody sensed the religious gap between the working and middle classes more acutely than Reinhold Niebuhr. Although by the 1940s he would become America's most revered theologian, in the 1920s, Niebuhr was serving his first pastoral appointment at Detroit's Bethel Evangelical Church. The emergence of an industrial working class loomed over Niebuhr's Detroit experience. "[T]he real moral issue Protestantism faces," he argued in the mid-1920s, "is whether it is simply a sublimation of the economic interests and prejudices of a certain class or whether it has vigor to qualify those interests and transcend them." In 1926, he took to the pages of the liberal *Christian Century*, attacking Henry Ford's claims of generosity and benevolence. What troubled Niebuhr so deeply were not just the observable social effects of industrial exploitation, but Ford's simple-minded self-delusion—his insistence that hard work alone solved all problems and dissolved hierarchies of class.[11]

Ford's naïveté was compounded by the moral apathy of the Protestant churches—the result, Niebuhr claimed, of churches being "too much of a middle class institution." Because the middle classes lacked "any high degree of social imagination" and never directly experienced class exploitation, they were unbothered by its existence and unmoved to confront it. I. Paul Taylor felt similarly frustrated with churches' class bias. "I went in to hear one of the most popular preachers of Detroit lately when he was scheduled to speak on 'America's Labor Problem,'" Taylor wrote in 1919. "His whole contention was that there were no classes and there was no real struggle and there would be no apparent one if everyone did his or her share and speeded up production." At its most prophetic, then, the social gospel recognized class as a reality of the social power structure and lamented religion's own complicity in making an ideology to support the system.[12]

The social gospel made important contributions to the quality of working-class life and opened up an important public debate on questions of economic justice. However, the social gospel did not arise from or reflect the religious consciousness of workers themselves; to the contrary, most of the thinkers and activists who founded settlements and shaped the social gospel were committed to a liberal, progressive, religious modernism, and were ill-at-ease with the seemingly alien religious cultures of working-class "others." Although devoted to the amelioration of industrially generated misery, social gospellers remained perplexed by—even hostile toward—workers' autonomous expression of religion. Consequently, working-class religion, when social gospel reformers addressed it, was commonly criticized via a shared vocabulary of culturally freighted keywords: cultish, clannish, docile, fatalistic, other-worldly, hysterical, mystical, authoritarian. These terms constructed a narrative placing working-class religion on the margins of modernity, and even questioned whether workers' religion posed a basic threat to democratic, open societies. In order to be an effective bulwark for democracy, social gospellers argued, religion needed to reflect the norms of modern, rational, social-scientific thought; working-class religion, social gospellers feared, was likely to foment fanaticism, divisiveness, and political corruption. In formulating these ideas, assumptions, and categories, the social gospel invented "working-class religion" and misread working-class religious consciousness.[13]

African American religion, with its long tradition of exuberant music and powerful preaching, was especially susceptible to charges of overemotionalism. In 1918, when large numbers of black migrants began settling in Detroit, mainline church leaders expressed alarm over "forms of religious fervor" among these newcomers. A mayor's report from 1926—chaired by none other than Reinhold Niebuhr—similarly worried that African American migrants suffered from a "lack of emotional stability." Consequently, working-class migrants found their spiritual needs met by "irresponsible religious organizations that experience mushroom growth in the city." Storefront churches, in particular,

> lack stability and discipline in their group life; the moral fruits of their religious fervor are frequently jeopardized by a type of hysteria which issues in social phenomena of dubious ethical value. The leadership in these groups is usually without adequate educational equipment and free of any kind of supervision or discipline.

In denouncing working-class black religion as "irresponsible" or "hysterical," the report reinforced the idea that "appropriate" religion should be both emotionally disciplined and socially beneficial.[14]

Critics of working-class Catholicism picked up the same theme. One sociologist described immigrant Hungarian Catholics as "emotionally unstable and very suggestible." Similarly, the supposedly "peasant mind" of Sicilian and southern-Italian Catholics found cathartic release only during celebrations of St. Joseph's Day, when boisterous brass bands marched with religious icons through Detroit's Italian neighborhood. Additionally, the institutional Church's strong support for devotional culture generated a deep emotional response among laypeople, who embraced patron saints with "gratitude and zeal," in the words of Detroit's Catholic newspaper. Southern white evangelicals, meanwhile, exhibited what one scholar described as a "deep drive for individualistic expression" in their religious lives, often through rollicking revival services.[15]

While working-class religion was denounced as overly fervent, it was also simultaneously accused of producing a sullen resignation toward the disappointments of earthly life. Polish immigrants, for instance, were described as suffering "low standards of living . . . revealed in fatalism." Southern whites were likewise "trained to a stoic concealment of their emotions" by a "rigid, patriarchal morality." In response, critics said, workers turned toward other-worldly superstitions, especially folk medicine. Various investigators found the use of charms, curses, herbs, and folk elixirs, along with a generalized acceptance of faith healing, widespread among Poles, Hungarians, Mexicans, African Americans and southern whites alike. The problem, as Reinhold Neibuhr told his friend Fred Butzel, was that this type of religion "excites the people but doesn't do them any good, doesn't give them any leadership." Reflecting the broader modernist belief, Neibuhr suggested that religion was "good" when it directly engaged with social problems. Churches that substituted other-worldly exuberance for social ethics were, in Neibuhr's words, "the lowest form of religious life."[16]

Middle-class social gospellers like Neibuhr drew a connection between a society's religious culture and its political order. In particular, the clannish insularity and authoritarian structure of some working-class religions seemed to present a major impediment to progressive advancement and enlightened social reform. Catholics were especially presumed to lack intellectual independence. Detroit's Hungarian Catholics seemed "sheep-like" to one observer, locked in helpless thrall to the parish priest. The lives of tens of thousands of Polish immigrants who surrounded the Dodge Brothers plant were "enveloped in religion," and the authority of the parish priest was rarely questioned. African Americans, too, formed "cults," built around the intense and supposedly authoritarian charisma of particular ministers. As Detroit Urban League president John Dancy described them, cults depended upon an "emotional attitude for holding on to its membership" and served "no real worth while purpose in the community." Dancy especially criticized the Church of God and Saints of Christ on these grounds; the congregations were "for the most part very poor . . . [and] made up of people who are tremendously emotional and usually below the average in intelligence." At its worst, modernists believed, such a "corrupted" form of religion threatened the very operating of the social order. And, as civil society fractured during the early years of the Great Depression, social gospellers fretted: how would these allegedly benighted religions form an adequate political response?[17]

The Churches, the Social Gospel, and Organized Labor

If social gospellers were critical of working-class religious consciousness, they were similarly suspicious of working-class labor activism and trade unionism. While they often supported movements to protect female and child laborers, and condemned corporate misdeeds, social gospellers largely rejected the idea that economic structures produced intrinsic divisions between classes. Rather, they felt that the major source of conflict during the industrial age was a breakdown in communication and regrettable loss of brotherly codependence between labor and capital. In 1919, confronting the most bitter labor conflict in a generation, pastor Charles Brent characteristically preached: "When both sides [labor and capital] accept the principle of partnership, which is the business aspect of brotherhood, the rest of the road will be smooth. Upon this it is the Church's duty to insist." Singling out labor radicals for condemnation, Brent concluded, "their worst enemies and sure conquerors are those who aim to make the social and industrial order conform in the broad and in detail to Christ's bold purpose of world-wide brotherhood." Similarly, Mac Wallace of Brewster Congregational Church argued that, "This country recognizes the unalienable rights of both labor and capital, and it demands not a limited brotherhood, but a universal brotherhood." Christianity, to social gospellers, called for a universality of common interests and a basic humanity shared by all people. If the churches could serve as neutral umpires and "consciences" for the community, then the labor question might be brought to a peaceful resolution.[18]

Trade unionists and working-class activists were duly skeptical of the supposed class neutrality of the social gospel—a movement that, after all, was firmly rooted in the educated middle class. Indeed, tensions between unionists and preachers emerged along with the first craft unions early in the antebellum era. Repeatedly over the course of the nineteenth century, ministers insisted that they respected the dignity of labor, but opposed unions as tyrannical or "un-Christian" conspiracies against the public; just as often, unionists insisted not only on their own personal religious zeal, but on the churches' betrayal of the principles of "true Christianity" and transformation into churchianity.[19]

Still, labor leaders in the early twentieth century recognized the potential for powerful allies and potent cultural resources in the social gospel movement. Finding a proper balance between the church and the union, however, proved tricky. When American Federation of Labor (AFL) Vice President Daniel Keefe addressed a meeting of the Detroit pastors' union in 1907, he emphasized the AFL's efforts on behalf of temperance, education, and moral elevation; little was said about the more controversial (but also more central) issues of strikes and boycotts, or the hotly contested judicial injunctions that were hampering the AFL's effectiveness. Moreover, Keefe's tone at times hearkened to earlier labor critiques of churchianity. "I do not hesitate to say," Keefe intoned, "that if the church had adopted the policy of today 20 years ago and preached the policy of love, instead of talking hell fire until it lost all its terrors and the smell of brimstone had a wholesome flavor, labor and the church would have been closer together long ago. . . . We [The AFL] want your advice and approval and help; but we want it to come from the heart, not the tongue." Likewise, when William Bailey, president of the Detroit Federation of Labor, addressed the Church League for Industrial Democracy in 1919, he pointedly observed that "I have attended a great many churches. . . . I have often thought of what a pleasure it would be indeed to have the opportunity to do the talking and have the ministers do the listening." Bailey's slightly sour distinction between ministers who talked and workers who quietly listened suggested a thinly buried resentment that some workers nurtured against their supposed social betters in the pulpit. For his part, AFL president Samuel Gompers, in an open letter that circulated among Detroit's clergy, sought to persuade religious leaders that unions and churches "have much in common." Both worked to protect women and children, and hence protect the family. Unions created a higher standard of living and more free time, and therefore paved the way "for the enlivenment of spirituality." Many unions, according to the AFL, advanced the cause of temperance, supported no-work laws on Sundays, and helped Americanize new immigrants. Yet, despite these commonalities, the AFL also clearly acknowledged that a good number of ministers supported union-busting industrialists—and, to that end, they "seem to be against us."[20]

The Detroit Council of Churches, meanwhile, did little to cultivate strong relations with labor unions. In 1922, the organization discussed bringing the famed New York social gospel preacher Charles Stelzle to speak on social evangelism, but it ultimately shied from the anticipated controversy, concluding that industrial matters should not be discussed for "at least a year." Again in 1923, representatives of the Department of Industrial Relations within the DCC hoped to bring together a major employer, a religious leader, and a labor leader for a conference on "Christianity and Industrial Relations" but could only aspire "in time to bring about a better understanding between the churches and the working classes." It was optimistic mainly in the modest, conservative goal of finding a labor leader "who can be trusted to present their case very acceptably to church audiences." Despite the enthusiastic support of Reinhold Niebuhr, who led the Industrial Relations division of the DCC in the 1920s, efforts to hold monthly discussion groups on industrial justice were considered by him only "a partial success."[21]

Events in 1926 further soured relations between unionists and church leaders and amplified the perception that the reigns of religion were held by the upper classes. In October of that year, the AFL declared it would hold its annual convention in Detroit, and it coordinated with the Federal Council of Churches (FCC) to arrange for speakers to blanket the local pulpits on

Labor Sunday—the Sunday corresponding to the AFL's convention. Initially, the DCC responded cordially, making all the usual arrangements to place AFL representatives in local churches. But suddenly and ignominiously, the DCC, along with the Young Men's Christian Association, rescinded its offer to the AFL. Labor was to be banned from the pulpit. William Green, president of the AFL, responded in slack-jawed shock that "sinister" forces must have been working behind the scenes. Newspapers across the country picked up the story. In short order, Green's conspiracy theory was confirmed: an open letter printed in the newsletter of Detroit's Board of Commerce warned ministers against hosting speakers who attacked "our government and our American plan of employment." Moreover, the Board of Commerce and Building Trades Association had threatened to withhold a $5 million donation to the construction of YMCA buildings unless the DCC turned AFL speakers to the street. Instantly, labor's bewilderment boiled into anger. When an embarrassed James Myers of the FCC arranged a last-minute meeting at a Congregational church, Green declined to attend. Instead, AFL delegates like Ohio State Federation of Labor President John Frey declared before a packed and cheering convention, "when mammon dominates the altar, then Christianity has passed away."[22]

Indeed, the conflict between the AFL and the churches reflected increasing levels of anticlericalism and "free thought" within working-class culture. At the heart of working-class anticlericalism were two related ideas. The first, as radical pamphleteer Bennett Stevens wrote, was that "doctrines and ritual of the churches are powerful means of developing attitudes of subservience among the workers. . . . The worker is taught to reconcile himself to poverty, for it is 'God's will.'" In other words, radicals echoed a typically Marxist analysis, arguing that working-class religious consciousness thrived on obscurantism, mysticism, and fatalism: ironically, the same discourse employed by the middle-class social gospel! (albeit for different ends).[23]

Usually, however, anticlericals focused less on religious ideology per se, and more on exploitative preachers. The "bad preacher," in fact, became a potent meme within working-class culture, symbolizing all the dishonesty, corruption, and greed of the privileged classes. Detroit's socialist speaker Joe Brown, for instance, loved to ridicule clerics in his lectures. "If his audience found his economic talk uninteresting or boring," Brown's friend Frank Marquart recalled, "Joe quickly switched to religion and told why men of the cloth chase after women: 'They don't work, they eat well, they have excess energy, and they have to get rid of it somehow.'" Brown took a satiric approach, but often, complaints against preachers were more serious and pointed. African American radicals associated with the Good Citizenship League complained throughout the 1920s, "We are tired of picked leaders [especially Second Baptist Church's Robert Bradby] meddling into cheap politics and selling the race out for the husks from organized graft under the guise of religion and sociology." More angrily, in 1922, the group lamented: "Every election the preachers sell us out to the highest bidder. . . . Politics messed up with the preachers, have got us where we are—political outcasts." The Catholic Evidence Guild—a lay-led body of street preachers generally sympathetic to workers' issues—confronted exactly this dynamic when it took to Detroit's parks to proclaim the Gospel in 1937. An audience of five hundred people clustered for two speeches, but

> [a]t the close of the two question periods, a swarthy worker arose and put the weasel query: "Why do the preachers eat the poor man's bread?" This produced a ripple of laughter, but it did not disturb the rather surprising respectfulness of the crowd. The question was clearly understood as but half sincere . . . and was answered in effect that the "Laborer is worthy of his hire."

While the Church dismissed this "swarthy" weasel, the incident sharply reveals a key tenet of anticlerical belief across working-class Detroit: churches and preachers lived like parasites off the toil of others while fashioning fancy apologias for the privileged classes. In the hothouse of the 1930s, the question was acute: would the emergence of the new industrial unions produce a decisive rupture between the working classes and the churches?[24]

Religious Consciousness and the Making of the New Deal in Detroit

Beginning in the 1930s, workers' political and religious consciousness shifted, broadened, and intertwined as Detroiters responded to the travails of the Great Depression. Although the Depression sent chills throughout America, it hit Detroit with special cruelty. In the early 1930s, 223,000 workers—nearly 50 percent of the city's labor force—were unemployed. By July of 1931, the Mayor's Unemployment Committee (MUC) bleakly reported to President Herbert Hoover that the "unwilling victims of unemployment" had virtually bankrupted the city. The federal government was consequently forced to fund the city's relief efforts for the next two months. The deterioration reached a new low after Detroit's banks were abruptly forced into a mandatory "holiday" in February of 1933, just weeks before Franklin Roosevelt's inauguration. Even the Urban League's optimistic John Dancy felt his nerves fray: "In the language of the street," he confided to a friend, "we are in a hell of a fix."[25]

While early New Deal programs offered some assistance, the typical fluc-
tuations of auto-industry employment combined with burdensome relief
caps for laborers employed on federal works projects ensured that the agony
of insecurity rippled throughout the entire decade. Indeed, after dipping late
in 1933, the number of unemployed auto workers shot up to 40,000 in July
of 1934. In December of that year, four and a half years into the Depression,
the Department of Public Welfare documented a record 66,000 families on
relief rolls. This volatility remained unrelieved until the Second World War
virtually eliminated industrial unemployment.[26]

Responses to the Depression fueled a real and dramatic change to Detroit's
political culture. Prior to the 1930s, Detroit had been heir to the tradition
of Lincoln, to the Yankee politics of the "bloody shirt," and to the Protes-
tant-Progressive synthesis of moral uprightness and "clean" government. In
1912, this Republican, Protestant elite formed the influential Detroit Citizens
League, which, by 1918, had successfully rewritten the city's charter along
typically Progressive lines. Yet, in the 1930s, this tradition found itself over-
turned by what one study described as a "bloodless revolution." In Franklin
Roosevelt's first presidential campaign, Michigan's urban centers increased
their Democratic vote by 190 percent. In the decade of 1930–1940, Detroit
Democrats swelled from a bare majority to a decisive 66.3 percent of the city.
Even openly radical candidates for city office, often backed by the aggressive
new industrial unions, became ubiquitous in political races of the late 1930s;
few won, but the Depression nevertheless fully remade the possibilities for
political discourse.[27]

Out of this background, Frank Murphy emerged as the apotheosis of religious politics in the New Deal era: committed to faith, community, and
social justice. Murphy rose from a local judge in the 1920s to become Detroit's
mayor in 1930. He later ascended to the governor's office in 1936, and finally
to the U.S. Supreme Court. A long-standing member of the Holy Name society, Murphy expounded a Catholic social doctrine throughout his political
career. Shortly after the First World War, for example, Murphy expressed his
belief in a "practical Christianity," noting that Christ "taught not only moral
righteousness, but social justice." According to many observers, this language
was not mere political cant. Thurman Arnold, assessing Murphy's career in
the late 1940s, described him as "deeply religious"; he "believed with Thomas
Aquinas that God had endowed men with reason so that they could make
their temporal law . . . conform to natural right."[28]

More to the point, Murphy clearly understood that his electoral success
in Detroit rested upon a working-class base and reflected a working-class
sensibility. Often, he issued broad appeals to the generic "Common Man"

with language rooted in a Catholic ideology that idealized organic corporatism and distanced itself from liberal individualism. In 1931, for instance,
Murphy celebrated the 40th anniversary of Pope Leo XIII's famous labor
encyclical, *Rerum Novarum*. According to the mayor, the pope's prolabor
encyclical demonstrated that "A GOVERNMENT'S WHOLE REASON FOR
EXISTENCE" was to promote the common good and, especially, to defend
the rights of working people. Murphy took care to position his Catholicism
in the broadest possible terms, singling out Jesus's "Sermon on the Mount"
(with its promise that the meek would inherit the earth) as the heart of his
civil religion: vaguely philosophical, deeply sympathetic to working people
and the victims of poverty, and utterly uninterested in the specifics of doctrine. Murphy even connected his own political quest for social justice to
a religious narrative, claiming that the common trauma of the Depression
had transformed Americans into "plain folks once more." In fact, Murphy
expected this economic shock to produce a spiritual renewal: "as the beautiful
beatitudes begin to roll and reverberate across great wastes of the country,"
the mayor intoned, "there will be an awakened people, following anew the
greatest Leader of mankind."[29]

Murphy's fusion of New Deal liberalism with a self-consciously "common folk" religiosity made him perhaps the most popular politician of his
era, and not only among Catholics. Murphy was also an important figure
in the incorporation of African Americans into Detroit's political life. His
performance as judge during the 1926 murder trial of African American
doctor Ossian Sweet was widely acclaimed in black circles, and his rise to
mayor's office helped encourage broader politicization. Maggie Gibson, a
socially engaged, working-class church matron, epitomized the sentiment
of many African Americans. "I am praying for you Mr. Murphy," she wrote
shortly after his mayoral victory in 1930; "You shall have our vote 10 years to
come." In 1936, the coalition that supported Murphy (and, at a national level,
Franklin Roosevelt) elected Charles C. Diggs as Michigan's first Democratic
African American state senator, a position Diggs would hold for many years.
Murphy's career helped decisively shift black party loyalties from Republican
to Democrat, and energized black political participation. Whereas only 27
percent of Detroit's eligible blacks voted in 1930, that number shot up to 57
percent just two years later, and continued to rise to 66 percent in 1938.[30]

Murphy's use of clergy in public service laid a critical bridge between
the social gospel of the Progressive Era and the state-building of the New
Deal. As long as the premise of religious pluralism was respected in making
their appointments, city and state leaders felt safe entrusting clergy with
public duties that revolved around the "labor question" or other matters of

social justice. When he created the Mayor's Unemployment Commission in 1930 to provide what he hoped would be a more dynamic and democratic supplement to the Department of Public Welfare, Murphy selected Dr. Frank Adams, pastor of First Universalist Church, as vice chairman. When Adams was forced to move on in 1932 (his congregation could no longer afford to pay him), Murphy replaced him with Father Edward Hickey of Sacred Heart Seminary as sole chair. Leon Fram, a prominent Detroit rabbi, headed the Labor Subcommittee. Meanwhile, Rev. Frederic Siedenburg, a Jesuit at the University of Detroit and nationally known supporter of the Catholic "social justice" movement, found himself in virtually constant service to the city and state. In April of 1934, Siedenburg chaired the Detroit Regional Board for the settlement of labor disputes, and when this body was replaced by the Detroit Regional Relations Board (the local branch of the National Labor Relations Board) in September of that year, he retained his appointment at the request of President Franklin Roosevelt. In 1935, Siedenburg chaired a committee to assemble "facts relating to the relief situation," and, again in 1937, Siedenburg and two non-Catholic clergymen served on the Emergency Michigan Mediation committee at the request of then-governor Frank Murphy, convened to address the dramatic Flint sit-down strikes. Indeed, Siedenburg emerged as something of a role model for the new public religion; when Norman Kinzie was appointed to lead the Social Service Department of the Detroit Council of Churches in the early 1940s, one minister encouraged Kinzie to emulate Fr. Siedenburg, "who represented his church in most every civic endeavor, and whose influence was felt by all who were fortunate enough to be associated with him."[31]

Murphy thus created a new political imaginary for working-class congregations, who increasingly came to fuse their religious identities with their civil identities as "makers" of the New Deal. Churches reciprocated the rhetoric of New Deal politicians, thus producing a symbiotic relationship between the transformed political identities of many worshippers and their religious consciousness. The *Michigan Catholic*, for instance, praised the New Deal as a "peaceful social revolution," and assured its readers that "the President's conception of the duty of government to aid the homeless and jobless" accorded fully with papal social encyclicals. Sometimes, the message was less subtle. Parishioners at St. Rose of Lima were instructed to "Vote Straight Democratic" in the 1934 elections. A full-page advertisement in the parish bulletin promised that Ray D. Schneider, a candidate for the U.S. Senate, would "complete the New Deal."[32]

Working-class churches ultimately created liminal spaces between the "public" realm of the citizen and the state, and the "private" realm of families and communities, spilling freely into each sphere. In Detroit's Depression-torn Black Bottom, for instance, future Detroit mayor Coleman Young recalled that "people turned to church and politics." More significantly, Young noted, "the two were symbiotic. Every pastor had a political position, and every address had multiple purposes." As civic actors, churches and religious leaders offered critical services, built public coalitions with like-minded groups, and served as important social spaces. Not just the practical coalition, but the very political culture that emerged in the 1930s depended upon and reflected this hybridity: politicians frequented local pulpits, secular social workers learned their trade at religious colleges, Catholic priests commiserated with Protestant ministers and Jewish rabbis on public boards, religious charities worked alongside public welfare providers, and a good many congregants were educated on government programs and policies on Sunday mornings. Religion consciousness had proved integral in constructing the identities and shaping the experiences of the working-class majority that eventually flooded into the New Deal coalition.[33]

Within this context, Detroit was completely transformed from "open shop U.S.A." to an unambiguous "union town," heart of the United Auto Workers (UAW). In working-class Detroit, the union joined the church, the neighborhood, and the amusement center as the nexus of social life and cultural expression. Churches, however, were often tepid toward the UAW in the formative years between 1935 and 1938. The organizer John Zaremba bluntly declared, "We did not have the church support." Sometimes, workers had to choose between their church and their union. Walter Dorosh, a Catholic activist in the Ford plant, admitted to having "a big fight with my minister. I just told him, 'You just go jump in the lake. I happen to know who is organizing the plants.'" Likewise, UAW activist Kenneth Roache declared, "I never went to church after I was eighteen years old." The Detroit Council of Churches, meanwhile, maintained a deafening silence on labor issues in the 1930s, which probably indicated its unwillingness to endorse the UAW. Owen Geer, a Methodist pastor at Mt. Olivet Community Church in Dearborn (a city created as the virtual political fiefdom of Henry Ford), provides the exception that proves the rule. One visitor described Geer as "stimulated by a profound spiritual conviction to spread Christianity in the community and particularly to the forsaken working men." In 1937, Geer backed the UAW's effort to unionize Ford, offering his pulpit to union leaders. Taking this stance in Henry Ford's very backyard constituted an unusually bold and risky action rarely found among Detroit's Protestant church leaders (a few years later, Geer successfully led the effort to rewrite Dearborn's city charter, effectively freeing the city from what he called the "economic over-lord-ship" of Ford).

The minister recognized that his congregants were directly affected by issues the union was addressing; many had been injured on the job and received paltry compensation, while others were terrorized by Ford's "security" specialist, Harry Bennett. But, even though he established the Detroit Religion and Labor Fellowship and recruited "a number of fine Christian leaders for the labor movement," Geer felt that he had done "nothing spectacular in the field of religion and labor reconciliation." In fact, throughout the UAW's critical, formative years, Geer felt "very much alone so far as the support of the general church goes" when it came to issues of working-class activism.[34]

UAW organizers found themselves caught between countervailing cultural currents. On the one hand, they could not ignore the promising appeals of the social gospel, which offered a powerful moral justification for unionism, potential political alliances with New Dealers like Frank Murphy, and the ever-enticing lure of respectability. On the other hand, they worried about becoming too embroiled in religious issues, which might balkanize workers along ethno-religious lines, or energize the individualistic, antiunion religious rhetoric of industrial elites. At the same time, anticlerical and antireligious voices were always whispering around working-class institutions, urging an abandonment of all religious pretenses as both diversionary and divisive. Nevertheless, religion played an important role in the public narrative that the UAW constructed in its early years, for a very simple reason: religion remained a very real cultural force among the working classes that the UAW could not ignore, even had it wanted to. The historian Peter Friedlander has analyzed the situation astutely: "the working class was not so much affected by the Left as the UAW was influenced by the church, the political machine, several kinds of rural Protestant conservatism, and a variety of local prepolitical subcultures." Moreover, religious consciousness was not merely persistent; it was also ambiguous. Therefore, UAW leaders employed several different strategies in their effort to construct a narrative of working-class identity that braided the idioms, themes, and symbols of religious consciousness.[35]

The union typically asserted that no conflict existed between organized labor and organized religion. To the contrary, the UAW (like the AFL before it) simply claimed that both shared the same values. To make this claim plausible, UAW leaders marshaled as much public support from religious leaders as possible. During the major General Motors strike of 1936–1937, the UAW applauded the "solidarity" expressed by an interfaith panel; Fr. John Ryan of the National Catholic Welfare Conference, James Myers of the Federal Council of Churches, and Rabbi Barnett Brickner of Central Conference of American Rabbis argued, much to the UAW's liking, for "democratic relations" between employers and unions, and offered to mediate the

GM strike. When New York's Episcopal bishop Francis McConnell spoke on "Why I Support the CIO," the UAW promoted the speech and broadcast it on its radio program. Likewise, Walter Reuther's *West Side Conveyor* quoted Pittsburgh's labor priest Charles Owen Rice, who announced, "I am for the CIO because it advocates help for the forgotten man of industry." And in 1936, Owen Knox, a Methodist minister deeply impressed by Harry F. Ward's radical interpretation of religion, moved to Detroit specifically to minister to workers. His "Labor Church of the Air" became a semiregular feature of the UAW's radio programming.[36]

Religion was, in fact, woven into the subtext of the UAW's breakthrough GM strike of 1936–1937. The strike was planned to coincide with former Detroit mayor Frank Murphy's election as governor; union leaders surmised that the liberal Murphy would be reticent to employ National Guard troops in breaking the strike. As predicted, Murphy refrained from ejecting the strikers, and after mediating a peaceful settlement, the Catholic governor proclaimed, "the voice of Him whom we know as the Prince of Peace has been heard in our community." Following the strike, Murphy delivered "A Profession of Faith," originally aired as a radio speech and reprinted by the UAW in 1938. In it, Murphy asserted that democratic self-rule was possible because of the fundamentally religious belief in the "essential goodness of men"; as the governor put it, "a self-respecting government possessed of a sense of moral responsibility for the welfare of those it was created to serve, has no higher duty than to safeguard the health and happiness of the poor, the humble, and the lowly." The UAW benefited both from Murphy's practical decisions and his rhetoric, which implicitly placed unionism on a par with Christian democracy.[37]

But with relatively few local ministers fusing unionism with religion, the union sometimes did it itself. When it was branded by industrialists as radical and anti-American, the UAW retorted in a religiously charged, Gospel-quoting panel of the *West Side Conveyor* that the great evangelist St. Paul was "**CALLED . . . A RED:** For we have found this man a pestilent fellow, and a mover of sedition. . . ." If even St. Paul could be Red-baited, the union implied, surely the accusation carried little meaning. In the spring of 1938, the *United Automobile Worker* printed a "Prayer" composed by a Packard worker. Like many prayers, this one took the form of a petition seeking aid and protection from enemies. Interestingly, however, the UAW prayer was entirely inward-focused, making no mention, for example, of employers or the government. Rather, the enemies that this supplicant sought protection from were bad members *within* the UAW—selfish, narrow, critical of the union but not constructive in building a better union, these internal Judases were perceived as posing the greatest danger. If God were to bless the UAW, the prayer added, he might bestow good members: eager to participate, prompt in dues payment, interested in the good of all workers.[38]

At its most ambitious, the UAW argued that membership in and support of a union constituted a basic part of religious commitment. Key to this line of thinking was the theme of "duty." In 1937, for example, James Myers of the Federal Council of Churches claimed that "it is the moral and religious duty of a worker to join a labor union." Myers reasoned that joining a union indicated unselfishness and the individual's commitment to the common good of all workers. Catholic leaders sounded much the same note. Texas bishop Robert Lucey appeared in the Catholic magazines *Christian Front* and *Commonweal* proclaiming it the "duty" of Catholic workers to join a "bona-fide" trade union and "get into the parade and go down the road with labor." Both pieces were picked up and disseminated by the UAW. While this exhortation was in some sense a clerical assertion of social power (clergy, after all, were claiming the authority to tell workers what they should do), it also reflected how traditional aspects of religious consciousness were intertwining with the newer awareness of political opportunities afforded by the labor movement. Workers had a duty to unionize because they had moral obligations to their fellow workers. Seeking an individualistic path to economic security was considered selfish and short-sighted. It separated workers from the sinews of community and reciprocity.[39]

Some pious autoworkers clearly had their doubts about the UAW, forcing the union to assert its compatibility with religion in more defensive tones. J. K. Paulson, shop steward at Local 156 in Flint, lamented that the union had "come into contact with a few workers who seem to believe that to be a member of a union . . . would conflict with their religious views." Paulson found this conclusion "rather absurd," and protested that the UAW possessed leaders "whose religious faith we cannot question but whom we know to be most sincere in worship of their Lord and Master." In fact, UAW leaders stood in marked contrast to the many ministers who abused their pulpits by criticizing organized labor. Of these antilabor ministers, Paulson "cannot believe they are even sincere in their own chosen field, but rather paid propagandists."[40]

Still, religion was ambiguous, and could be wielded as a cultural weapon against the UAW as easily as for it. In 1937, Henry Ford appropriated religion for his defense by sponsoring a shadowy union "Based on Christian Principles." Calling it the Workers Council for Social Justice (WCSC), Ford hoped to diffuse the UAW's effectiveness by channeling his employees into the more paternalistic confines of a company union. More cynically, he also hoped that workers might join the WCSC after confusing it with Fr. Charles Coughlin's National Union for Social Justice, which formed late in 1934; Coughlin denied knowing anything about the WCSC and did not support it. When Ford meddled in religion, the UAW decried it as a ploy and distraction that threatened to split the labor movement.[41]

During the UAW's ambitious attempt to organize Henry Ford's River Rouge plant in 1937, unionists learned of a shadowy competitor called the Ford Brotherhood of America (FBA). Much to the UAW's irritation, the FBA's masthead proclaimed a quote from the Gospel of John: "Know the truth and the truth shall set you free." "The use of such quotations and slogans inevitably implies that the UAW is unchristian, that it is irreligious," the UAW newspaper complained. "Such demagogy is not necessary for a union like the UAW, which is made up of Catholics, Protestants, nonreligious workers, Negroes, white men, German-Americans and every variety of race, color and creed." Religion, when ecumenical and socially progressive, benefited the UAW and was applauded for its virtue and wisdom; but when religion was particularistic and conservative, it threatened the UAW's "culture of unity" and needed to be denounced.[42]

When such conflicts arose between organized labor and organized churches, the UAW countered by declaring that labor, not the church, embodied "True Christianity." In this, it picked up a hallowed rhetorical tradition that first arose in the industrial revolution of the 1830s and was later promoted by the Knights of Labor in the 1880s and in the socialism of Eugene Debs between the 1890s and the 1920s. Few union leaders in the country were more adept or credible in this role than the UAW's first president, Homer Martin. Martin, after all, became involved with the auto union after his career as a Baptist preacher in Kansas abruptly ended in 1932. The UAW newspaper conscientiously highlighted Martin's biblical background, both to deflect accusations of radicalism and to ease the worries of Protestant autoworkers suspicious of the new organization. Shortly after he became UAW president in 1936, the paper reprinted a rabble-rousing sermon that had caused Martin trouble in Kansas: "The man who pays workers less than a living wage and takes advantage of depression to drive down living standards and then comes to church on Sunday is no Christian but a carping hypocrite!" Martin's church grew as working people responded to his message, but the well-heeled donors "stormed out," bankrupting the congregation and leaving Martin to work at a local Chevrolet plant.[43]

Martin's irascibility and incompetence eventually brought his career as a union leader to an inglorious end. Some organizers were unimpressed by Martin's religious background; John Zaremba, for example, felt that "A man who would leave the pulpit and try to go after something else would never qualify him to be a leader for a just and honest cause." But in the late 1930s, Martin's rhetoric hit a deep cultural nerve. B. J. Widick recalled that Martin "made men feel that in organizing a union they were going forth to battle for righteousness and the word of God." Late in 1938, Martin took this very message to the UAW's radio program. Organized labor, according to Martin, sought "the highest aspirations and ideals of man," but unfortunately "the church has in many instances failed to realize the importance of the labor movement in accomplishing the ends to which the church itself is fundamentally dedicated." To the contrary, Martin insisted, "[t]oo often . . . [the church] has joined the chorus against organized labor." According to Martin, organized religion suffered from a basic disconnect: while churches supported the lives of the poor and downtrodden in the abstract, whenever a specific action to correct these problems was advanced—as in striking, organizing, and so forth—the church decried labor. Martin warned against the continuation of such attitudes. "If the church does not face these problems realistically and adopt a position in keeping with its expressed ideals, then labor will turn more and more away from the church as an instrument for a solution of its problems and a means of realizing its hopes for making this a better world in which to live."[44]

Conclusion

The story of working-class religious consciousness in Depression-era Detroit played out along perilous fault lines between competing identities, conflicting cultures, and clashing interests. Middle-class proponents of the social gospel critiqued labor exploitation and hoped to bring a measure of peace and justice to the factory, but they also criticized working-class religion itself as culturally primitive and socially destructive. New Deal politicians like Frank Murphy experienced more success in uniting social Christianity with an increasingly politicized working class, but the relationship between religion and the UAW remained an open question in the union's formative years between 1935 and 1938. Ultimately, as the next chapter demonstrates, pious workers came to embrace the new culture of the CIO from the perspective of a remade religious consciousness. The critical, 1930s-era transformation in working-class religious consciousness was not *imposed* on Catholics, African Americans, or the increasing numbers of poor white southerners by social gospellers or labor organizers; rather, it was rooted in an imaginative rethinking of work, class, and politics from *within* these religious communities.

FIGURE 4. Sweetest Heart of Mary was an epicenter of Polish Catholicism. This service from the 1930s was typically well attended. Courtesy of Walter P. Reuther Library, Archives of Labor and Urban Affairs, Wayne State University.

FIGURE 5. Proponents of worker religion attempted to intertwine religious culture with a form of class identity. For Catholics, "St. Joseph, the Workman" became a major object of devotion. Copy in Association of Catholic Trade Unionists Collection, Box 4, Folder Labor Day Mass 1956, Walter P. Reuther Library, Archives of Labor and Urban Affairs, Wayne State University.

3. Making Worker Religion in the New Deal Era

Late in 1936, as the industrial centers of Michigan exploded in a wave of strikes, pickets, and protest, Fr. Erwin Lefebvre of St. Monica's parish in Detroit contemplated how to reach his working-class congregation with the Church's message for labor. Ultimately, he hit upon the idea of replacing his usual Sunday sermon at the late-morning mass with a reading of and commentary upon Pope Leo XIII's labor encyclical, *Rerum Novarum*. Lefebvre's audience was primed for the priest's message. Workers in Depression-era Detroit had accumulated generations' worth of resentment, and by 1936, the lid was beginning to come off. Throughout the 1930s, the workplace had become steadily more dangerous and stressful. Aiming at ever-higher production rates even with a diminished workforce, Detroit's automakers introduced one of the most hated of all management tools: the "speed-up." Welders and machinists doubled their production numbers by 1932 while punch-press operators tripled production, even as wages stagnated or declined. The cost of this pace, according to one study, was "notorious." Sickness and injury became widespread. "In working-class Detroit," the novelist Erskine Caldwell surmised, "you are known by your hands": the more missing appendages a worker suffered, the more of an outcast he became. Beginning in 1933, strikes at Detroit factories "just burst like lightning," according to one historian. These early strikes were largely unsuccessful, but a second and more lasting series of strikes followed passage of the National Industrial Relations Act and the formation of the Congress of Industrial Organizations (CIO) in 1935, and continued on and off for the next several years. The Flint sit-down strike of 1936–1937 unleashed a torrent of similar job actions. Between January and March of 1937, over 100 Detroit plants were hit by a sit-down.[1]

Fr. Lefebvre's labor mass, therefore, hit a nerve with the factory workers that dominated the pews. Where the late-morning service was usually sparsely attended, Lefebvre observed, "now the church is crowded every Sunday at this Mass." The priest's experiment quickly became developed and integrated into the official devotional calendar of the Detroit Archdiocese, joining the important cycle of Lent, Advent, and Holy Days in Catholics' routine living of their faith. Beginning in the late 1930s and continuing into the 1950s, at least one of the masses celebrated on the Sunday preceding Labor Day was dedicated as a "labor mass," and often featured a noted speaker on a labor theme. Fr. Raymond Clancy, a leading Detroit "labor priest," captured the cultural cross-current between religion and labor with a pithy phrase: mass, he explained, was "collective bargaining with God with Christ as our Business Agent."[2]

As the labor mass demonstrates, the centrality of the labor question in Depression-era Detroit—and its apparent resolution through New Deal politics and CIO-style industrial unionism—challenged the religious consciousness of a new generation of Detroit workers. During the 1930s and early 1940s, powerful ideas and idioms regarding the social meaning of work reshaped the religious practices and identities of many Catholic, African American, and southern white evangelical workers; as I mentioned earlier, I refer to these new formulations of religious consciousness as *worker religion*. The role of worker religion remained vitally important throughout this period because, ultimately, the UAW was not attempting to organize workers. It was attempting to organize Catholics steeped in devotional culture: ordinary people of immigrant stock who regularly attended Mass at St. Florian's or Sweetest Heart of Mary or Holy Trinity or any of several dozen other working-class parishes, who sent their kids to parochial school and participated in a church-based fraternal league. It was attempting to organize African Americans who sang in the choir at Hartford Avenue Baptist Church or served as deacons at Bethel AME or rocked in prayer at any of the dozens of Detroit's storefront churches, people who knew their Bible well, but had been Jim-Crowed out of labor unions and were just beginning to engage in the formal political process. It was hoping to organize poor white evangelicals from the South, whose sense of fairness, justice, dignity, and community was rooted in their experiences of Bible reading or prayer meetings or the occasional urban revival. The UAW succeeded not so much because they were able to pull workers into the culture of the labor movement, but because religious activists emerged from *within* these communities to retrofit the social gospel for their own purposes, articulating a vision of worker religion that braided secular concerns of politics, unionism, and work with the preexisting idioms of devotional Catholicism, African American church life, or evangelical culture.

Even so, the process of creating worker religion was contentious, divisive, and often measured or incomplete. Worker religion became hotly contested cultural territory, both between religious communities and within them. While the architects of worker religion excitedly attached their own religious cars to the liberal train of Progressivism, opponents viewed worker religion as far too modernist, far too pluralistic, and far too close to the orbits of communism and radicalism. Worker religion, in fact, came to be seen by its adversaries as a type of antireligion, insidiously eating away the foundations of the "true" faith. The struggle was political, of course, but it reflected more than that. At its heart, worker religion proposed a fusion between ambiguously related threads of social, political, moral, and cultural identity, and it opened new possibilities for the historical agency of ordinary believers. The question was how durable such a fusion might be.

The Making of Catholic Worker Religion

The Great Depression shook the social world of Catholic Detroit. Insecurity and turmoil flowed from the workplace into the Catholic neighborhoods of the city. The pastor at Our Lady of Help raised a common lament when, in 1931, he noted that, "Of the 286 families who are represented in our school, 150 are in the 'bread line.'" Churches could hardly escape the effects of this vast social disruption, and parishes struggled to survive. St. Florian's parish in Hamtramck, built through such sacrifice on the part of its working-class parishioners, received only eight tithes of more than $30 in 1933—nearly 75 percent of the congregation summoned less than $1 in support of their church that year. Pastors at St. Rose of Lima parish pleaded with parishioners in 1934, "Who is there so poor, that he cannot by some little sacrifice on his own part" find a way to support the parish? After a month of gentle chiding, all tone of friendliness vanished, as St. Rose's newsletter declared, "It is manifestly improper and even sinful on the part of a Catholic to refuse assuming a proper share of support of the Church and Catholic school." Such language may sound callous and insensitive. One might expect that some hard-pressed parishioners would be angered or insulted by the demands and perhaps even leave the Church entirely. But, in contrast, Sunday collections by late February jumped to the highest point since 1930. Were these Catholics motivated by guilt, or habit, or a noble devotion? Did they skimp on meals or clothing in order to sustain their parish? Clearly, these working-class Catholics accepted the legitimacy of their Church's demands, and likely sacrificed mightily to meet the call. Their behavior suggests the power of Catholic culture and the importance of the parish.[3]

Still, it was not possible for church leaders to ignore the human cost of the Depression (although it is revealing that the diocesan newspaper failed to acknowledge virtually any social or economic disruption until the late 1930s, close to a decade after the city's economy first faltered). Eventually, perhaps grudgingly in cases, leading Catholics were pushed by the external forces of the Depression, the New Deal, the UAW, and what scholar Michael Denning has called the "laboring" of American culture more generally. Denning has argued that, throughout the 1930s, images and stories of workers, the poor, and "common people" infiltrated and decisively shaped the mass culture—and consequently the political values—of the era. So, too, in Detroit's Catholic parishes, the remaking of religious consciousness consisted in prioritizing labor itself, in forthrightly acknowledging the new social and political influence of Catholic workers *as workers* (more specifically, as *male* workers). Attending mass, worshippers were suddenly alert to the importance of papal labor encyclicals. They knew of novenas held for striking workers, knew about devotions to workers' patron saint, and worshipped shoulder to shoulder with newly unionized autoworkers. Reinventing Catholicism within the teeth of the Depression, Catholics drew upon the tools of religion—symbols, rituals, myths, and texts—to create a new narrative that featured working people as central actors in the history of the Catholic Church and the unfolding of Christ's divine message for Earth. From Charles Coughlin's reactionary corporatism, to the anarchic impulses of the Catholic Workers, to the liberal unionism of the Association of Catholic Trade Unionists, working-class Catholics were inundated with religious messages and symbols addressing the importance of labor to traditional Catholic worship and identity.[4]

Remaking this religious consciousness required communicating in a vernacular that was well-established and widely understood. For Catholics, the world was populated with sacred characters that served as mediators to God. During the 1930s, these characters were increasingly portrayed within a social context common for Catholic working people. In 1937, for instance, the *Michigan Catholic* published a characteristic example with a poem entitled "The Workman." "Within the factory's fiery maw," the poem begins, "The workman toils mid sweat and grime." But Catholic workers were never alone:

> For here beside each workman stands
> An angel pure with outspread wings
> And high above the deafening roar
> A heavenly alleluia rings

And so wherever workmen toil
At honest tasks through endless days
The angels weave their hours of pain
Into immortal songs of praise

In many ways, the poem encapsulated and celebrated traditional elements of a Catholic laboring religious consciousness: hard work was divinely ordained; suffering and sacrifice, especially when undertaken on behalf of the family, were noble before God; God would elevate common labor onto a redemptive, glorified plane. These themes stand rather starkly beside the rhetoric of the UAW, which, after all, intended to *alleviate*, not revel in or romanticize, the miseries of the workplace. Underneath a shared respect for working people, the Catholic acceptance of organic hierarchy, natural law, and man's inherent depravity rubbed uncomfortably against the secular optimism of a union movement much more confident that the world could be shaped to its own ends.[5]

Saints and sacred characters also embedded Catholics within a somewhat mythic understanding of their own history—not the Enlightenment history of human rights and liberal progress so important to the UAW, but a romanticized version of the Middles Ages. In the Catholic imagination, the medieval Christian West was hardly a "Dark Age," but rather a harmonious era far removed from the harsh divisiveness of modern nations, classes, and sects. Medievalism united Catholic theologians, architects, laborites, and radicals of differing social and political orientation. In intellectual circles, the philosophy of Thomas Aquinas struck many Catholics as the perfect expression of the divine mind (and will). For architects, the embrace of neo-Gothicism bespoke an urge to re-create the organically united medieval village in the midst of sprawling, polyglot industrial metropolises. Catholics compelled by labor themes also situated themselves within a medieval mythology. Indeed, perhaps no group created a more "invented tradition" of the Middle Ages than the Catholic Workers, which imagined a rural world of peasants and saints, a great familial commonweal cooperatively and peacefully working together. The Association of Catholic Trade Unionists also came from this tradition; its banner depicted an industrial machine gear drawn in a style evocative of the medieval aesthetic. In its "Industry Council Plan," the ACTU consistently praised the corporate ideal of the medieval guild and pushed the UAW to emulate its ancient ancestor (future CIO President Philip Murray, himself a Catholic, attended Mass with ACTU members whenever he was in Detroit and was another staunch supporter of the ICP). By grounding the laboring of Catholicism in a common past, the Workers and ACTU helped legitimate the novelty of its organization and offered a compelling set of symbols rich in Catholic meaning.[6]

Just as stories, characters, and narratives united an "old" Catholic culture with the new world of working-class Detroit, Catholic ideology also combined these currents. Prolabor Catholics were deeply suspicious of economic liberalism, an attitude that came to parallel an enthusiasm for industrial unionism. But Catholics also typically exhibited a disapproval of *social* liberalism (thus, its condemnation of Hollywood movies and birth control). Above all, Catholics distrusted liberalism's incessant celebration of the individual. Thus, when a Catholic Ford worker denounced the perceived despotism of Henry Ford, he revealingly described the auto magnate as a "monster individualist." Freed from duty and obligation to his fellow man, the liberal individual of the Catholic imagination was freed as well from the moorings of tradition. He was arrogant, self-indulgent, pleasure-seeking, and cutthroat. In stressing the inverse of liberalism—deference toward others, fulfillment of duty, acceptance of societal interdependence, the wisdom of tradition—the new socially activist Catholic groups of the 1930s echoed the essential elements of a much older, everyday Catholic culture. In short, the story of Detroit's working-class Catholics in the 1930s is a story of both change and continuity; or, put another way, a story of new social, political, and spiritual identities emerging within a broader culture deeply linked to a coherent tradition with long-established rituals and habits of mind.[7]

The making of a Catholic worker religion, however, was unpredictable, unstable, and contentious. No single figure better illustrates the contradictory currents within religious culture, and its relation to class identity, than Detroit's radio priest, Charles Coughlin. While Coughlin at times espoused a progressive religious vision of ecumenism and social justice, these pronouncements were uneasily nestled within his countervailing tendency toward demagoguery and intolerance. Coughlin's early championing of the New Deal gave the UAW cause to hope for his support; the priest's fame and moral credibility among so many workers only added to his allure as a potential promoter of the UAW. But Coughlin's religious populism was mercurial and fickle; if the UAW needed a lesson in the unpredictability and volatility of religion, Coughlin was an ideal teacher.[8]

Beginning his broadcasting career in 1926, Coughlin's radio sermons of the late 1920s were strictly religious in nature. But after 1930, Coughlin's preaching reflected the broader "laboring" of American culture, and his subject matter shifted almost entirely to political and economic topics. Coughlin correctly assessed the nation's moral mood, and his fame and influence skyrocketed. Future UAW President Douglas Fraser recalled that "Coughlin's

Sunday broadcasts were sacred in his family. When the radio priest came on, everything in his home came to a stop. . . . [T]his was true of his entire neighborhood." So, too, UAW stalwart Leonard Woodcock remembered walking Detroit's working-class neighborhoods in 1936, hearing "Father Coughlin in every house." Broadcast on over thirty radio channels across the country, Coughlin was, for a time, the most famous and popular person in the country, allegedly receiving more mail than even the President. Coughlin's popularity, particularly between 1930 and 1933, rested on a blend of personal charisma and his linkage of religious piety with an anti-banking populism. This consciousness-in-the-(re)making emphasized the "common-folk" origins of Christianity, the government's responsibility to ensure this religious vision of social justice, and a moral universalism.[9]

In articulating his Christian populism, Coughlin described a Jesus who "remembers how He was born in the cradle of the laboring class." Workers in the 1930s, Coughlin intoned, knew that Jesus defended their interest, for they "still hear the words leveled at Him by the greedy despots of His day when He mingled with the common man." Likewise, Coughlin cited scripture to show that the Sacred Heart of Jesus protected and offered succor to the worker: "*Come unto Me all ye who labor and are heavily burdened and I will refresh you.*" Coughlin's understanding of class was vague but clearly corporatist; his "working class" included essentially everybody who was not wealthy, stressed the mutuality of social obligations and the organic nature of social hierarchy, and repeatedly defended the plight of homeowners. These themes may explain why Coughlin's most enthusiastic supporters seemed to be the Irish and German upper-working or lower-middle classes, people with some stake in society—a home, a farm, a small business, or a skill. Early in the 1930s, Coughlin even promoted specific political solutions to the labor question that might have encouraged budding unionists. "A philosophy of industrialism which looks askance upon the organization of the laborer into peaceful unions or Christian societies must be scuttled," he asserted. Late in 1934, Coughlin went further and argued explicitly that "labor should have a voice in the management of the business." In fact, Coughlin argued that "men and women of the laboring class" not only had a *right* to form unions, but that unionizing was in fact a consecrated "duty."[10]

As the UAW began formally erecting an organizational network, therefore, Coughlin loomed as an important figure. He was, without question, ubiquitous. The job of building a relationship with Coughlin fell to Richard Frankensteen, an ambitious activist in the embryonic UAW. With Coughlin's support, Frankensteen helped created the Automotive Industrial Worker Association (AIWA) in the Dodge Brothers' massive Hamtramck plant. In 1935, Frankensteen and Coughlin addressed 30,000 autoworkers in Detroit's Belle Isle Park; at the time, the AIWA had attracted over 10,000 workers, while the UAW claimed only a few hundred (eventually, AIWA would be absorbed into the UAW and become the important Dodge Local 3). Given the Dodge plant's reliance on the labor of tens of thousands of Polish Catholics, Fr. Coughlin offered the AIWA a desperately needed moral legitimacy. In May of 1936, at the first UAW convention in South Bend, Indiana, Frankensteen urged Coughlin to the stage. To a cheering crowd, Coughlin declared, "Away with independent unions!" in a pitch for coordinated labor action.[11]

Later in 1936, Coughlin veered into more strident, conspiratorial, and intolerant terrain. His early sympathy to unionism became clouded by an ever-greater hostility to strikes and an obsessive anticommunism. His violent opposition to Franklin Roosevelt, and his partnership with Huey Long's fundamentalist and anti-Semitic operative, Gerald L. K. Smith, caused liberals and laborites to recoil. Most ominously, Coughlin increasingly began to conflate his two archetypal enemies—the scheming banker and the atheistic communist—into a single caricature: the sinister Jew. When, in 1938, his newsletter *Social Justice* began printing the anti-Semitic forgery, "The Protocols of the Learned Elders of Zion," Coughlin's xenophobia was fully exposed and his incompatibility with the UAW unquestionable.[12]

Yet, if Coughlin had come to symbolize a Catholic worker religion based on suspicion, resentment, and intolerance, many thousands of Detroit Catholics pushed their faith in a countervailing direction. Beginning in 1937, the pressures of working-class life, the political opportunities afforded by the New Deal, and the insurgency of the UAW shattered the dams of Catholic insularity. Lay Catholics were spurred by the call for "Catholic Action" emerging from church leaders; as Detroit's Archbishop Edward Mooney described it, Catholic Action would "have Catholics know their faith better, live it more intensely and apply it more effectively in all its phases." Subsequently, Catholic activism spilled out in a flood of movement-founding, institution-building, and social activism. The two short years between 1937 and 1939 witnessed the emergence of Detroit's Catholic Worker movement, the establishment of Houses of Hospitality, the founding of the Association of Catholic Trade Unionists, the erection of an Archdiocesan Labor Institute, the launching of two Catholic labor newspapers, and the formal censuring of Charles Coughlin's anti-Semitic and antiunion diatribes. Many Detroit Catholics in this period (including a number of clergy) participated in major strikes or demonstrations—including the violently repressed Ford organizing drive of 1937, the Federal Screw Works strike of 1938, and the especially important Chrysler strike in the autumn of 1939—embraced the UAW, and braided their new identities within a remade Catholic culture.[13]

This culture grew observably on a nearly month-to-month basis. In March of 1937, many Catholic workers participated in their first sit-down strike at the Dodge Main plant in Hamtramck. A month later, the Franciscan labor priest Sebastian Erbacher began offering free lectures on the papal labor encyclicals at Duns Scotus College, and Detroit-area priests launched plans to attend Social Action summer schools sponsored by the NCWC. On May Day—the communist international holiday for workers—Fr. Clare Murphy of the Federation of Catholic Study Clubs and a team of Catholic activists took to the streets, armed with copies of the *Catholic Worker* and similar publications, to offer a religious counterpoint to the communist celebrations. When Edward Mooney became Detroit's first Archbishop in August of 1937, the UAW correctly surmised that Mooney would be friendly to overtures from the union. Two weeks after the archbishop assumed his duties, the UAW took out a full-page advertisement in the archdiocesan newspaper, welcoming Mooney and "cordially [inviting] into our ranks, all Roman Catholic automobile workers." Mooney himself declared shortly thereafter that "no Catholic Church authority has ever asserted that the C.I.O. is incompatible with Catholicity." By the end of the year, Catholic priests and laymen had become semiregular guests on UAW radio programs and hundreds of Catholics were attending labor forums at various parishes.[14]

The intensity and excitement surrounding Catholic Action reached a new level with the emergence of Detroit's Catholic Worker movement. In September of 1937, Catholic Worker cofounder Dorothy Day attended a conference on Social Action at Detroit's Marygrove College, where she found a crowd eager to learn more about her movement and its aims. Day urged Detroiters to establish a House of Hospitality, the community homes promoted by the Catholic Worker movement to house and serve the poor. A follow-up conference held two weeks after Day's visit, hosted by the priests Sebastian Erbacher and Clare Murphy, drew in unionists, teachers, housewives, and "'jacks of all trade,'" provoking what one witness called a "lively discussion." Again in November of 1937, Catholic Worker cofounder Peter Maurin visited Detroit, where he provoked vigorous discussion with unionists at a UAW meeting. Joe Zarella, another Catholic Worker from New York, spoke at Detroit's Catholic high schools, where students "bombarded him with questions, and promised support for the Catholic Worker ideal." A teaching sister wrote Dorothy Day to announce that, at her school, "All the girls are greatly enthused" over the possibilities of the movement.[15]

Within two months of Day's visit, Detroit layman Louis Murphy had established the St. Martha House, Detroit's first House of Hospitality. Soon, the House was a neighborhood social center. It also quickly began hosting classes on union protocol and parliamentary procedure. The men and women populating Detroit's House of Hospitality intertwined material lives shaped by working-class concerns with spiritual lives enmeshed in Catholic devotionalism. On an average day, up to 600 neighborhood women streamed in and out of the House for food and supplies. Unemployed men—a painter, a brewery worker, a sailor, and others—lived at the House with Louis Murphy and assisted in its maintenance and charitable works. Meanwhile, in the dining room, a large statue of St. Anthony adorned the table, votive candle burning at its feet. Animated meetings and discussions, held around the statue, could last past midnight, yet many of these men rose early in the morning to attend 6 o'clock Mass. Cultural form and social experience began blending in the late 1930s to remake Catholic consciousness.[16]

But it was the Association of Catholic Trade Unionists (ACTU)—a lay-led fraternity of workers encouraging Catholic activism within existing unions—that most successfully united the rise of the UAW in secular society and the push for Catholic Action within the Church. Describing their Catholicism as "social" did not require much innovation, for the religion had always stressed the importance of community and social reciprocity. Characterizing Catholicism as "action," however, represented for Actists (as they called themselves) a creative departure from the Catholicism of the immigrant generations. Laborite Catholics linguistically transformed their faith from a noun ("the Church") to a verb, an activity to be performed (Actists pronounced their group's acronym, "Act, Too!"). Significantly, Catholicism to these believers was no longer defined by a place—the parish, the church building, the school—but by what one did in the world. In their consciousness, lay activists believed they were "making" Catholicism by building the union—and that in the absence of action lay agnosticism. Staunch anticommunism was another critical element of the ACTU, but previous scholarship has often reduced the group to a merely anticommunist political bloc, or a "right-wing" obstacle to be hurdled by "progressive" unionists, an analysis that is deeply reductionist, unimaginative, and ultimately inaccurate.[17]

The ACTU originally developed in New York as an outgrowth of Dorothy Day's Catholic Worker movement. But where the Catholic Worker might be described as a "radical movement"—involving a loose organizational structure, an ascetic embrace of poverty, an ideological commitment to personalism, and absolute pacifism—the ACTU could best be called a "liberal organization"—clearly structured, dedicated to practical action in the labor movement, and espousing a corporate vision of society. John Cort, one of the ACTU's New York founders, felt that his experience was typical of other Actists: in the late 1930s, he "[c]ame to the Catholic Worker and didn't buy the whole schmeer but nevertheless got involved in various aspects of social justice and social action."[18]

In mid-July of 1938—just weeks after R. J. Thomas replaced Homer Martin as UAW president following near-fatal divisions within the union—Catholic workers in Detroit formed their own ACTU chapter. Like the original New York group, the Detroit ACTU first grew out of the Catholic Worker movement, operating out of the St. Martha House of Hospitality before establishing independent offices and a distinct operational mission. The Detroit chapter benefited from an especially talented and dedicated lay vanguard in leadership positions. The first ACTU president, Paul Weber, was an experienced journalist, well-versed in union practices from his association with the Newspaper Guild; in the 1940s, he would attain a leadership role in the Michigan CIO and serve as press secretary for Michigan's liberal Democratic governor G. Mennan Williams in the 1950s. Weber, described by one observer as "brisk and confident," personified the ACTU in Detroit for at least the next decade, and his background in journalism proved particularly valuable in producing the ACTU's newspaper. Launched as the *Michigan Labor Leader* in 1939, the paper was renamed the *Wage Earner* in 1942 and became a widely read and nationally respected source of labor news until its closure in the mid-1960s.[19]

Meanwhile, in January of 1939, a vanguard of priests met at the University of Detroit to craft a clerical complement to the ACTU. They devised a series of parish-based labor schools under the auspices of yet another new organization, the Archdiocesan Labor Institute (ALI). The ALI reveals the Church's view of its own mission—if the ACTU was predicated on "action" within union locals, the Church itself continued to hold the authority to teach "correct" principles. The ALI would educate, the ACTU activate. Furthermore, the clerical formulators of the ALI declared that parishes would sponsor the schools and host meetings, and priests act as de facto directors, but they also recognized that lay leaders would do most of the legwork in organizing meetings. The meetings themselves were tightly structured and rather demanding, consisting of two hours' worth of instruction. The first hour, led by a priest, drew heavily from papal encyclicals to instill within unionists the Church's understanding of the moral issues at stake in the labor movement and to connect the religious with the economic; the second hour, led by a layman, instructed students in the "A B C of Parliamentary Law," the standard protocol governing UAW meetings.[20]

The ACTU's first vice president, Paul Ste. Marie, was also a prominent UAW organizer and the first president of the critical Ford Local 600, which eventually became the largest and one of the most radical union locals in the world. Thomas Doherty, first ACTU recording secretary, was another UAW activist. In 1939, Richard L. G. Deverall and Norman McKenna, publishers of the liberal *Christian Front* newspaper, relocated from Philadelphia to Detroit to reestablish their newspaper as *Christian Social Action* (the name *Christian Front*, the paper explained, had been "stolen and disgraced" by anti-Semitic Coughlin followers in New York). McKenna would work periodically for both the *Wage Earner* and the *Michigan Catholic* through the 1950s. Deverall, besides publishing his paper and lecturing throughout Detroit, would also lead the UAW Education Department in the early 1940s, developing the UAW newsletter *The Distributor*. In short, Detroit's liberal Catholic vanguard possessed many of the attributes essential for successful social action: an Archbishop broadly supportive of the movement's aims, a cadre of priests ready to work with an involved laity, the technological and intellectual skills necessary to disseminate ideas and information, a range of social spaces—parish halls, schools, and colleges—in which to meet and work, and the network of a larger organization (the UAW) to further spread the group's aims.[21]

At its height in the early 1940s, the ACTU claimed around 2,500 members. Given the hundreds of thousands of workers who belonged to the UAW, the ACTU was always a decided minority within the union. Nevertheless, as the labor historian Philip Taft has argued, the ACTU's "effectiveness cannot be measured by numbers"—and Taft especially points to the Detroit chapter as "very significant." Moreover, as John Cort observed, while the ACTU's formal membership may have been small, the Communist Party in Michigan at the same time claimed only 1,000 members, yet there is little disputing the importance of communists in building the UAW and shaping the "cultural front." Given the fact that nearly 40 percent of Detroit's practicing Christians were Catholic during the UAW's formative years, given that the majority of these Catholics were working class, and given the ubiquity of Catholic institutions and activities, it seems fair to propose that Catholic activism operated within a broader "spiritual front" that impacted the wider culture and transcended the formal membership numbers of the ACTU.[22]

What was happening in Catholic Detroit, however, was more significant than simply the creation of new institutions. Catholic culture itself had come to echo the broader laboring of American culture and politics, and this shift was influencing the laity to remake elements of their religious consciousness.

Lay Catholics were increasingly encouraged to harmonize their social engagement, class identity, and religion. Emblematic of this shift was the earnest, grass-roots efforts of lay parish leaders to recruit fellow Catholics into the ACTU. During the summer of 1939, parish-based newsletters throughout the Archdiocese called on Catholics to join the ACTU. From Blessed Sacrament parish's "Hour" to St. Florian's Polish-language "Florjanowo"; from Holy Rosary parish's "News-Lite" to the Italian-language *La Voce Del Popolo*, local bulletins announced: "CATHOLIC WORKERS! *God needs you in your labor union!* Labor's fight for justice is in vain unless labor follows the principles of Jesus Christ." Citing Archbishop Mooney's plea not to be intimidated by false reports about unions in the corporate press, the newsletters urged— "Catholics! Get in the labor parade. Don't just stand on the sidelines and find fault." In September of 1939, *St Vincent's News* tried to ease the skittishness of Catholics toward organized labor. "As part of a United Christian Front in the unions, you can change the un-Christian conditions that you think exist. We as Catholic workers have sound principles; we must see that they are carried out."[23]

When the ACTU chapter of Chrysler UAW Local 7 met for the first time in July of 1939, the group's newsletter argued with enthusiasm for bringing the religion of ordinary Catholics into the labor movement. "WE, AS CATHOLICS, HAVE A SPECIAL RESPONSIBILITY TO SEE THAT OUR UNIONS ARE EFFECTIVE, MILITANT, AND RUN PROPERLY," its missive blared (caps in original). Reciprocity and communal obligations had long been major elements within Catholic culture, and ACTU leaders stressed these themes. "[T]he welfare of Local 7," leaders declared, "is PART OF OUR RELIGION!" One senses a liberation and excitement appropriate for people newly confident in their agency and newly self-aware of the forces shaping their lives and identities. The ACTU, leaders promised to potential members, meant the following:

> You can do *your* part to carry out the injunction of our leader, Jesus Christ, "Go forth and teach ye all nations . . ." *You* can share with the bishops and priests of the Church the task of converting the world. And *you* can do more than any priest, bishop, or Pope toward bringing your non-Catholic fellow-worker back to the faith of their fathers!

Workers were no longer background players in the Catholic vision of history; they were, in fact, the main sites.[24]

Michael Lucas, captain of the ACTU chapter at St. Gregory parish, offers a fine example. Exuding initiative, Lucas contacted his pastor, arranged speakers, and announced a rally for a coming Monday evening in the parish hall.

The meeting was announced at every Mass on the prior Sunday, resulting in 50 new members. The minutes of Lucas's St. Gregory chapter, which first met in August 1939, reveals both the earnestness of lay leaders as well as the struggles of maintaining a grass-roots organization committed to social action. In January of 1940, membership stood at 63, but meetings became bogged down in disagreement over whether a section of the Dodge bulletin was "Communistic." Poor attendance remained a problem, but plans continued for a Labor Day rally in 1940, and the chapter survived to seat new officers in January of 1941. Clarifying the importance of religious consciousness to the ACTU's mission, the chapter's new president explained that the "first duty of the worker is to save his soul and then bring Christianity into the factory." Again, this sentiment came from a working-class lay leader, not a priest.[25]

In fact, Actists often appeared more moved by worker religion than clergy—perhaps not surprising, given that the social experiences of priests were not themselves shaped by industrial labor. But clergy remained important allies. "Tell your parish priest about the ACTU," the Actist bulletin informed its members. "Invite him to a meeting. Ask him to one of our speakers' committee talk to the Holy Name society or other parish group." Although parish priests were nominal leaders of ACTU chapters, in reality lay parish captains scheduled meetings and publicized Actist activities. Most parish captains held modest expectations for priests' contribution to the organization; they hoped that priests might at least announce meetings from the pulpit, publish information in the parish bulletin, and meet with Actists on a monthly basis.[26]

But a number of priests were, in fact, just as excited by the prospect of Catholic Action and the importance of remaking Catholic consciousness. Fr. Clare Murphy, for instance, urged militancy upon lay unionists. The importance of Social Action, he wrote to lay unionists in 1938, "can scarcely be overestimated." Committed laymen were essential "to save souls" and "convert minds to Jesus Christ. The masses know almost nothing about the strict practice of Christ's Gospel and how His principles are to be applied to working conditions and our business methods." Murphy sought to enlist "one solid group, men who are above all thorough Christians, profoundly in love with God, who will work not for mere human praise but for higher purposes, and men who have zeal, courage and real attack like the great St. Paul." During the Dodge Main sit-down strike early in 1937, Fr. Clement Kern and some of his fellow priests visited the plant in a show of support. As Kern later remembered, "We went to the outside, and here were these Catholic fellows on the inside. And they wanted us there and we wanted to be there. . . . They said, 'Father, come on in and celebrate Mass for us in here; tomorrow's Sunday.'" Although at the time Kern felt unable to perform a service outside the church building, this association of religion with separate, churchly space was exactly what Catholic Action eventually eroded—as Kern happily acknowledged. Sebastian Erbacher, the ACTU's first chaplain, noted with some self-consciousness that his own father was an underpaid cabinetmaker, and that he had personally labored alongside his father in the shop. "But not until this year [1938] have I had an opportunity as a priest to get down among the workers," he wrote to *Christian Front* coeditor, Norman McKenna. Fr. Neil O'Connor reflected this theme, writing in the *Christian Front* that he "would never forget the looks of gratitude and respect" that he and another priest received when they attended a UAW meeting in Saginaw. "It's good to see you here, Father," the workers told O'Connor, some "with tears in their eyes." Erbacher claimed that he encountered the same response. Before attending a union meeting, one worker approached him, "took my hand, and said that I do not realize what it means to see a priest interested in the workingman." Meanwhile, for skeptical clergy, "summer schools" offered in Detroit by the National Catholic Welfare Conference hoped to nurture "a new social consciousness which will clamor for action."[27]

The most effective tool at priests' disposal in the laboring of Catholic consciousness was the parish-based "labor school" movement supported by the ALI. Labor schools quickly fanned throughout the Detroit archdiocese, counting twenty-seven units within metropolitan Detroit by the end of 1939 and topping off at 41 schools in 1941. Given the names of the parishes that hosted them, it is clear that the labor schools reached widely into ethnic and industrial Detroit; heavily Polish and Italian, as well as more assimilated Irish and German parishes, all had access to the labor schools. Of course, one of the most important questions that could be asked of these schools is: what kind of impact did they actually have on working-class Catholics? Fortunately, the ALI surveyed both priests and students at the labor schools following one of the first school terms, providing some insight into this issue.[28]

Most of the priest-directors surveyed were laconic in their responses, but they nonetheless seemed generally pleased by the performance of the labor schools. Critically, the ALI labor-school surveys claimed a general increase in what it termed *Catholic-mindedness* among Catholic union members. Indeed, contrary to many popular interpretations, the Depression, New Deal, and industrial trade-union movement did not secularize the ethnic working class, despite the major inroads that secular culture made in the 1930s. For a significant number of Catholic Detroiters, these events actually heightened religious consciousness at the same time that they reinforced class identity.[29]

The priest-directors recognized both the successes and failures of the labor schools. Predictably, the biggest challenge faced by the schools concerned attendance. The students, after all, were working long hours at difficult jobs; they likely spent much of their free time attending union meetings, socializing with friends and family, or, if they were disciplined Catholics (and, for obvious reasons, we can believe they were) attending Mass and perhaps even participating with any of the myriad Catholic clubs, leagues, and charities. While priests recognized these practical difficulties, there was little they could do. An average attendance at school sessions hovered between 20 and 30, though some parishes clearly embraced the schools more enthusiastically; Assumption Grotto parish, for example, enrolled 151 students, although only 54 attended regularly. Altogether, priests had enrolled over 1100 students by early 1940, although probably one-third of this number constituted regular attendees. Still, even if students attended irregularly, priests recognized that many were developing practical skills and enhancing their knowledge of Catholic principles. At the Annunciation school, the director praised the "better acquaintance of men with Church's attitude on social and economic positions" that courses engendered. The priest at the St. Charles school said the courses had helped his students "to become more articulate in their respective Locals." Other priests responded more generally that "many" benefits accrued from the courses.[30]

Student responses to the ALI labor schools offer some insight to the thinking that laity was bringing to the ACTU. Of 69 available student responses, 56 claimed that ALI courses met or exceeded their expectations; only two claimed to be disappointed. More than half of those who enrolled in the courses were members of trade unions, but some of the students were unemployed; others feared the reactions and reprisals of antiunion employers and hence had stayed away from the union; a few resisted becoming unionized because they disagreed with the union's leadership. All but two of the students were Catholics, though it is worth noting that the non-Catholics responded very favorably to the classes' content (at least to the practical elements of public speaking and parliamentary participation).[31]

After being "Activated" by the ACTU and "Educated" by the ALI, Actists were expected to become prominent citizens in their union locals—promoting or blocking resolutions, debating issues, and voting on union business. Leonard Pinkowicz, a second-generation Pole and a welder at the Detroit Parts Company (DPC) in Hamtramck, exemplified the fondest hopes of the ACTU. Devoutly religious, Pinkowicz was also an early activist working for the unionization of his workplace; he became a role model for other Catholic workers at the company and a strong voice in union matters once UAW Local 229 was established. Similarly, Pinkowicz became the driving force in the small but active ACTU group at the DPC. Thirty-eight students claimed that they had acted on what they learned in the classes by participating more confidently and vigorously at the meetings of their locals. Some added that they had begun discussing Catholic principles with coworkers on the shop floor, and others claimed to be recruiting friends and coworkers to attend future sessions of the labor schools. One student at the Holy Rosary school epitomized the increasing Catholic-mindedness so heralded by religious leaders. When asked how the classes had made him a better unionist, the student replied that he was committed to building "a Christian platform in the U.A.W."[32]

The Catholic Workers, ACTU, and ALI did not see themselves primarily as *political* actors; rather, as one student of the ACTU observed, most members considered the group to be "primarily a 'religious movement.'" Thus, they aspired to infuse secular rituals of the working class with Catholic meaning, and to likewise weave issues of the workplace into Catholic ritual. Breaking down the meaning of "Associated Catholic Trade Unionists" on a literal basis, a typical ACTU speech-maker argued—like many secular organizers before him—that "we can't stay associated on only a bread-and-butter basis." Rather, unionists "need to 'Associate' our 'CATHOLIC' interests. This organizing of our 'Worship' and our 'Prayer' will draw us closer together from the INSIDE; it will keep us rallied 'round the Divine Worker." Christ himself, according to the speech, was "not just a great Labor Unionist, but an Organizer of Worship of Prayer." Therefore, just as the ACTU expected its members to take an active part in the maintenance of their union locals, so they expected members to participate in its religious equivalent: the Mass. "YOU are going to say Mass WITH the Priest," the speaker insisted, for the Mass is "an ACTION, and if YOU and YOU and YOU don't play YOUR part, the Mass is MISSING SOMETHING." The religious practice was not in itself new to Catholic workers; rather, the meaning of practice had been remade by the context of the late 1930s.[33]

Like the specific ritual of the mass, the broader Catholic devotional culture sometimes adopted labor-conscious idioms. Novenas—popular nine-day series of intense, directed prayers—sometimes expressed these currents. St. Rose of Lima parish, for instance, announced a novena in 1934 for St. Philomena, "The Patron of Working People" (the more ubiquitous novenas for St. Jude, the patron saint of hopeless causes, addressed working-class concerns also, albeit less explicitly). On the very personal level of everyday prayer, too, the ACTU and its allies linked class identity with devotional religion. ACTU prayer cards, distributed through the Catholic Extension Society, displayed a romantic familial image etched in the artistic style of Norman Rockwell.

A muscular, haloed St. Joseph sits at his workbench painting a toy donkey and gazing at his precocious, haloed divine son; young, blond-haired Jesus, shoulders folded upon the workbench, smiles broadly up at his father. On its backside, the card conveys New York Archbishop's Patrick Cardinal Hayes's "Prayer of the Worker," which includes a petition to Jesus:

> You were a worker as I am, give to me and all the workers of the world the privilege to work as You did, so that everything we do may be to the benefit of our fellowmen and the greater glory of God the Father. Thy Kingdom come into the factories and into the shops, into our homes and into our streets. . . . To us who labor and are heavily burdened send speedily the refreshment of Thy love. May we never sin against Thee.

The imagery and rhetoric of this prayer obviously reflected the specific concerns of workers but blended into the broader world of Catholic devotionalism. Such blending was the essence of worker religion for Catholics of the New Deal generation.[34]

Remaking the Black Church

Since the first all-black denominations formed in the early nineteenth century, African American churches had been centers of community action, voices for social justice, and catalysts for public involvement. However, the actual practice of African American religion at the beginning of the 1930s appeared remarkably traditional. Worship revolved around preaching and singing. The twin impulses toward emotional exuberance and social respectability remained intertwined elements of religious life. An often-literal commitment to the Bible, and a palpable belief in the embodied power of God, permeated the churches. The congregation itself bound black communities together.[35]

As the social and political context evolved, so, too, did the meaning and significance of religion. At the dawn of the 1930s, African American workers were almost entirely unorganized, deeply suspicious of labor unions, and loyal to the Republican Party, attitudes that were strongly reinforced from the leading black pulpits. But by the early 1940s, African Americans had become stalwart supporters of the Democratic Party and the CIO and articulated a consciousness that fused religiosity, labor activism, and race-based rights. Slowly over the course of the 1930s, black workers' hopes and expectations climbed upward on the back of the labor movement. A growing sense of political empowerment meshed with dreams of workplace equality and a general cultural celebration of common workers to reorient black workers' identity. Meanwhile, within churches, a "prophetic" message shaded in tones of the social gospel began tugging the traditional world of the black church into the orbit of the New Deal. Charles Hill, minister at Hartford Avenue Baptist Church and partisan of the labor movement, celebrated this transition. In 1943, he happily reported that "the colored clergy tell their flocks to obey the Lord and obey the CIO." The NAACP's Gloster Current agreed with Hill, observing that "Many colored deacons who were previously anti-CIO have now swung around and are all out for the CIO." The "remaking" of religious consciousness in the 1930s and 1940s reconciled black workers to the world of the UAW, and reinterpreted the union within the prism of the black church.[36]

This change is especially dramatic considering the deep connection between many black churches and Detroit's industrialists, specifically Henry Ford. Beginning in 1919, Ford established a relationship with the Rev. Robert Bradby of Second Baptist Church, a pattern he extended with Father Everard Daniel at St. Matthew's Episcopal. In both cases, Ford relied on the recommendations of these pastors in hiring black workers, especially at his massive River Rouge complex. Despite the fact that the work of most blacks at the Rouge consisted of dangerous and difficult jobs in the foundry, recent arrivals nevertheless quickly realized that Ford hired far more blacks than the other plants, and some even earned the opportunity to enroll in Ford's mechanical school to acquire valuable skills. Bradby and Daniel, already sympathetic to Ford's ideology of self-help and individualism, also profited from the arrangement as membership in their churches soared in the 1920s. Without the protection of organized labor, a paternalistic, if practical, relationship evolved between white industrialists looking for cheap labor (and hoping that a racially diverse workforce would deter efforts at unionization), black ministers seeking to solidify their roles as intercultural power brokers, and black workers eager for a job.[37]

The Great Depression deeply undermined the stability of this relationship between Ford and the ministers because no Detroit community was harder hit by the economic disaster than African Americans. Well over half of the city's African Americans were jobless; in 1930, only 364 out of 5,593 men who came to the Detroit Urban League were able to find work. Instead, African Americans filled Detroit's welfare rolls in a percentage far higher than their overall population; in 1933, a representative year, 30 percent of the 40,249 families receiving public assistance were black, even though African Americans constituted less than 10 percent of the total city population. By 1934, the Department of Public Welfare—anxious not to have what it called "a preponderance of Negroes" on its rolls—was pleading with employers to hire black workers, but these efforts were largely rebuffed with the answer that blacks were "lazy" or caused difficulties with white workers. Meanwhile, federal efforts to prop up declining wages even produced a cruel backlash for African Americans. Immediately after the National Recovery Administration (NRA) issued a wage code in 1933, African American workers found themselves laid off in droves. At least four Detroit hotels fired several hundred black workers rather than pay them a higher, mandated wage. As a state investigation of the NRA morosely but accurately concluded, "every opportunity is used to exploit Negro labor." Homes became dilapidated; "For Rent" signs dotted neighborhoods; despair took root. Truly, as John Dancy surmised, the Depression presented "a very dismal picture of Detroit's Negro situation."[38]

Churches, of course, were also "very vitally affected" by the Depression, in the words of John Dancy. In 1932, every black church in the city except Ebenezer AME was mired in debt. A number of church buildings faced foreclosure by banks. At Shiloh Baptist Church, the Depression brought "bitter-and-thin times," and the church "kind of fell apart," according to member O. Devene Ross McKinney. Even Second Baptist, Detroit's largest and oldest black church, faced crisis and economic paralysis in the 1930s. As early as 1929, Second Baptist minister Robert Bradby was mailing out letters to various creditors, explaining that "the economic depression came upon us" and asking for leniency. In 1930, as he solicited charitable donations from prominent Detroiters, Bradby shared the shocking statistics of his congregation: out of 4,300 members, 90 percent were unemployed.[39]

Churches bravely struggled to structure everyday life and hold communities together. Looking back on the Depression, Ernestine Wright remembered "times when I didn't have my meal for the next day, but I didn't cry. I did come to the church," where she secured some food and a small cash gift. Shiloh Baptist member Mary O. Brookins Ross recalled that her church "kept the faith and served many people in need of food and jobs." On Detroit's heavily black east side—an area of 100,000 people, in which over 50 percent of housing was deemed uninhabitable by one city worker—residents continued to support nearly three dozen Protestant churches. Likewise, John Dancy observed that Detroit's west-side African American churches were "filled to capacity at all services." Songs and sermons, meanwhile, reiterated traditional messages. The problem of unemployment, according to Rev. Solomon Ross, flowed from "sin" (although Ross allowed that sin might be social as well as individual). He argued that ministers should "get hungry sinners jobs" to demonstrate the power of Christ, an attitude that demonstrates both the desperation of the Depression-era jobless and abiding confidence in divine intervention. Spiritualist churches established food banks with uncharacter-istic social aplomb, but most also remained focused on the world beyond and offered what one minister described as "Divine Healing."[40]

But other African Americans were attracted to extreme and unorthodox religious options. In the Nation of Islam, African Americans found a revised version of Garveyism, a fervent linkage of racial pride with religious separat-ism, and a rejection of all pluralistic and politically liberal appeals. Founded in Detroit by W. D. Fard, an "Arab peddler" who lived in the Motor City from 1930 to 1934, the Black Muslims found most of its converts among the poor blacks suffering from the worst that Depression-era Detroit had to offer. Deeply resentful of their poverty and the perceived sanctimony of city welfare workers, converts to the Nation of Islam discovered a closely knit, highly disciplined community that inculcated the habits of worldly success. In 1930, as one student of the movement discovered, practically all of the 5,000–8,000 members were languishing in Detroit's slums and surviving on welfare checks; by 1937, none were on welfare and most were working steadily and maintain-ing a healthy standard of living. Such solidarity required Black Muslims to strongly distinguish between community insiders and outsiders. Although they lived in African American neighborhoods, converts remained isolated from the larger black community. The practice of the religion highlighted this process of separating an "elect" from the "fallen"; converts received new names (which they paid for), accepted dietary laws to remind them of the exile from their "homeland" of Africa, and obtained a new sacred book and sacred clothing.[41]

The Black Muslims made plenty of enemies. Detroit's police force, insensi-tive if not hostile toward African Americans, derided the sect as a "voodoo cult," and even accused the group of human sacrifice (Fard allegedly claimed to require the sacrifice of four white "devils" every year to allow him to return to Mecca). Fard's description of himself to police—that he was the "Supreme Ruler of the Universe"—did little to smooth these tensions. But the Black Muslims, despite their social roots among the poor and working class, likewise found few friends among liberal leaders in the African American community, or in the labor movement. The ecumenical John Dancy, in a moment of exasperation, complained that the "Moslem Cult" was "hard to reckon with. They will listen to nobody and they are unafraid." A.N. Hen-niger of the Detroit Board of Education employed even stronger language; he accused the Black Muslims' schools of teaching "race hatred, untruth, and mysticism." Shelton Tappes, an important African American organizer for the UAW, simply dismissed the "Muslim movement" by claiming it "didn't seem to call for an activity. And the people in those days [the 1930s] seemed to want to be actively involved or engaged in something." However, Tappes dissimilated; as a race-based sect with a vision of exclusivist black nationalism, the Black Muslims actively competed for the loyalty of African Americans and radically rejected the pluralistic and progressive vision essential to the UAW's mission. In fact, one study of the movement found that Black Muslims spoke "violently of the war of the C.I.O. against Allah and the need of removing from Planet Earth all Union organizers." When racial and ethnic consciousness mixed deeply with religious idioms, shared class interests with other groups became hazy and indistinct.[42]

The experience of black church life was, thus, in a state of tremendous ferment as the cultural tone of the Depression, with its sympathetic images of workers and "common folk," began slowly infiltrating religious cultures and institutions. In late 1931, the Detroit Urban League—known for its symbiotic relationship with the churches and promotion of a middle-class ethic of respectability, not for social or economic radicalism—joined with the Fellowship of Reconciliation and the League for Industrial Democracy to hold a mass protest against unemployment. By 1937, the Urban League's John Dancy, long a skeptic of organized labor, noticed that the course of the decade had produced a rising "union consciousness" among black workers. That Dancy, a figure of considerable influence within church circles, had begun to sympathize with and endorse the CIO signaled the beginning of a major shift in the political aspect of black religious life.[43]

Sure enough, "union consciousness" began slowly penetrating churches. In July of 1937, Bethel AME Church—one of the largest and most prestigious black churches in the city—hosted a major industrial conference around the theme, "The working men and their union." Delegates from "union, fraternal, civic, church, veterans, women and youth organizations" attended. Even more suggestively, when construction jobs began opening on a government housing project that same month, Bethel's minister William Peck was asked to inform all unionized "painters, plasterers, carpenters, brick layers and latherers" in his congregation to register at the Detroit Urban League. Obviously, the Urban League must have known that a good number of Bethel's congregants were unionized workers; many more were likely weighing the benefits of the UAW, and Rev. Peck felt the issue deserved serious attention.[44]

To some extent, black ministers were pushed into a more "social" interest because they could feel the winds of change and worried about a secular backlash from workers who felt deserted by their ministers; perhaps, clerics fretted, the urban angst of the Depression would ignite this tendency into a wildfire that churches couldn't put out. In 1931, Second Baptist's Robert Bradby complained of "the peculiar approach that people have today of what you call the Gospel, and the lack of confidence that is clearly manifested on the part of the masses for what we call leadership. Long coats and high collars have no more influence now." Fissures even began emerging between African American institutions once closely joined. Bradby, a one-time president of Detroit's NAACP, was shocked to hear that NAACP President Walter White made a "very scalding attack upon the church" and offered dismissive remarks about Christ during a visit to Detroit in 1931. Bradby threatened to quit the organization wholesale. White eventually assuaged Bradby and kept the illustrious minister within the NAACP, but clearly the forces of the Depression were eroding traditional cultural pillars.[45]

Bradby was due for more shocks to come. In 1938, George S. Schuyler, a highly regarded black intellectual associated with W. E. B. DuBois's journal *Crisis*, described anti-UAW ministers like Bradby as "Uncle Toms." Schuyler sarcastically derided the "gentlemen of the cloth, reverend gentlemen who are eager to sell out their people for filthy lucre" by choosing the interests of an auto magnate over black working people. Such rhetoric tapped the latent suspicion among many ordinary working people that ministers abused their lofty positions for personal gain. Other secular, grass-roots organizations also challenged the traditional primacy of the church in African American society. The Ford Hunger March of 1932, organized by "unemployed councils" affiliated with the Communist Party, brought some African Americans into a broad coalition of social groups. The brutality of Ford's response to the peaceful march—four people died when police responded with violence— also caused many blacks to question their normally unshakable loyalty to the auto giant. One black worker, writing the UAW's newspaper in 1937, claimed that the brutal conditions in Ford factories killed two of his brothers. He ridiculed Ford's unwillingness "to practice among his employees the piety he glibly preaches when he condescends to visit certain churches in our alley"; ministers who remained committed to Ford, it might be concluded, were similarly hypocritical. Meanwhile, Snow Grigsby, an activist African American postal worker, organized the Civic Rights Congress, and castigated "our Negro political leaders, ministers" and NAACP for failing to develop "a constructive program, and uniting our forces . . . for the advancement of the Negro masses." The Civic Rights Congress was not overtly antireligious—indeed, two ministers served on the committee—but it offered discontented African Americans a venue of social protest detached from clerical leadership, critical of clerical failures, and preoccupied with a populist advancement of the "Negro masses."[46]

Outside these social forces, some ministers also worried that Ford's financial grip on black churches was strangulating and perverting the spiritual core of congregations. As one African American observer concluded, "The fact is that the possibility of getting a job at the Ford Motor Company has been the incentive in many instances for Negroes' joining the church." The Rev. Malcolm Dade of St. Cyprian's Episcopal Church resented precisely this influence. "It was pitiful to see how men would come to you and beg you to just give them a letter," he later recalled. Dade pointed out that one of his parishioners attended religious services at his church, but also belonged to the St. Matthew's Men Club because it was the only way to get a foot in the door at Ford's. Dade even "had a man offer me $50 for a letter and all I had to say was just that I recommend the bearer of this letter for employment at Ford Motor Company."[47]

Pushed by secular currents, generational divisions, and their own interpretation of religious mission, new religious leaders emerged in the 1930s to promote a remaking of African American religious consciousness. In 1936, Horace White, a 27-year-old graduate of the Divinity School at Oberlin College, arrived in Detroit and assumed pastoral duties at Plymouth Congregational Church. White's decision to take up the pastorate at Plymouth indicated the minister's gumption. Just one year earlier, John Dancy opined that anyone interested in serving as Plymouth's minister was taking a "big chance," for the church was "not a going concern" despite a congregation of 200 prominent black Detroiters. White accepted the challenge, perhaps viewing Detroit as just the right place to "remake" black religious culture. Deeply impressed with the legacy of the social gospel, White quickly became a fixture in Detroit's political, civic, and civil rights scene. In 1940–1941, he would serve two terms in the state senate, and he maintained a politically oriented column in Detroit's African American newspaper, the *Michigan Chronicle*.[48]

In the late 1930s, White, like most liberals, was impressed with the social potential of the labor movement, and he immediately turned Plymouth Church into a meeting place for aspiring black unionists. In 1938, White broadcast his views in the *Christian Century*—the nation's preeminent journal of liberal Protestantism—assailing the black churches' willful captivity to Detroit's industrial elites. White's position, however, remained controversial. H. Easton Jr., a black worker at Ford's, attacked the minister as a UAW "agitator" and an outsider unfamiliar with the reality of most black peoples' working lives. Mockingly, Easton asked, "Has the learned ecclesiastical brother, who has seen fit to step down from his lofty pulpit to advise the Ford employees, done as much for his congregation?" Interestingly, Easton attacked White for precisely the traits that George Schuyler assailed in pro-Ford ministers like Robert Bradby: elitism, arrogance, and presumptuousness. The anticlerical blade thus cut both ways. And, in a sense, Easton was correct; White was certainly better educated and promoted a more sophisticated theological vision than Detroit's many black storefront preachers. His congregation, likewise, was unusually well-educated and financially stable. And, coming as he did from the sober Puritan tradition of Congregationalism, White may have lacked some of the Baptist, Methodist, or Pentecostal spark that typically attracted black worshippers. Nevertheless, White had begun to change the perspective of black workers and ministers alike.[49]

Malcolm Dade's story neatly paralleled White's. Like White, Dade had received advanced theological education, and his view of religion, like White's, was obviously tinged with the ideology of the social gospel; as he described to an interviewer, Dade became a UAW partisan because "the church had to be relevant to whatever was good for people in all phases of their life, whether it was economic, political, or social." Like White, Dade was not a Detroit native but arrived in the city from New England in 1936—the same year as White's arrival, Frank Murphy's election as governor, and the beginning of the UAW sit-down campaign. Dade's reaction to the life of black Detroiters mirrored White's; he remembered coming "into a community and here was a situation having to do with the working life of people that was just flagrantly bad, wrong, certainly not good." Like White, Dade also served a mainline church in which African Americans occupied a small minority; whereas White was a Congregational minister, Dade was an Episcopal priest. Dade's church, St. Cyprian's Episcopal, "was a store front" when he arrived in Detroit, but, like White's church and only a small handful of others, St. Cyprian's survived without the philanthropy of Henry Ford. As newcomers to Detroit, White and Dade were less entangled within the existing order and felt freer to offer criticism. Their education, theology, and congregational independence added to their self-assurance.[50]

Yet, where White's congregation consisted mainly of sympathetic middle-class African Americans who were already involved in the NAACP, the YM/WCA, and social welfare service, Dade's congregation contained a "good many" Ford workers (one of whom, Horace Sheffield, would become an important black unionist). Almost none of these workers had attained advanced positions at the plant, a dilemma that bred a sense of dependence. Dade's social pronouncements thus carried a greater personal risk for his own security at St. Cyprian's. And not all of his parishioners were responsive to Dade's positions; one of them, Dade recalled, accosted him, declaring "it was a terrible thing for a pastor of the church, particularly, to take a stand against Mr. Ford." Another disturbed parishioner, in more explicitly theological language, argued that "it was a sin to go or do anything that would hurt Mr. Ford" (though after the UAW triumphed, this man did join the union).

Likewise, as a priest in a hierarchically arranged church, Dade risked upsetting his superiors and incurring reprimands or transfer. When Dade hosted UAW speakers at St. Cyprian's, fellow priest and Ford loyalist Father Everard Daniels complained to the Bishop that Dade was hosting "political meetings." Dade, in short, was forced to remain clear-eyed: "if the union had not succeeded at Ford's I would . . . no longer be the minister of St Cyprian's. . . . I would have had to resign." But Dade also understood his own significance; union leaders, Dade explained, "wanted to put their finger on Negro life. And, Negro life . . . is in the Negro church."[51]

More representative of black church life, and probably more influential than White and Dade, was the Baptist minister Charles A. Hill. From the late 1930s into the 1960s, Hill combined a universalistic vision of human rights, a commitment to radical politics, and the passion of his Baptist pulpit to become black Detroit's preeminent prophetic voice. Hill was born in Detroit in 1893, the child of a black father and a white, ethnically German mother; his parents never married, and Hill apparently knew little of his father. Although baptized in the Catholic faith of his mother, Hill shopped around Detroit's religious marketplace, eventually landing at Robert Bradby's Second Baptist Church. After completing correspondence coursework from the Moody Bible Institute, Hill attended seminary at the Presbyterian Lincoln University in rural Pennsylvania. Upon graduating in 1918, Hill returned to Detroit and became assistant pastor at Second Baptist under Bradby.[52]

In 1920, Hill left Bradby to establish Hartford Avenue Baptist Church. And, although Hill never publicly denigrated his mentor, the two men stood on opposite sides of a generational divide that was reshaping the political life (if not the religious message) of the black church. Bradby, a longtime benefactor of Henry Ford's self-interested philanthropy, never broke his ties with the powerful industrialist. But Bradby's notions of individualism and self-help, and his hostility toward industrial unions, seemed increasingly out of place in 1930s-era Detroit. Hill, on the other hand, became one of the earliest and most vocal black supporters of the UAW and a ubiquitous presence in labor-liberal political circles. Like the disagreement between Fr. Everett Daniels (another loyal Ford supporter) and Malcolm Dade, the division between Hill and his mentor did not represent a fundamentally new approach to religious life—but it did signal a deep shift within the political culture of the black church, in which an older consciousness molded around a new social identity.[53]

The process was not seamless or without conflict. From an initial membership of thirty-five, Hill's church grew to become, by 1926, one of the ten largest black churches in the city, and many of these new members were

Ford workers. When Hill first spoke out against Ford, over one hundred members left the church. Most of these members, according to Hill, returned to the church and joined the union after the strike concluded, but their action reveals the deep ambivalence and discomfort some black workers had with the new world of the CIO. Many of those worshippers who temporarily abandoned Hartford likely feared for their jobs, but they were also not yet comfortable with the idea that the church—traditionally the source of order, respectability, and contemplation of eternal verities—should involve itself in controversial political matters. Hill himself obliquely commented on this point, noting that many of those who left Hartford later "admitted that, after all, the church ought to be interested in all areas here on earth, as well as talking about going to heaven." Part of Hill's significance was the ability to fuse these elements together, weaving New Deal politics into the religious consciousness of many black workers.[54]

By early 1941, the UAW's efforts to transform Detroit into a "union town" approached a defining crisis point. Having established contracts with Dodge and General Motors, the UAW desperately needed to receive recognition from the last unorganized auto giant, the Ford Motor Company. Failure at Ford's risked creating a precedent that might allow the other two automakers to void their contracts, hence dooming the union. Ford also contained by far the largest number of African American employees. Quite simply, if these black workers resisted the union, Ford could not be organized. As early as 1937, the union had hired the worker-preacher William Bowman—a molder in the Chevrolet Grey Iron factory as well as pastor of Detroit's Christ Community Church—to advocate on its behalf among other ministers beginning to tire of Ford's paternalistic stance. White, Dade, and Hill continued Bowman's work by participating in the Negro Ford Organizing Committee (NFOC), a group that brought together a broad cross section of workers, unionists, and sympathetic professionals.[55]

The timing for committee meetings—Sunday mornings—was imperfect. UAW organizer Shelton Tappes observed that "many of the ministers weren't able to come," although he remained well aware that the "ministers were important" because their participation represented a breakdown in the paternalistic system of black church support coming from white industrialists. Still, even if the NFOC appreciated clerical support, the timing of their meetings suggests that some members may have accepted such support at arm's length. Perhaps NFOC participants saw their own Sunday morning meetings as a more masculine counterpart to church, where black women dominated the pews. Perhaps some remained suspicious of religion and preferred to limit the ministers' involvement. James Boggs, a black activist on the UAW's left wing, hinted at the possible tension between secular and religious cultures among black workers when he recalled that, in the early 1940s, "Guys stopped going to church and go to the union meetings." However, Boggs continued, "then it wasn't long before people was back at the church and the union meetings was down." Whatever the explanation for Sunday morning meetings, prophetically inclined ministers remained publicly associated with the NFOC and offered the organization an aura of respectability.[56]

Ultimately, in April of 1941, the labors of UAW organizers and their clerical allies were finally put to the test when a strike was launched against the Ford Motor Company. Horace White delivered speeches and sermons from the UAW's sound truck that constantly circled the plant. When a contingent of black workers resisted joining the strike, Hill "went out to the Ford factory and I pleaded with them to come out; I told them that they could not afford to make any advance by themselves; they had to learn to work with other workers." Hill was happy to host union meetings in Hartford's basement, making it "difficult for [Ford spies] to prove that we were just discussing union matters. And so . . . [unionists] got together regardless of their race and nationality." Hill's entreaties were appreciated by his secular colleagues. Carl Winter, a communist labor leader, later claimed that Hill "played an important and a very likely decisive role in bringing the workers in the Ford Rouge plant to support the union. . . . Reverend Hill played a very active part in appearing in the picket lines and talking to black workers and inviting them to come out and join the union."[57]

Ministers who supported the UAW not only sought a renegotiation of power arrangements between workers and managers: they also connected the union with the ethics and idioms of the black church. Sunday after Sunday, black workers absorbed a message of empowerment through the story of Exodus; they asserted dignity, self-respect, and a measure of equality through the public performance of worship. When the UAW itself stressed these goals—the dignity of work, fair treatment, a semblance of personal consent with one's daily environment—ministers and workers alike responded positively from their *own* frame of experience. Though it likely did not realize the connection, the UAW was essentially proposing to extend some of the social values of church life into the workplace.

This connection, to some extent, explains perhaps the least acknowledged aspect of Detroit's socially activist black clergy: the utterly routine nature of life in their churches. Underneath the genuinely new secular commitments to industrial unionism and progressive politics, Hill, White, and Dade all remained popular, first and foremost, as pastors. Hartford Avenue Baptist Church, for instance, consistently hosted a laundry list of social clubs and activities, including children's groups, choirs, a missionary society, and prayer services. St. Cyprians, too, built its reputation around the variety of activities it offered; indeed, Malcolm Dade's first and abiding priority, upon arriving at the church in 1936, was the development of a strong network of extracurricular pastimes for young people. Horace White's major achievement in 1936–1937, aside from his public excoriation of Henry Ford, was purchasing an organ to improve the musical offerings for his congregation. It was from *within* this dense social and spiritual context that radicals like the communist singer Paul Robeson would make periodic appearances at Hill's church, blending old-time spirituals with the newly emerging political identity. The unionists meeting in the church basement were made all the more normal and legitimate by blending into the established network of church-based social ties and the broader African American religious narrative of exodus, survival, and justification.[58]

White Southerners and the Remaking of Evangelical Culture

As the Great Depression shook Detroit's social firmament, a third large migrant group struggled for a foothold among the city's working class: poor white evangelicals from the South. Southern whites, like Catholics and African Americans, were highly religious; and southern evangelicals, too, remade religious consciousness in the volatile factories of the North. Estimates of Detroit's southern-born white population fluctuated substantially. One detailed study asserted that more than 100,000 southerners entered Detroit in the 1920s, lured by the promise of high wages. A Wayne State sociologist argued that the number was close to 80,000 in 1930, although Louis Adamic found only 15,000–30,000 when he examined the city in 1935. The onset of the Great Depression likely explains the discrepancies between these numbers, as many southern whites fled Detroit's decimated labor market and returned to subsistence farming in Appalachia. One study conducted between 1937 and 1939 found that most of its subjects had migrated back and forth between Michigan and Tennessee at least four times, and often as many as eight times. Industrial waged work in the fall and winter combined with subsistence farming in the spring and summer.[59]

Southern whites, as a largely seasonal workforce, only sporadically settled in Detroit before World War II. But some southerners could be found working at small hamburger joints, gas companies, or dairies. Most shared the experiences of Andrew Cotham, who grew up on a hardscrabble farm in

Tennessee and moved to Detroit via Missouri in 1928, following a word-of-mouth path already blazed by others from his district. Typically, Cotham found work in the auto industry, bouncing around a number of plants before eventually moving up to semiskilled work. While exact numbers are unclear, contemporaries estimated that 20–30 percent of all autoworkers by the mid-1930s were southern-born whites. In some factories, southerners could occupy as much as half the workforce.[60]

Like most migrant groups, southern whites were deeply conscious of their "outsider" status in Detroit. Elmer Akers, researching the world of southern whites in the 1930s, found that employers, labor agents, and landlords alike disdained southerners as dishonest, lazy, and clannish. Erskine Caldwell, himself a son of the South, painted a grim picture of southerners' lives in the urban north. On any given night, Caldwell claimed, an underclass of homeless teenagers roamed downtown Detroit, "slipping into and out of beer parlors, hovering in the shadows of alleys, and whispering together in the all-night movie houses on Woodward Avenue." These were the refugees of the southern diaspora, "the working-class families that left their homes in Tennessee, in Texas, in Kansas. . . . don't be a sucker and remain a hillbilly all your life," Caldwell imagined them hearing—"on to Detroit!" Many workers, meanwhile, viewed southern whites as labor competition. The acerbic Louis Adamic captured this animosity when he dismissed the southern newcomers as "hill-billies . . . 'white trash' or a little better," who took jobs away from seasoned workers more amenable to unionization. Margaret Collingwood Nowak—wife of Stanley Nowak, the UAW's liaison to Detroit's Polish workers—observed that important plants like GM's Ternstedt on Detroit's west side hired "easily exploited groups—southerners, foreigners, and women." In the eyes of management, "Any U.S. born worker was dubbed a 'hillbilly,'" and social distance between European-born and southern-born workers was used to forestall bonuses and wage increases.[61]

Nevertheless, by 1937, more than 7 percent of white Detroiters had been born in southern states (nearly the same percentage as black Detroiters). A few "colonies of southern people"—such as the so-called "Cass Corridor" (running along Cass Avenue)—became well known as sites of southern taverns and honky-tonks. More significantly, the religious culture of the South was physically reshaping the religious geography of the city. By the late 1930s, southern migrants had built 3 Pentecostal Assemblies of God congregations, 41 non–Northern Baptist congregations, and at least half-dozen other enterprises, including the Detroit Foursquare Gospel, Detroit Gospel Tabernacle, and Missionary Tabernacle. At the same time, radio channel CKLW, broadcasting from Windsor, Ontario, targeted Detroit's southern whites with what one analyst called "reactionary politics, old time religion," and various commercial appeals.[62]

The religion of poor white southerners has long been caricatured or derided for its supposed overemotionalism, provincial narrowness, and antiintellectualism. Indeed, as poor white southern religion swelled into Detroit in the 1930s, it fit neatly into the Progressive-modernist discursive category of "working-class religion" already constructed to assess immigrant Catholics and southern-black migrants. Liston Pope, a leading liberal theologian of the period and ally of the labor movement, could thus dismiss poor white southern religion in 1942 as serving chiefly to make "this present life more endurable" by offering "escape from it in otherworldliness and emotional excitement." It was, in short, an opiate, one typically wielded by church-building employers to dull any threat from labor activism. Scholars following Pope's lead have offered a variety of "deprivation" theories to explain the religious culture of poor southern whites, seeing religion as a type of psychological "compensation" for the abject poverty endured by so many rural southerners. The folklorist D. K. Wilgus, meanwhile, assessed poor white southern religiosity in northern cities some thirty years after Pope, and found a "rigid, patriarchal morality . . . accompanied by a deep drive for individualistic expression." For Wilgus, transplanted southern society "was one of extremes: sobriety and drunkenness, piety and hellraising, daily stoicism and orgiastic religious revivals."[63]

Recent scholarship has altered and deepened our understanding of poor white religion, moving away from Pope's dismissiveness while complicating the dualistic portrait offered by Wilgus. The religious worlds of the poor southern whites arriving in Detroit had witnessed profound and rapid changes dating back to the late nineteenth century. Just as the southern economy was jarringly remade by the incursion of industrialism and the rise of the tenant-farming regime, and just as the southern political system was violently reshaped into racist, single-party Democratic rule after the collapse of the Peoples' Party, the religious worlds of southerners were rocked by the explosive spread of holiness, Pentecostal, and fundamentalist movements, on the one hand, and the rise of religious modernism on the other. Many poor southern whites embraced the various evangelical insurgencies of the early twentieth century as a way to claim authenticity, meaning, and community for themselves, in response to social elites who exploited them and cultural elites who denigrated them.[64]

While the various new evangelical movements of the early twentieth century were distinct from (even hostile with) each other, certain main elements characterized poor white southern religion. Perhaps most important was the deep and lasting cultural imprint of Calvinism, which had defined southern religiosity since the mid–eighteenth century.[65] Calvinism could be a demanding, exacting faith. It entreated Christians to vigorously prepare themselves for salvation, even as it assured them that most people—including many of themselves—were hopeless sinners, sure to be damned. The Calvinist temperament enabled a cool stoicism, a certain quiet resignation to the difficulties and iniquities of the world. According to the northern missionary Elizabeth Hooker, the southern religious mentality envisioned life as a "stupendous tragic drama," in which "trouble and suffering" was the normal lot. At its worst, this mentality might lead to fatalism or apathy. Because Calvinism stressed the salvation of a small "elect," it lead some believers away from broader social action and toward a "separated," purified, exclusivist community. From the perch of these islands of holiness, the wickedness of others might seem all the more apparent, and the temptation to judge outsiders harshly proved hard to resist.[66]

But this same Calvinist culture also provided poor white southerners with meaningful scaffolding for making religious consciousness. In urging each individual Christian to prepare her/himself for salvation, Calvinism suggested a deep well of internal spiritual possibilities. Southern Calvinism's highest ideal was the attainment of a "born again" moment of joyous release and rapturous reinvention, where the individual soul fused with a divine essence and emerged from the encounter a new spiritual creature. Moreover, the insurgent Holiness and Pentecostal movements of the early-twentieth-century South radically altered the Calvinist notions of predestination by preaching "perfectability" for all who opened themselves to God. The possibility of personally serving as a vessel of the Holy Spirit, even if the larger world dismissed you as ignorant and disposable, was an empowering possibility for many. The emphasis on human sinfulness, meanwhile, elevated humility, honesty, and sincerity as key social values.

Likewise, the injunction to build godly communities compelled southerners to take the virtues of friendliness, neighborliness, and communal well-being very seriously. Many southern congregations essentially became extended, fictive families, uniting "brothers" and "sisters" in Christ and providing working-class people with a vital source of social capital. These spiritual kin-clans were sometimes transplanted to the North nearly intact. The roster of one Southern Baptist church, built just east of the Packard Motor Plant in Detroit, contained 160 members from the same cluster of neighborhoods in Mayfield, Kentucky. Revivals and preaching in the Appalachian vernacular were common; the church served as these migrants' main vehicle for "preserving . . . the spirit and outlook of their native southern community."[67]

The creation of these deeply knit congregational communities supported a final important element of poor white religious culture: a deep, intuitive sensitivity to matters of fairness, justice, and mutual respect. Although southern whites often appeared to outsiders as an easily exploited proletariat (the Calvinist stoicism, perhaps, serving as a deceptive survival mechanism), workers' seeming passivity could quickly dissipate if employers were perceived to violate a community's sense of just treatment. After all, if *spiritual* equality prevailed in Christ's Kingdom, and if any believer might be saved, then a certain respect was due even to the least of those on Earth. Most southerners were convinced that fairness and justice were explicitly ordained in the Bible, and one of the long-standing consequences of the revivals of the early nineteenth century was the firm belief that the Bible offered a plain, uncomplicated truth, comprehensible to any who could read a text or hear a sermon. As Elizabeth Hooker noted in her extensive Depression-era study of Appalachian religion, the Bible reigned as "the ultimate source of authority regarding truth of whatever kind." This profound attachment to the notion of common-sense biblical justice shaped two key components of poor white religious life: first, it helps explain the attraction of fundamentalism, with its insistence on the inerrancy of scripture, to many southern migrants; and second, it nurtured an antiauthoritarian, antielitist populism with open-ended political possibilities.[68]

Many of these threads within southern religious consciousness were picked up by the most famous and notorious southern religious transplant of the 1930s: J. Frank Norris. In 1934, Norris accepted the pastorate at Temple Baptist Church in Detroit. Always a swirl of energy (as suggested by his preferred nickname, the "Texas Tornado"), Norris energetically set out to transform Temple Baptist into a thriving epicenter of plain-folk fundamentalism. Missionary teams canvassed the neighborhood around the church, expertly honing in on recent arrivals from the South. Visiting committees went door to door, chatting up potential congregants. Meanwhile, Norris broadcast blistering, hellfire-and-brimstone sermons over Detroit's WJR, the most powerful radio signal in the city. He moved his newspaper, *The Fundamentalist*, from Texas to Detroit in order to highlight activities in the North. Entrepreneurial and opportunistic, Norris was fantastically successful; in five years, he built Temple Baptist's membership from 800 to over 6,000. Upward of 75 percent of these additions were transplanted southerners.[69]

Combative and crusading, Norris had emerged as a fierce partisan in the divisive struggle between modernism and fundamentalism that first emerged in the 1910s. For Norris, modernism was a cosmic force irresistibly pledged to the destruction of Christianity and needed to be vigorously resisted. Even the

Southern Baptist Convention (SBC) seemed, to Norris, too accommodating. By the 1920s, Norris had built a minor Baptist empire out of his mega-church in Fort Worth, which he used as the base for his own independent organization, the World Fundamental Baptist Missionary Fellowship (WFBMF). Norris exemplified what historian Joel Carpenter has called the "separatist impulse" in American fundamentalism: the desire to disentangle the church from a hopelessly lost world and build an alternate society for God's faithful remnant. The WFBMF published its own newspaper, which in turn revolved around Norris's personality and reflected his own interpretation of scripture. Immediately upon arrival at Temple Baptist Church, Norris pulled the congregation out of the Northern Baptist Convention and into the separated world of the WFBMF.[70]

While Norris was obsessively antimodernist, he was also steeped in Texas populism (like the more famous William Jennings Bryan, who also fused populism and fundamentalism). In 1911 and 1912, Norris ran off wealthier members of his congregation because he preferred "the more virtuous common folk." He criticized billionaires like John D. Rockefeller and praised the dignity of labor. Norris's populism clearly appealed to southern transplants in Detroit. When Beauchamp Vick, Norris's music director from Fort Worth, arrived in Detroit in 1936, he approvingly noted that Temple Baptist's congregation was composed of "what we call in Kentucky 'real folks.'" In many northern congregations, working-class southern whites were denigrated as uncouth, unsophisticated hillbillies; it is not surprising that so many chose the affirming, community-building characterization they received at Temple Baptist.[71]

But Norris's populism would undergo a profound change in the northern, urban milieu of Detroit. He arrived in the city during the same volatile upsurge of CIO activism that pushed Catholic and African American congregations into rethinking the relationship between religion, labor, and politics. Whereas many Catholic and African American figures began to see the union as a truly just "people's movement," Norris moved in the diametrically opposite direction. Partly, this shift can be attributed to Norris's chummy relationship with Detroit's leading industrialists, many of whom came to finance his religious efforts. Ideologically, however, Norris became obsessed with communism, which he saw infecting both the New Deal and the CIO, and this fear of communism propelled the preacher far to the right. It was, for Norris and other fundamentalists, an almost talismanic term: communism would end liberty and usher in dictatorship; it would replace the local rule of common folk with a bureaucracy of atheistic elites; it would end marriage and unleash sexual libertinism; it would erode white supremacy and promote "race mixing"; it would replace belief in God with the cult of Man; and, most importantly to Norris, it was the final realization of theological modernism and, as such, a harbinger of the end-times.[72]

Norris's anticommunist denunciations likely shaped the thinking of less prominent ministers such as Elmer Rollings. In 1937, Rollings declared that the reading rooms at Detroit's YMCA were filled with communist literature and accused the organization of supporting presentations by communist speakers. Rollings demanded Detroit's Community Fund to immediately halt all funding. The YMCA, of course, was perhaps the preeminent institutional expression of social gospel modernism in Detroit. It was a major recipient of Community Union funds and widely seen as a source of civic and political progress (in the classic "Progressive" sense). The Community Unions' response to Rollings, therefore, was very revealing. As the organization's investigation stressed, Rollings was "*not* an ordained minister," but was rather "a 'self-styled' preacher" operating out of a makeshift tabernacle church. Among all "respectable" churches, the Community Union reported, Rollings was "thoroughly despised." His congregation—mostly workers at the Hudson and Chrysler plants—was characterized as "below the average in intelligence and low in the economic scale." Like Norris, Rollings fit neatly into the modernist religious discourse as the prototypical religious demagogue, manipulating the uncritical masses: his preaching "borders on evangelism, appealing to their emotions." The force of the Community Union's rebuttal suggests the escalating cultural tension unleashed within all religious communities by the lingering effects of the Depression, the explosion of CIO organizing, and the early cascade of troubling news from Europe.[73]

However, while Norris was an influential force, the migration from south to north did not automatically produce a fervent, politically reactionary fundamentalism. Norris could not monopolize the religious consciousness of southern whites any more than Coughlin could monopolize the consciousness of Catholics. For some southerners, religion simply became a less urgent matter in the pluralistic environment of an industrial city. Eva Anderson, for instance, moved to Detroit from a pious community in the rural South where "[i]t was simply expected" to stop work on Saturday night and find the nearest church or biggest revival. Working in Detroit interrupted this schedule and, as an investigator found in 1937, "gradually she began to lose the feeling of having to go to church every Sunday." Jim Hammitte, who migrated from Kentucky in 1942, shied away from discussing religion with his mostly Catholic coworkers; but he also began finding excuses for missing church services. Still, as the researchers who interviewed Eva Anderson noted, northern life may have altered traditional patterns of church going, but "it would be morally and spiritually impossible for [southern whites] to identify themselves with any but the narrower Fundamentalist Churches." In other words, even as the new context of Detroit altered the practice and meaning of religion, the template of evangelicalism remained elemental to shaping social identity and provided an essential framework for interpreting the world.[74]

Given this fluidity, and the long history of populist religious politics, it is hardly surprising that some southerners responded to the UAW with enthusiasm. Sociologist Erdmann Beynon noted, "To many [southerners], the appeal of the CIO became a revival movement." Largely because of their deep sense of common-folk equality, southerners "embraced the cause of union labor with a religious fervor not shown by other employees," according to Beynon. One factory manager angrily reported in 1937, "The first ones to cause us labor trouble are always the southerners." Indeed, southerners emerged as key UAW leaders. Martha Strong, for instance, became one of the most important female leaders in the UAW at Local 174; in the late 1930s, she helped stage the union's first "slow-down" strike and successfully organized GM's Ternstedt plant. One investigation from 1937 deduced that, even at Temple Baptist Church, where thousands of southern factory workers absorbed the violently antiunion sermons of Frank Norris, "most of them are in the C.I.O."[75]

The unrest of the late 1930s unsettled the social and political meaning of southern evangelical consciousness every bit as much as other workers. Some southern whites actively explored the long-standing idioms of evangelicalism, and began to remake them within an overtly working-class narrative. Lloyd T. Jones, president of UAW Local 2 (Murray Body) in the late 1930s, offers a telling example. Under a blaring, confessional title in the union newspaper, Jones admitted, "I Was a Ford Preacher." Describing himself as "one of those Southern boys who came to Detroit when we of the South thought Henry Ford was the only man in Detroit," Jones explained that he had served as pastor of the only church in the Ford-controlled coal mines of Harlan County, Kentucky. There, Jones was tempted by the special privileges that he received as a man of the cloth; mammon seduced him into believing Ford's benevolence. In 1925, Jones moved to Detroit with idyllic visions of the future: he would post a quick profit before returning to the South, buying a gas station, and "just coast along on the station's profit and preach the good gospel to all the mountain folk."[76]

But, like all sinners blinded to the truth, Jones's false reality crumbled when he entered the Valley of the Shadow of the assembly line. He quickly learned the hard reality of making crankshafts. The physically exhausting work caused men to pass out all around him. Lunch allowed a mere fifteen-minute break—no time at all to recover from the backbreaking pace of labor. By the mid-1930s, the scales had fallen from Jones's eyes: "I thank God I have now found a way through the great organization of the United Automobile Workers to turn the lash of Ford's whip" back upon those who had tormented and dehumanized him. Pharaoh could no longer drive his slaves; the Lord had turned the tables and offered deliverance.[77]

Jones's essay constitutes a classic, self-conscious conversion narrative, a story of a born-again religious experience central to the life of southern migrants. However, the rebirth he recounts is not one from sin to Christ, but from "false" to "real" consciousness. After enduring the inferno of the Ford plant, Jones was saved by the labor movement. But, while his evocation of these evangelical motifs was clearly deliberate, Jones was not simply putting on a pleasing affectation. Like many fellow autoworkers, he remained a Bible-believing Christian. Jones argued sincerely that Ford's dictatorial treatment of his workers corrupted the "true" Christianity that the auto giant cynically presumed to finance. Admitting his own sinfulness, Jones showed that, when preachers like himself (or, one might add by implication, like Norris) drifted too far into Ford's sphere of influence, they corrupted the spirit of the "people's" religion with the treasures of mammon. Jones utilized the easily recognized conventions of the southern religious experience to tap into the basic sense of fairness, dignity, and justice that always underlay evangelical culture and attached that consciousness to southerners' new identities as unionized workers. In many ways, the earthquake in poor white religious consciousness that began in the 1890s came to fruition in northern cities like Detroit in the 1930s and 1940s.

Conclusion

Worker religion opened new imaginative possibilities for fusing religious, political, and class consciousness within the context of the labor movement. But the ultimate social effects of this religiosity remained contested and ambiguous. Antimodernist and conservative religious voices became increasingly strident as the United States prepared for entry into the Second World War, prompting new fears about working-class religion's susceptibility to overly emotional, authoritarian demagogues. With Detroit transformed by a massive southern diaspora, and with racial conflict exacerbated by the exigencies of war, the political shape of working-class religions suddenly loomed as one of the most urgent cultural issues in the struggle for democracy.

FIGURE 6. The congregation of Bethel A.M.E. Church, like many African American churches, believed in its ability to conjure God's presence in history; as the sign in the upper-right declares, "Prayer Changes Things." Courtesy Bentley Image Bank, Bentley Historical Collection, Bethel A.M.E. Church Collection.

FIGURE 7. Protestors in Detroit criticize the politicized religion of Rev. Gerald L. K. Smith. Note the heterogeneous character of the protestors and the rhetorical linkage of Smith's religious message to fascism. Courtesy of Walter P. Reuther Library, Archives of Labor and Urban Affairs, Wayne State University.

FIGURE 8. While religious leftists opposed the "fascism" of Gerald L. K. Smith, supporters of Smith—like these protestors at Bushnell Congregational Church— equated religious liberalism with both race-mixing and communism. Courtesy Bentley Image Bank, Bentley Historical Collection, Gerald L. K. Smith Collection.

4. Race, Politics, and Worker Religion in Wartime Detroit, 1941–1946

In 1938, Zygmond Dobrzynski, director of the Ford organizing drive for the United Automobile Workers (UAW), attended a religious revival. Leading the service was the pugnacious Southern Baptist J. Frank Norris. At his 1938 revival, Norris, flanked by the Flint police sheriff and a prominent member of the Ford Motor Company, produced a typically ebullient performance, burning the Soviet flag, denouncing unionism, and celebrating a nationalistic "Americanism." To a stunned Dobrzynski, Norris seemed a "Raving Minister," using the "Pulpit as a Mask to Promote Dictatorship." Dobrzynski countered that the UAW contained "thousands of churchgoers who recognize the putrid character of the Norris falsifications." Indeed, Dobrzynski turned the rhetorical tables, denouncing Norris as a Judas who "sold out the ONE who had led the oppressed peoples of those days in protest against human bondage."[1]

Dobrzysnki's close encounter with revivalism reveals a great deal about the shifting relationship between religion, politics, and class as the United States drew ever closer to the maelstrom of the Second World War. Religion remained a potent force within working-class culture, and the UAW knew it. Indeed, the UAW was urgently struggling to assert its own moral discourse—grounded in the modernist liberalism of the social gospel—against Norris's fundamentalist doctrines of individualism and biblical literalism. But even more, Norris's revival reveals the interpenetration of religious and political ideas in the context of a world sliding toward catastrophic, ideologically driven warfare. Dobrzynski's language indicates that religion held political consequences: that it might promote "Dictatorship," or, alternatively, that believers might reject Norris's "falsifications" and embrace a progressive democracy. Critically, Dobrzynski recognized the intended target of Norris's politically charged religion: Detroit's working classes.

As the Second World War loomed, the discourse surrounding working-class religion reached new ideological extremes. For the UAW and its liberal allies, the political chaos of the 1930s had fueled the dangerous growth of what Harry Cruden, a worker from Local 227, called the "Three Little Stools": Charles Coughlin, Frank Norris, and Gerald L. K. Smith (a Disciples of Christ minister and acolyte of Huey Long, who moved to Detroit in the late 1930s). Collectively, these three religious leaders reached tens of thousands of Detroit-area Catholic and Protestant workers through radio programs, newspapers, social organizations, and sermons. All of them condemned the New Deal and lambasted the UAW. "Their Bible is not the Word of God," Cruden forcefully insisted, "but an Americanized version of 'Mein Kampf.'" The choice of language is highly revealing. Within the categories of modernist religious discourse, working-class religion had metastasized from mere obscurantism or escapism; it now engendered fascism and threatened western democracy. T. McNabb, a worker at UAW Local 227, made the argument explicit: working-class religion, if corrupted, enabled "the mass mania that precedes totalitarianism." Yet, on the shop floors and across the neighborhoods of Detroit, religious consciousness remained central to working-class identity. Therefore, shaping the *political* character of working-class religion— as a bulwark for democracy, a wedge for fascism, or a stalking-horse for communism—emerged as one of the most urgent cultural projects of the war years.[2]

The new idioms of worker religion had emerged, in part, to counter modernist criticisms and to infuse the traditional religious worlds of working people with a heightened social and political consciousness. As liberal concern over fascist religion peaked, Catholic laity in the ACTU and clergy involved with the Labor Institute rushed to emphasize their rejection of Charles Coughlin and their commitment to both the labor movement and American democracy. They presented the new idioms of "worker Catholicism" as a meaningful articulation of the faith, fully rooted in the two-thousand-year tradition of the broader Church, while simultaneously providing a socially engaged movement of "faith in action."

Meanwhile, hundreds of thousands of working-class southern whites poured into area war-production plants in the early 1940s, and, as Dobrzynski's coverage of J. Frank Norris suggests, liberals and laborites especially fretted over the fascism they perceived within southern workers' fundamentalism. By 1942, the story of southern religion in Detroit had taken a dramatic turn with the arrival of the Presbyterian Church's "minister to labor," an

Arkansas-based firebrand named Claude Williams. Williams fully agreed with the UAW that a corrupted form of fundamentalism would lead to fascism; but he also possessed a deep biblical faith, and yearned to transform the idioms of southern evangelicalism into a profoundly activist worker religion. As the ACTU had built a Catholic worker religion upon the larger edifice of Catholic history, Williams aggressively promoted an agenda for political engagement within a fully reenvisioned, class-conscious reading of the entire evangelical experience.[3]

Ideas about race ultimately formed the sharpest matrix of ideological forces within working-class religion during the war years. Over the course of the early 1940s, racial tension in Detroit stretched to—and, in some instances, past—the breaking point. Throughout the war years, black and white workers struggled tensely over access to housing, jobs, and social respect. During 1942, "hate strikes"—in which white workers refused to work alongside blacks in the same department—momentarily halted war production in local factories. In 1943, these tensions exploded in the worst race riot of the era. Within this volatile context, advocates of worker religion pushed their political commitments beyond support for the labor movement; they also came to define racial equality as a fundamental component of the newly emerging, postwar democracy. Naturally, this idea gained its most potent expression among African Americans themselves, who forcefully asserted that the war would be fought in vain if it did not achieve a "Double V for Victory" against fascism abroad and racism at home. Placed in the broader discourse of the period, it followed that, if "democratic" religion supported unionism and racial equality as coeval goals, then religion that *opposed* unionism or racial equality (such as the religion of the "Three Little Stools") could be understood only as fascist.[4]

Of course, Coughlin, Smith, and Norris articulated a potent counter-narrative diametrically opposite that of progressives. According to this alternate discourse, working-class Christianity was indeed under deadly assault: by secularists, unionists, modernists, and communists. Most insidious, for religious antimodernists, was the pernicious influence of clerical progressives like Fr. Raymond Clancy, Claude Williams, and the Rev. Charles Hill on American workers. A corrupted religion, rightists were convinced, prepared the working classes for the eventual political triumph of communism or a similar anti-American statism. Particularly within the dispensational, premillennial worldview of Norris and Smith, communist tyranny was foretold by scripture, and represented not merely a flawed economic system, but a portent of the end-times. For fundamentalists, *communism* was synonymous with both religious modernism, which denied the literalism of scripture, and the overstretched hand of government, which threatened God's chosen remnant. As such, a minister suspected of smuggling communism into America through the guise of religion threatened the destruction of both democracy and Christianity. "All patriotic Americans are agreed that we must win this war," Gerald L. K. Smith conceded in 1942; but he insisted, "We are not agreed on what must follow."[5]

"Worker Catholicism" and the Meaning of Democracy

When war erupted between the fascist states of Europe and the western democracies, American Catholicism found itself straddling a series of ideological chasms. One especially difficult legacy confronting Catholics was the long history of American anti-Catholicism, an intellectual tradition that stretched back to the colonial period and had long juxtaposed supposed Catholic tyranny to Protestant liberty. Catholics, according to the typical American anti-Catholic discourse, slavishly followed the orders of a foreign prince (the pope), groveled before authoritarian priests, thoughtlessly imbibed a superstitious catechism, and dangerously undermined the separation between church and state; post-Enlightenment Protestantism, in contrast, was celebrated for its supposed elevation of individualism, reason, self-discipline, and liberal democracy. Protestantism was thus regarded as quintessentially American and Catholicism as always slightly foreign.[6]

This ideological antagonism developed a new manifestation with the rise of fascism in early-twentieth-century Europe. Not without reason, American liberals looked on warily as Pope Pius XI signed a series of friendly concordats with the government of Benito Mussolini in 1929—a settlement greeted triumphantly by Catholics in the United States, especially by Italian immigrants. In 1933, the pope solemnized a pact with Hitler designed to mute Catholic criticism of the Nazi regime. Meanwhile, Catholics around the world rushed to support the insurgency of General Francisco Franco as civil war exploded in Spain in 1936. To American liberals, Catholic collaboration with the most illiberal forces in Europe only confirmed the traditional narrative of Catholic "tyranny."[7]

In Detroit, Charles Coughlin embodied these fears. To liberal unionists in the UAW, Coughlin welded an authoritarian religious culture to a socially destructive current of emotional religiosity. When UAW organizer Joseph Ferris sought to explain Coughlin's popularity with workers, he concluded that the priest "was an outlet for [people's] emotions." Another UAW organizer, John Zaremba, noted Coughlin's authoritarian power, complaining that

Polish autoworkers obstinately viewed him as "infallible." Ferris agreed with Zaremba, noting, "It was surprising how [Coughlin] controlled the people from the pulpit, from the radio." Wyndham Mortimer, the UAW's first vice president, frankly described Coughlin as a "fascist demagogue." The UAW newspaper offered an elegant indictment after Coughlin's anti-Semitism was fully exposed in 1938: "Fascism brazenly hurls defiance at Christianity and crucifies the faithful. The bible is being rewritten to conform with what Hitler 'thinks' of God. And in Detroit, a priest looks at this modern spectacle of Christ being crucified in Europe and applauds the barbarian horde." The radio priest had come to seem, in labor's imagination, an American shadow of Hitler and an opening wedge for European-style fascism.[8]

Prolabor Catholics, both clerical and lay, thus struggled to prove their opposition to fascism and their dual commitments to unionism and democracy to sometimes-skeptical outsiders. When, in November of 1939, Coughlin defied his ecclesiastical superiors and broadcast a bitterly antiunion radio sermon during a critical strike of Chrysler workers, the prolabor contingent needed to respond vigorously. Fr. Raymond Clancy, with the endorsement of Archbishop Mooney, broadcast a stinging rebuke. According to Clancy, Coughlin had "misquoted" and "misinterpreted" the Pope in his address, implying that a papal declaration on the obligations of ownership applied equally to workers as well—meaning that Catholic workers were obligated to return to work, when in fact they were not. More sensationally, Clancy averred, Coughlin confused the Pope's *description* of Italian fascism (wherein the state was empowered to resolve labor disputes) with an *endorsement* of such a system.[9]

The UAW obviously approved of Clancy's address. George Addes, the union's secretary-treasurer and himself a nominal Catholic, wrote to Clancy expressing gratitude and hoping to expand the Catholic "social justice" message to further recruit Catholic workers. But responses to Clancy's speech also indicated the contested nature of worker religion. Frank Boucher, a one-time parishioner of Clancy's at Epiphany parish in Detroit, wrote his ex-pastor to express "disappointment" at the address. "Pray, where are all our Catholic Priests when we need them so badly to fight for the workingman's rights?" Boucher asked. "Can you not obtain a voice on radio . . . except when you are willing to act as a Judas?" For Boucher, Coughlin's anticommunist and anti-Semitic conspiracy theories, not Clancy's legalistic economic treatises, explained the true threat to the working class: "How the Communist element in this town . . . must have enjoyed [Clancy's speech], which all makes factual that part of the Jewish Protocol which instructs the Jews to work on Gentiles by pitting one against the other." Clearly, worker religion remained very much contested; Boucher's understanding of Catholicism was not dormant, just as Clancy's was not universally embraced.[10]

Both Coughlin and Clancy invoked religion—indeed, the same documents from the same church—to defend what they considered to be the interest of the working class, both spoke from the mantle of religious authority, both utilized a rhetoric of social justice, and both found receptive audiences. Their disagreement suggested how religion might serve reactionary conservatism as well as democratic progressivism. This volatility explains the force of Clancy's rebuttal. For Clancy—who began his address by describing himself as first and foremost "an American" (secondarily, as "a Detroiter," and lastly, "a Catholic priest")—it was essential to distance his church from the taint of an odious, reactionary, and un-American ideology. He intended not merely to check Coughlin's errors, but to declare in unambiguous terms that *his* version of Catholicism was the true faith: a reliably democratic religion and friend of the American worker.[11]

In articulating their commitment to democracy, worker-religion Catholics faced an additional challenge, for they not only opposed the fascist strain in American Catholicism: they were also strident and absolute anticommunists. In the CIO-dominated world of the late 1930s, this placed liberal Catholics in a curious position. Prolabor activists of the time often accepted the cultural assumptions of the communist popular front, and formed working relationships with communist organizers, even if they were not communists themselves. Catholic laborites dissented vigorously and hoped to chart a third course: one that celebrated democracy and unionism while unequivocally opposing both fascism and communism. Thus, while the ACTU newspaper outlined a detailed plan for what it termed "economic democracy," the group also frankly rebuffed potential alliances with communists. "[A]ny deluded Catholic who accepts [communist] support," read an ACTU resolution from August of 1938, "must inevitably pay for it by acts contrary to his religion and the welfare of his country." The communist influence in some of Detroit's most important union locals therefore put the ACTU in a rhetorically difficult position. "No good thing need be opposed because it happens to have the unsolicited support of Communists," the group delicately declared. "But no reciprocal political relations can rightfully exist between Catholics and the Communist Party for any cause."[12]

Communists and their leftist allies, meanwhile, retaliated against Catholic laborites. To radicals, there was little distinction between a Charles Coughlin and a Raymond Clancy: the Catholic Church was, by definition, an oppressive and totalitarian institution, and thus was innately sympathetic to fascism. The accusation plainly grieved liberal Catholics. In 1938, Detroit's ACTU chaplain Sebastian Erbacher complained that "laborers are being filled with hatred for the church," and accused communists of painting all Catholics with the brush of fascism. Two years later, the ACTU warned its members that a "fake [ACTU] handbill" insinuating a link between the Catholic labor group and European fascism had appeared in various factories. And again, in 1942, former *Christian Social Action* editor, Richard L. G. Deverall—at the time, an official in the UAW Education Department—was accused of being a closet fascist. When *In Fact* magazine published the charge (after the UAW executive board had already dismissed the accusation), Deverall wrote to the magazine's editor with a barely contained rage. "As a member of the liberal element within the Catholic Church," Deverall fumed, "I very bitterly resent being attacked as a fascist, when I have suffered for years because of the fact that I HAVE battled Fascism."[13]

Tensions were especially stark in those locals that contained large numbers of both Catholics and communists. The preeminent example was Ford Local 600, the largest and most influential of all UAW locals. In the run-up to the highly contentious UAW presidential election of 1946, in which the ACTU backed the anticommunist platform of Walter Reuther, an unattributed letter (likely from *Wage Earner* reporter Norman McKenna) acknowledged that "Commies have been stirring up feeling against the Catholics" within Ford Local 600. Horace Sheffield, an African American activist at Local 600 who enjoyed a positive relationship with Paul Weber and other Actists, agreed that "the left wing beat them down and called them fascist." Nevertheless, Local 600 contained bastions of ACTU influence. The local's president, Joe McCusker, was "friendly" to the ACTU, and McCusker's brothers, one of whom headed the aircraft unit at Ford, were ACTU members.[14]

Reuther's eventual victory in the bitterly fought 1946 UAW presidential election solidified what one scholar has termed an "informal alliance" between the ACTU and Reuther's administration. But this association also fueled the suspicion and resentment of some non-Catholics (and certainly most radicals). When the Archdiocesan Labor Institute asked its students, "Have you heard any criticisms of these classes from your fellow-workers" on course evaluations, the question suggests that leaders knew their religion could provoke hostility. In general, ALI priests must have been satisfied that most students heard no such comments, but some certainly did. One student at the St. Leo labor school wrote succinctly in large print: "The Catholic Church (50 years late)." A student at the Holy Rosary school noted that his coworkers pressed him on why the Catholic Church was suddenly "interfering" in labor matters, when the need for intervention had been apparent for many years. Another student heard his coworkers complain that the Church "was trying to control unions." Paul Weber knew that, in the wake of Reuther's victory, outsiders would accuse the ACTU of acting as a "Catholic bloc" within the UAW, and see sinister, clerically driven forces conspiring against union democracy. He argued forcefully against this perception, claiming, "This choice was made freely, and individually, without direction or pressure from any source." Moreover, Weber pointed out that the ACTU's bottom line remained the fact that "Reuther's policies have been consistently in harmony with the principles laid down in the Papal Encyclicals" and offered the best chance of enacting something resembling the ACTU's cherished industry council plan. In an interview after Reuther's election, Weber explained that the ACTU did not push a "Catholic line," although sometimes the group democratically decided to support various positions. "We are not campaigning for the election of Catholic officials but for the adoption of Catholic principles," Weber asserted.[15]

In the long run, prolabor Catholics did make strides in distinguishing themselves from reactionary Coughlinites and building alliances with secular unionists. UAW socialist Frank Marquart, for instance, appreciated the activism of the ACTU in defending "democratic unionism." African American unionist Horace Sheffield added, "There's no question about it . . . [the ACTU] made some positive contributions." Meanwhile, Coughlin's political views became increasingly anathema within Catholic circles. By 1943, two well-regarded priests asserted, "90% of the clergy [in Detroit] have no use for Coughlin."[16]

Nevertheless, Coughlin had not disappeared from Detroit's cultural landscape. One visitor to his Shrine of the Little Flower on a Sunday morning in September 1943 reported, "The whole vast church was crowded. . . . There must have been 4,000 people." War workers had become a crucial part of the congregation, compelling the church to hold eight masses a day (with each mass drawing nearly 3,000 worshippers). Ever the religious entrepreneur, Coughlin had supplemented the popular regular novenas to St. Therese and St. Jude with a Shrine of St. Sebastian. As described by one observer:

It has become the custom for some time to hang on the walls of the Shrine the names of the soldiers, members of the Guild of St. Sebastian, the patron of soldiers. The number of members became so huge that it covered all the walls of the Shrine, obscuring the beauty of the marble and carving. . . . There are now some 130,000 names recorded. . . . Of much greater significance is the political value of this St. Sebastian fellowship. It ties several hundred thousand parents in with Father Coughlin.

While even Coughlin admitted that he was "as good as finished" in Detroit's political circles, he remained a popular parish priest in Royal Oak and found new vitality across denominational lines with like-minded Protestant anti-modernists. And Coughlin's embrace by the Protestant far right continued to provoke the most paranoid fears of war-era liberals: that a "corrupted" religion provided an incubator for an American fascism.[17]

Fundamentalism and Fascism

Throughout the 1940s, Detroit remained a predominately Catholic city. But during World War II, Detroit experienced a profound demographic revolution, becoming one of the central destinations of the "southern diaspora." Between late 1941 and 1944, as war-industries jobs proliferated in Detroit factories, over 250,000 southern-born whites flooded into the Motor City. The surge of southern evangelicals into Detroit's booming war-industries plants left religious modernists stunned and puzzled. Edward DeWitt Jones, one of Detroit's leading Protestant luminaries, announced with bewilderment in 1942: "No other city . . . has so many flourishing 'Tabernacle churches' as Detroit." Ellsworth Smith, director of the Detroit Council of Churches' (DCC) War Emergency Commission, was initially optimistic about the "church-minded" migrants, but was worried by 1945. "It cannot be said too emphatically," he warned, that "Detroit is a center of terrific religious energy." Moreover, a "very disturbing proportion of this energy is being drawn off by independent groups which offer a poor and often destructive religious education." Smith feared that "vast areas of population" might be "surrendered to these non-denominational, but very energetic, groups." The Civil Rights Congress of Michigan (CRC) agreed, noting that only 400 of the city's 1,600 churches belonged to an established denomination. In sum, the CRC concluded, Detroit "is in a 'Bible Belt' . . . just as devout" as the more famous southern cousin.[18]

Southern religiosity quickly became visible, not only in neighborhoods but on the shop floor as well. In May of 1942, an interdenominational assembly calling itself the Peaceful Valley Tabernacle began holding services in Detroit-area Chrysler plants. By April of 1943, fellowships were meeting in two plants, and the group was hoping to expand to five. Charles Allen, leader of the Tabernacle, claimed to have distributed 850 New Testaments among fellow workers during that time and, beginning in December of 1943, had launched a half-hour radio show. Significantly, Allen noted, his ministers were "not trained preachers by any manner of means—just men of the shop who love God and like to study His Word and talk about it." Allen's was a church of working-class autodidacts who claimed the power of biblical interpretation for themselves and brought their religion directly into the workplace. By late 1943, sources estimated that between 3,000 and 3,500 similar shop-floor preachers—self-taught, often semiliterate southern fundamentalists—were working in defense industry plants. UAW President R. J. Thomas counted more than 1,000 preachers in Ford factories alone.[19]

Leftist commentators quickly attributed political implications to the spread of working-class evangelicalism. Wilbur Larremore Caswell, writing of Detroit in *The Churchman*, worried that "fanatical sects," once under the influence of a Frank Norris or Gerald Smith, represented "one of the most serious perils to both our religious and our political life." Most leftists had two specific so-called "fascists" in mind: J. Frank Norris (introduced in Chapter 3) and Gerald L. K. Smith. Smith, a Disciples of Christ pastor, became a sycophant and acolyte of Louisiana senator Huey Long in the 1930s. After Long's assassination, Smith relocated from Louisiana to Detroit, where he founded the America First party—perhaps the first explicitly political program premised on Christian fundamentalism since the schism between modernists and fundamentalists in the 1920s—and the Christian Nationalist Crusade to promote religious revival. In 1941, he launched a newspaper (*The Cross and the Flag*), and a year later ran for Republican Senator from Michigan. Polling 100,000 votes, Smith lost, but subsequently ran for president three times as a candidate of the Christian Nationalist Party. In 1942, Smith announced that he received support from 50,000 Detroit-area CIO members—proof, Smith averred, that there are "still millions of Bible-reading, church-going prayerful workers in America" who remained untouched by "Communists" like the UAW's Walter Reuther. Detroit's Civil Rights' Congress was shaken: "There is probably more American fascist, reactionary, and downright sedition propaganda generated in Detroit than in any other city," it concluded in 1943.[20]

Smith eagerly highlighted his commonality with Charles Coughlin and sold Coughlin's *Social Justice* at his own gatherings (despite Coughlin's own wariness toward Smith). Smith's willingness to publicly embrace the causes of a Catholic priest suggested—to both supporters and opponents—a new social possibility: religious alliances, Smith signaled, were now to be primarily *political*, not denominational. "We Christians must continue to enjoy our liberty to disagree theologically," Smith wrote in 1945. However, "when it comes to Communism and Atheism the lovers of Christ must stand together as one solid body." Coughlin's right-wing populism and anticommunism were, to Smith, far more substantial than deviations on doctrinal points. Given the deep and historic antipathy between Catholics and conservative Protestants, Smith's openness to Coughlin foreshadowed a major restructuring of American religion throughout the remainder of the twentieth century. Smith was not alone; Denver's "cowboy minister" Harvey Springer, who often appeared with Smith in Detroit, agreed. "A lot of people in my audiences are Catholics," Springer explained, because "Good Catholics as much as good Protestants resent having their sacred Bible pulled apart by a lot of Jews."[21]

Faced with a new, working-class population practicing a largely alien religious culture, a small corps within the Presbyterian Church was determined to find a missionary who might speak the newcomers' language while conveying a socially positive message. They hoped, in other words, to remake the religious consciousness of southern whites in accordance with the social and civic norms of a northern, industrial metropolis. The most important supporter of this approach was the Rev. Henry Jones, director of the Dodge Community House in Hamtramck. Given his position as the leader of a settlement house, Jones directly witnessed the lives of working-class believers and sought to turn his settlement house into a space for cultural and political action. In February of 1941, Jones heard a bracing talk by a radical southern preacher named Claude Williams. Intrigued, Jones brought Williams back to Detroit for a speech at the all-black Lucy Thurman branch of the YWCA. The Detroit Presbytery had found its "minister to labor": one of the most colorful, radical, and divisive figures in Detroit's religious history.[22]

Williams recalled that, when he first received the call to preach in 1921, he was a typical and unremarkable southern fundamentalist, believing it his "religious duty to 'preach salvation to the lost souls of a dying world.'" But the closer he read the Bible, the more Williams felt moved by "the victims of unrighteousness and injustice." Williams's developing social conscience provoked a spiritual crisis that was finally resolved by a profound moment of divine intervention: "Angels administered unto me and I received direct revelations from the 'God of the Living.'" Williams was "born again." Convinced that he could be "free in struggle or a slave in comfort," Williams concluded that his role in the world was to share the lives of sharecroppers and coal miners. Shortly after this second conversion experience, Williams began excoriating the dismal poverty he encountered on sojourns throughout the South. He worked fervently on the part of labor unions, developing especially close ties with the Southern Tenants Farmers' Union. Perhaps even more threatening to many in the South, Williams attacked racism directly, organizing interracial fellowships wherever possible.[23]

Not surprisingly, Williams encountered hostility—and sometimes endured violent attacks—from both townspeople and local police during his southern efforts. He often wound up in jail or threatened with the end of a noose. Indeed, southern Presbyterians defrocked Williams for his disruptive activities in 1934. Liberals in Detroit might be persuaded that these incidents were simply the outbursts of unreconstructed rednecks, but Williams's combative personality and his radical political beliefs nevertheless made his selection as "chaplain to labor" a high-risk decision. Even his supporters recognized that Williams easily, and perhaps recklessly, threw his passions against any perceived injustice. One investigator who visited Williams on behalf of Yale Divinity School reported that Williams's temper was "fanned quickly to a white heat by unnecessary injustice." Even Williams's Christmas cards to friends presented jeremiads on "the evils of tyranny." According to this observer, "if ever the term 'fanatic' is to be used accurately, it can be applied to Claude Williams"; nevertheless, even this writer acknowledged that Williams's program was "very effective" and the minister "can hold his own intellectually in any gathering." Williams himself, after two years of bruising battles with his opponents in Detroit, admitted that he often came across as excessively bitter or doctrinaire, but he responded in typical fashion that injustice was nothing to be complacent about.[24]

Despite his colorful and tumultuous past, by November of 1942 Williams was tutoring Jones on a two-pronged approach to class-based ministry: reach the new migrant workers with one hand, and reach labor leaders with the other. On the latter goal, Williams seems to have genuinely developed ever-closer ties with the UAW. When Williams's initial six-month tenure was reviewed in April of 1943, Henry Jones argued to the Board of National Missions that the southern minister had forged significant in-roads among the ranks of the auto union. Besides meeting with labor leaders twice monthly in a "Church and Labor Fellowship," Williams had also arranged for Fred Sweet of the UAW to address "forty-three pastors who . . . reach 15,000 people each Sunday morning in various services." Discontinuance of Williams's mission "would be disastrous since labor groups have been encouraged by Claude Williams's ministry. A hopefulness has been created in the minds of Labor which must not be dashed out." Jones's argument proved effective: Williams's work was extended for three years, with diminishing funds each year as Williams was expected to establish his own self-supporting organization. In March of 1944, Williams reported that he was performing the invocations at previously all-secular meetings, such as the Michigan Women's Labor Auxiliary-CIO and the Women's Auxiliary of UAW local 247. And after Cedric Belfrage's celebratory biography of Williams was published in 1944, William Levitt, the International Education Director of the UAW, agreed that "pushing the book" among union members was a high priority.[25]

But Williams's key work consisted of his ministry to working-class southern migrants. He insisted that an "all out offensive for justice and goodwill" be taken directly to the poor, the unlettered, and the uprooted—immediately and in their own language. To focus on what Williams termed "the more sophisticated groups" of skilled workers would only create an isolated minority that would "diminish into utter ineffectiveness" and stand as "pathetic examples of the unrealism of present-day liberal religion." If action was not taken, and if appeals to these groups were made only by secular bodies, Williams warned, "to that extent will religion be further discredited among the people and considered irrelevant by them." In articulating the significance of his efforts to evangelize Bible-believing laborers, Williams consistently reiterated a powerful narrative. Since the late nineteenth century, Williams argued, America had witnessed a mass populist religious movement embodied in the rapid rise of Pentecostal churches. Mainline churches, ignoring this spiritual ferment among the lower classes, promoted a "pipe-organized, stained-glass and silk stocking religion," which alienated and oppressed the masses. According to Williams, ordinary working folk responded by transforming their repression into virtues. Denied good clothes, they scorned worldliness as wicked; denied good schools, they castigated learning as the devil's work; denied good doctors, they accepted faith healing; with no time for leisure, leisure became evil; denied the rights of citizens, the state became evil.[26]

In time-honored evangelical fashion, the Bible—not sacraments, rituals, or clergy—rested at the center of Williams's cosmological imagination, as it did for most southern white Protestants. Williams's unique approach to ministry involved numerous visual aids, instructional charts, and posters. Williams developed these theatrical props, he explained to Studs Terkel, because they "translated the democratic impulse of mass religion rather than its protofascist content into a language [common people] understood." The idea of "translation" was vitally important to Williams and his allies. The Bible contained life's essential truths, but these insights could be easily misrepresented and abused. The purpose of the visual aids was to take the obscure language of biblical stories and reveal the true meaning of scripture.[27]

For example, in a handout titled "The Galilean and the Common People," Williams taught that the "religion OF the prophets and the Son of Man is a religion OF, BY, and FOR the toiling masses of humanity. That is why the rich pay doctors of religion to think out a religion ABOUT the prophets and 'Jesus' and the NEXT life." In another lesson, titled "The Carpenter," Williams contrasted the "false" religion of rulers and priests with the "true" religion of Moses, Jeremiah, and the prophets. These lessons were frequently rendered in quasi-mathematical formulas. Typically, one chart equated a progressive nationalism with Christianity: "the Labor Movement: Government = True Religion: Real Democracy." Always, Williams attempted to ground his political points with scriptural references or biblical parallels.[28]

As he told the great oral historian Studs Terkel, Williams viewed the Bible "as a workingman's book." Thus, all of Williams's social critiques were placed within a biblical context. The best example comes from the title of one of Williams's most widely read tracts: "The Scriptural Heritage of the People." The slave revolt of Israelites in Egypt, Williams pointed out, established a precedent for social action "against conditions not unsimilar to the conditions in the South from which many of our newcomers to Detroit have escaped." Employing typically loaded language, Williams declared that Jesus was "lynched" for advocating a people's world; how, then, could true followers of Christ support lynching or the ideology which lay behind it? Traditionally Protestant hymns, too, remained vital in Williams's efforts at religious "translation." Typical efforts included "Round and Round Hitler's Grave," "A People's World" (sung to the tune of "Bound for the Promised Land"), and "Give Me That Old Time Religion" (which would "end all racial hatred").[29]

While he was unabashedly biblical, Williams resisted sectarian trappings with militancy. In a particularly vivid example of this mind-set, Williams casually remarked in a lecture describing his ministry that "the word 'christ' is a sectarianism." Indeed, Williams's writings often refer to Jesus as the "son of Man," "the Nazarene," "the Carpenter," or other such titles, but never as "Christ." Williams's antisectarian leanings produced a deep suspicion of institutional religion (despite the financial support he received from and alliances he forged with fellow Presbyterians). According to Williams, Protestantism had become a "'puppet' church" serving the interests of "economic royalists who stand for wage slavery, industrial arrogance, [and] racial bigotry." Some of this antipathy was fueled by the difficulty Williams confronted in securing meeting space for his growing fellowship within any of Detroit's finer establishments. Horace White's Plymouth Congregational Church was often opened for Williams, but many other churches declined. One minister allegedly feared that his membership "would catch syphilis the next Sunday morning by sitting in the pews where these workers and Negroes sat the previous Sunday evening," while the prominent minister Benjamin Bush stunned one of Williams's African American colleagues by earnestly asking whether "the Negro culture and the white culture could exist harmoniously side by side." Walk into any Detroit church, Williams claimed, and behold the baleful influence of industrial benefactors: "Are these churches serving the people?" Williams asked. Although he claimed that he offered his critique not out of "antagonism" but so that the church might "fulfill its mission," the depth of his anger and the personal nature of many of his attacks likely made it difficult for other ministers to accept this caveat.[30]

Williams sought to take his biblical radicalism directly into the workplaces of the new southern migrants. Indeed, given the flowering of conservative evangelical fellowships on the shop floor, Williams had little choice. By 1943, he had identified a number of so-called "shop tabernacles" at Dodge Truck Mound Road Plant, Dodge Lynch Road Plant, Chrysler Bomber Plant, DeSoto Gun Plant, Dodge Main, and other plants. Many believed these tabernacles were established with the support of management, and the UAW rightly worried that industrially sponsored religion countered the union's own religious discourse. Williams agreed that employers had been "attempting to take advantage of the religious sentiment of their employees and of the uncritical preachers among them to foster under the guise of religion" an antiunion scheme. Williams sought to counter this influence by establishing what he called a "Gospel Preacher's Council of Applied Religion." The initial group consisted of twenty-five preachers employed in war plants, but members believed "there are hundreds of us preachers who toil with their hands as we do." Joining together for fellowship, Bible study services, and publication of a newsletter ("The Toiling Parson"), Williams intended for the Gospel Preacher's Council to serve as his main conduit into working-class religious communities. In 1943, Gospel Preacher's Councils were operating at General Electric, Hudson, U.S. Tire and Supply, and Murray Body, with efforts underway at Briggs and Ford. Among whites, Williams allied with the UAW's Lloyd Jones and a storefront pastor named RaLue Cessna. With this like-minded nucleus, Williams created a bimonthly meeting at the Dodge Community House for labor and religious leaders to discuss the challenges posed by Frank Norris and Gerald L. K. Smith—or, as Williams put it, "the Detroit apostles of fascism," who perverted the gospel and used "the King James Bible as their *Mein Kampft* [sic]."[31]

In 1944, Williams launched his most ambitious effort: the Detroit Council of Applied Religion. In May of that year, he hosted an "ordination" ceremony for his working-class ministers that unabashedly mixed radical politics and religious ritual. Held at the African American Lucy Thurman branch of the YWCA, participants constituted an interracial fellowship. Williams provocatively chose to host the ceremony on May 1st, the day of international workers' solidarity. In his sermon, he urged the church to "return to vital religion" and "return to the people." While receiving their ordination, Williams's ministers were instructed not to kneel as if before a bishop "in a submissive way," but to stand as ready to fight. Music and song had long been key to Williams's ministry, and "old tunes with new content" were liberally used on this day as well. Appropriately, the ceremony's closing "hymn" was the labor ballad, "Joe Hill."[32]

A month later, in June of 1944, Williams convened a "Peoples' Congress of Applied Religion (PIAR)," which sought to fuse together representatives from four groups: organized labor, youth groups, the "grass-roots preacher" of the "mass religious movements," and the "middle-class preacher and laymen." To further its ministerial aims, the Congress designed Bible study courses to teach that the "history of the labor movement will never be completely written until it begins with Moses," and labor "will never enlist and retain the bulk of American workers until it recognizes and approaches them in terms of their deep religious conditioning."[33]

The Peoples' Institute acted as the organizing arm of local "councils" of applied religion. After a council was organized, cards were sent to factory stewards seeking to enroll those that were "democratically inclined." The cards were returned, sorted into zones, and new chapters were encouraged to form within these zones; in Detroit, 10,000 cards were returned from the Ford local alone. The Detroit council typically met on the first Monday of each month; songs and scripture opened the meetings. Next, members reported on social tensions or democratic violations that required attention. Following this, a research committee established the facts, prepared a resolution which included a list of actions to be taken, and mailed its findings to pastors, union secretaries, the UAW research committee, the American Jewish Congress representative in Detroit, Charles Hill, the Inter-Faith Chairman of Detroit Council of Churches, and Henry Jones.[34]

Tellingly, Williams measured the success of the first annual convention of the PIAR against the near-simultaneous Michigan convention of Gerald L. K. Smith's "America First" party. Williams was heartened by the fact that, after only two and a half years of work in Detroit on a shoestring budget, his congress attracted 214 delegates from 25 states, while Smith, after more than seven years in Detroit and generous support from Henry Ford, had drawn only 200 delegates from 27 states. But Williams's obsession with Smith was really the most revealing aspect of this comparison, for it was the political shape of working-class religion that most concerned both men. "Smith would distort and pervert the Bible, exploit the faulty religious conditioning of the masses and prostitute religion to develop shock troops at the behest of an industrial baron who aspires to be the Thyssen of an American fascism," Williams emphatically wrote to one of his supporters in the Presbytery. Contrarily, he hoped to "appeal to the very deep and genuine religious sentiment of the masses, to enlist them as democratic elements in the dynamic movements of a free society."[35]

Williams's religious radicalism was hardly uncontested. To the contrary, the right-wing evangelicals that Williams attacked so vigorously as fascist responded in kind, accusing Williams of serving as a communist front. And communism, for these ministers, presented just as grave a danger to the intertwined future of Christianity and democracy as fascism posed for liberals and leftists. To Frank Norris, Williams was part of a "MODERNIS-TIC, COMMUNISTIC ECCLESIASTICAL CONSPIRACY" and "one of the rankest Communists in America." Closer to Williams's home, the National Laymen's Council of the Presbyterian Church described him as a "militant agitator for a *new social and economic order*" (which, indeed, he was). The Laymen's Council claimed to have a copy of a document, obtained from the files of the House Committee on Un-American Activities (HUAC), proving Williams's connection to the Communist Party, and even claimed to know Williams's party name.[36]

Gerald L. K. Smith likewise began his campaign against Williams by describing him as the "Communist on the Presbyterian payroll," and claimed to possess a "Confidential Memo" showing that Williams received checks straight from the Soviet Union. Smith knew that Williams had referred to him as a fascist, and he warned his fellow fundamentalists to be alert to Williams's friends at *The Protestant*, a magazine whose contributors and editors constituted "compromisers and shifty-eyed traitors to the true cause of Christianity." By 1945, Smith had upped the rhetorical ante, referring to Williams as "Satan's Apostle to the American Church." One of Smith's followers, infiltrating a conference Williams held at St. Paul's Episcopal Church in Detroit, decried the presence of "Satan in God's House," and claimed that Williams's followers "crawled over the pews and actually saturated the place in a most undignified manner." It bears repeating that Smith took his own rhetoric quite literally, as did many of his followers. Communism was not understood as simply a misguided or flawed economic system but actually evil—the antithesis of both democracy and Christianity; as such, a minister suspected of smuggling communism into America through the guise of religion threatened the destruction of both democracy and Christianity.[37]

It is striking and deeply ironic that Smith and Norris used virtually the same ideological language as Williams and the UAW to draw diametrically opposite conclusions. *Both* parties claimed to speak for and defend democracy, both warned against the dangers of fascism, and each saw the other as democracy's greatest threat. The idioms of worker religion remained very much contested, among evangelicals as much as among Catholics. And, as the war continued, the growing salience of race within Christian discourse added a potent new dimension to the struggle between reactionary and progressive visions of working-class religion.[38]

African Americans, Racial Ideology, and Religious Politics

In the late 1930s, worker religion revolved primarily around issues of unionism and class identity. But by the early 1940s, racial ideology had emerged as perhaps the most crucial piece of this discourse. For those who had built or supported the UAW, fascist religion became inextricably linked with racist and anti-Semitic religion. Contrarily, for right-wing religious leaders who condemned the UAW and its liberal religious allies as communist, *communism* became virtually synonymous with promiscuous race-mixing. African Americans were, of course, at the heart of these changes and debates, and African American ministers played a decisive role in bringing racial injustice to the forefront of Christian discourse. In particular, Horace White, Malcolm Dade, and Charles Hill hoped to diminish the stereotype of overly emotional and obscuritanist black religiosity, and to more deeply link the cause of black workers with the UAW. By presenting black religion as fully invested in the broader movement of the working class, these clerics linked it with the culture of contemporary liberalism. Such a connection, especially made in the context of the Second World War, permitted the ministers to make an additional contribution to the discourse surrounding the politics of religion: "fascist" religion was really "racist" religion.[39]

For black ministers of the 1940s, the most important concept linking Christian religion and democratic citizenship was captured in the ubiquitous word *Brotherhood* (utilized as shorthand to represent the more cumbersome phrase, the "Fatherhood of God and the Brotherhood of Man"). Brotherhood was both a religious and a civic concept: an assertion of reciprocity, a belief that, because blacks and whites shared the same Father in heaven, so they shared the same rights on earth. If equality was divinely ordained, neither residential segregation nor employment discrimination could be tolerated. Horace White articulated this view in an especially politicized analysis of the crucifixion during Easter, 1944. Jesus "was a man who had arrived at the point in his thinking and feeling, that he could look upon all men as brothers, and that they were the children of one God." Charles Hill was even more explicit during Brotherhood Week in 1946, criticizing those who told Detroit's African Americans to maintain patience, and wait until their rights could be duly doled out.[40]

In addition to equality, Brotherhood also asserted universalism and non-violence. The ministerial generation coming into prominence in the 1940s hailed integration and rejected Black Nationalism. During the 1943 riot, Hill and other ministers issued a press release urging both black and white ministers "to express a militant determination and a positive spirit of goodwill which will refuse to let Americans be divided by racial lines." Brotherhood meant celebrating human unity, not ethnic or racial specificity. Fittingly, Hill explained his participation in labor and civil rights circles by saying it "was right to help all of humanity." And most black churches in Detroit united in recognizing "Brotherhood Week" every February, thus incorporating both the political and theological justifications for equality within the lived experience of church life. Often, black and white ministers exchanged pulpits for the occasion, offering sermons on the moral implications of equality. Without fail, articles and editorials on Brotherhood filled the city's black press, celebrating the churches that most enthusiastically commemorated Brotherhood Week.[41]

The Brotherhood concept allowed African American churches to intertwine moral appeals for equality with political demands for action on behalf of working-class congregants. As early as 1943, several Detroit churches were hosting an FEPC Sunday to demonstrate support for fair employment laws. These Sundays were named for the Fair Employment Practice Council, an ecumenical organization that viewed equal-opportunity laws as an opportunity for "translating Judeo-Christian principles and democratic ideals into practice." Both Hill and White dedicated specific services at their churches to protest racially restrictive real estate covenants. Annual membership drives for the NAACP were routinely kicked off on Sunday mornings (in 1952, Bethel AME church hosted the service, with the sponsorship of Ford Local 600—yet another indication of the braiding of racial activism, union consciousness, and black church culture). Race Relations Sunday and, for some churches, Labor Sundays were celebrated as well. The impact of these symbolic performances is, of course, hard to measure, but at the very least, they indicate the ways in which African American religious culture was attempting to incorporate and express a political consciousness transformed by the rise of the UAW and the experiences of the Second World War.[42]

The rhetorical connection between racism and fascism, forged by leaders in the African American church, was quickly embraced by white Catholics and Protestants who had been instrumental in the creation of a worker religion in the 1930s. ACTU president Paul Weber, for instance, acknowledged in 1943 that the "race problem in Detroit is rapidly becoming the most critical problem facing the people of this great industrial city." Speaking for his fellow Actists, Weber grimly detected "a growling, subterranean race war going on in the City of Detroit," and he placed the "greater part of the blame . . . upon white people who persist in a totally un-democratic and un-American attitude of discrimination toward colored people." Fr. Raymond

Clancy utilized what was emerging as typical language to describe racism: it was un-American as well as un-Christian, attributes that had become, for liberal Catholics, mutually reinforcing.[43]

Weber's language suggests that the wartime struggle to define Catholicism as democratic and tolerant was already pushing Catholic worker religion past its initial formulation as a specifically Catholic set of working-class identities, and toward a broader, less class-specific, vision of social justice. Indeed, in the early 1940s, Catholic Action spurred the growth of religiously based antiracist organizations, just as it had spurred prolabor groups in the 1930s. In May 1942, Detroiters established a small but lively chapter of the Catholic Interracial Council (CIC), which distributed thousands of pamphlets and lectured before tens of thousands of Detroit-area Catholics in a variety of organizations during the mid-1940s. The growing antiracist discourse even shaped some of the idioms and performances of Catholicism for CIC sympathizers. At a remarkable service in 1943, Sacred Heart Church dedicated an "interracial shrine," followed by a program on Catholic Action and Race Relations, which was in turn cosponsored by the ACTU and Ford Local 600. In the process, the worker-religion practices of the late 1930s were pushed to include a specifically antiracist component.[44]

Claude Williams, meanwhile, had been radicalized on issues of racial justice in the poverty-torn rural South in the 1930s and always viewed racial equality as a central part of his vision for class-conscious evangelicalism. Immediately upon his arrival in Detroit, Williams formed alliances with two African American ministers, Charles Hill and the Congregationalist John Miles. Both of these ministers had already been utilizing some of Williams's more innovative teaching methods for months before the minister's arrival. Williams's propaganda constantly invoked racial tolerance as a religious value. In a pamphlet on "Anti-Semitism, Racism, and Democracy," Williams described Caesar as "the Hitler of Rome"; reminding his listeners that Jesus stood opposed to Caesar's empire, Williams claimed that Rome's decree of world taxation without representation found its modern equivalent in the poll tax. Thus, Williams argued, to advance democracy and advance the Gospel, one must end the antiscriptural poll tax. "Prejudice or discrimination against any group because of race, sex, or color," Williams declared, "is a transgression at the very heart of true religion." African American ministers looking to promote civil rights easily recognized Williams as an ally; little wonder that Williams's "lessons" soon began appearing in Detroit's African American newspaper, the *Michigan Chronicle*.[45]

Leading mainline Protestant ministers, who had sometime supported the social gospel but rarely embraced the labor movement or worker religion, quickly moved to denounce war-era racism. In 1942, Protestants took a leading part in the Metropolitan Detroit FEPC. In 1944, the DCC boldly issued an "interracial code" for the city's Protestant churches, the first of its kind in the country; in telling language, the code sanctioned member churches that excluded African Americans, citing "Christian, democratic, and scientific principles." An interracial "workshop," sponsored by the city of Detroit in 1945, demonstrates the pervasiveness of the discursive strategy linking democracy, Christianity, and interracial justice. Representatives of 100 churches attended, and many speakers expounded the theme that had come to define the war for many: democracy needed Christianity, and both needed to advance an agenda of racial equality. Herbert Hudnut, pastor of Woodward Avenue Presbyterian Church, claimed that America's lack of racial "brotherhood" had undermined both its religion and its politics. Hudnut made the obvious connection explicit: "We are Nazis to the extent that we possess degrees of hate within us against our fellow men."[46]

Nevertheless, just as worker religion itself always remained contested in the 1930s, this broader interracial religion failed to erase racial divisions, which remained raw and powerful. Louis Martin, editor of the *Michigan Chronicle*, observed in 1944 that Detroit supported many interracial committees, but complained that they "function almost in a vacuum." Malcolm Dade recalled that African Americans attempting to attend white congregations "were told very frankly, with blunt boldness, of the fact that there were black churches in the diocese," and were pointed toward St Matthew's or St Cyprian's. During Brotherhood Week in 1947, Dade argued that "The Church has an inescapable imperative to witness the Brotherhood more than any other segment of society." But unfortunately, Dade complained, the church's brand of brotherhood was too often "specious," making Brotherhood Week one of "penitence and shame." Horace White, in his 1944 Easter message, voiced the same frustration, complaining that too many of his fellow black preachers have "removed the real significance of Jesus' death on the cross from the common people." Rather than utilizing the resurrection as an invigoration in the struggle for freedom, White felt that most preachers reduced Easter to "just another festive occasion with meaningless sentimentality."[47]

The urge to articulate a worker religion that conjoined racism and fascism pointed to very real social tensions simmering within workplaces and neighborhoods throughout the city. At the volatile Packard plant, for instance, J. Frank Norris received the support of company officials to host popular Packard Days services on Thursday and Friday nights at Temple Baptist Church, in which he excoriated communism, the UAW, and racial integration. According to Claude Williams, Norris operated sixteen different religious programs at Packard, plus a shop-floor radio show. Williams described the content of Norris's gospel to a CRC investigator:

> Sunday after Sunday, both from his pulpit and on the air, [Norris] preaches that it is an insult that white men should be compelled to work along side of "niggers" in plants. For the "protection" of white women, he demands that the whole Negro population of "rapists" and "primitives" be separated in schools, in homes, in theatres, in parks, in shops, in jobs.

Yet, at the same time, Norris sought to cultivate a handful of African American preachers on the shop floor. The case of the African American Pentecostal preacher and Packard worker Robert Hill vividly illustrates the cultural trench warfare being waged over religious ideology. Hill, described by Williams as "the most dynamic speaker in the plant," had been courted by Frank Norris and even appeared on Norris's radio show. Williams's protégé, the African American Packard shop preacher Virgil Vanderburg, approached Hill and apparently convinced his fellow evangelist that "he was being used." Hill was flipped to Williams's position, and, because Hill was "the most influential speaker, the anti-Negro forces are check-mated in their religious programs."[48]

The cultural struggle between Williams and Norris was, in the end, a struggle over the ways in which working-class people juxtaposed their religious and political identities. Such ideas and identities mattered, an importance demonstrated by the Packard "hate strikes." In October of 1941, white Packard workers launched an unauthorized strike over the transfer of two African American metal polishers to the "white" work on defense products; the strike spiraled on for six months. When 25,000 Packard workers launched a second hate strike in June 1943, working-class unity seemed, at best, elusive. Religion exacerbated these disputes. Offering his considerations on the troubles at Packard, *Michigan Chronicle* reporter Theodore Wood observed, "Conflicts in plants between whites and blacks were more frequent where revivalist influence was strong."[49] Nor was such incendiary religious conflict limited to Protestants. According to Leroy Spradley, an African American committeeman in the UAW, one Polish American priest also visited the Packard plants, and urged an alliance between white Protestants and ethnic Catholics in an effort at "maintaining Christian civilization there." In practice, this translated into creating a black/white dyad that would thwart the promotion of blacks into previously all-white shop departments. The politics of race, not the boundaries of denomination or even the social experiences of work, was increasingly shaping working-class religion.[50]

Meanwhile, outside of the workplace, the social geography of religion in Detroit remained etched along racial and class lines. Many Catholics—especially ethnic Poles—viewed home ownership as virtually a sacred duty. This impulse was thoroughly supported, from the highest level of the Church to the local parish. Auxiliary Bishop Stephen Woznicki, the highest-ranking Pole in Detroit's Archdiocese, acknowledged to interviewers that "he personally, and the Polish priests generally, encourage the Polish people to buy and own their own homes." Perceived threats to these Catholic communities, often established through heavy sacrifice on the part of working-class parishioners, were greeted with open hostility. Catholic worker religion—never a universally embraced practice within Catholic communities—exposed even deeper rifts between working-class Catholics as its message expanded to include racial equality.[51]

The small-scale riots surrounding occupancy of the Sojourner Truth Housing Project in February 1942 offer the most vivid example. Designed to house two hundred of the tens of thousands of African Americans laboring in Detroit's defense industries, the Sojourner Truth homes—federally funded, but locally administered—were designed for a northeast section of the city near previous black settlements. Whites in the adjacent neighborhoods reacted swiftly. Led by the Polish American realtor Joseph Buffa, residents formed the Seven Mile-Fenelon Improvement Association (SMFIA). This organization, and individuals associated with it, lobbied local and federal officials to keep "their" neighborhoods—and public housing in general—all white.[52]

To the dismay of worker-religion Catholics, priests and parishioners became a driving force in the SMFIA. In December of 1941, well before the anticipated move-in date of black workers, the Detroit Council of Social Agencies complained that one Fr. O'Mara was "one of the most bitter factors" opposing the housing project. Even more important than O'Mara was Fr. Constantine Dzink, whose overwhelmingly Polish parish, Saint Louis the King, became a headquarters for SMFIA meetings. Described by one reporter as "an aged bald, Polish peasant," Dzink personified liberal fears that working-class religion nurtured fascism. Employing long-standing discursive categories, the report described Dzink as "a virtual dictator over the lives and thoughts of several thousand Poles." Once again, for progressives, the supposed authoritarian culture and emotional susceptibility of working-class Catholics had morphed into something political and downright dangerous.[53]

Detroit's most prominent Catholic Workers, Louis Murphy and Marie Conti, visited fellow Catholics protesting the Sojourner Truth homes, and came away from the experience deeply troubled. Given the ubiquity of American flags on the protest line, Conti wondered whether "the Negro can help but doubt democracy." Encountering actual Catholics was even more disturbing than the symbolic displays. Although Murphy and Conti tried to stimulate peaceful conversation and calm reflection, they instead found themselves in bitter disagreement with other "good Catholics" from St. Louis the King. "I said to a Catholic, self-called, that Christ died for both white and Negro—and he actually denied it," Conti lamented. Tellingly, another "good Catholic" accused the Workers of not being "real" Catholics, but "Communists" and "nigger-lovers"—a painful contrast to Conti's own dismissal of a racist as a "self-called" Catholic, and a revealing conflation of communism with racial pluralism. As Murphy and Conti retreated in shock, a group of men followed them menacingly, one uttering threats. "I have never in my life seen hate personified as I did in the persons of these Catholics," Conti concluded. For her and other liberal Catholics, the actions of her coreligionists provoked a deep crisis of psychic dissidence. Indeed, Conti may have been feeling a rupture in her preexisting sense of a universal Catholic peoplehood and the recognition that working-class religious identity could not necessarily be contained by the idioms of worker religion.[54]

The issue was, of course, much clearer for African American clerical leaders, who naturally supported the Sojourner Truth homes and used their churches as spaces to hold rallies and discuss strategy. Anticipating some of the protest strategies made famous in later battles for civil rights, fifteen black Baptist ministers circled City Hall on January 28, 1942, singing the spiritual "We Shall Not Be Moved." They hoped to pressure Mayor Edward Jeffries to keep his word that the homes would shelter black workers (Jeffries, instead, became increasingly conservative and race-baiting). After the mini-riot accompanying the first move-in on February 28, a mass meeting of 3,000 gathered at St John's CME church, and some dislodged black families actually wound up living in churches until the matter was settled in April of 1942. Having seeded the African American surge into the UAW in 1941, black churches during the war were building on that legacy of political activism in the direction of civil rights.[55]

Charles Hill was a good example of this development; the preacher who hosted union meetings in his church basement in 1941 became leader of the Sojourner Truth Citizens' Committee in 1942. His letter "To Loyal and Patriotic Polish-Americans" perfectly encapsulates the emerging universalism characteristic of worker religion during the war. African Americans and Polish Americans "are in the same boat together," Hill wrote. In another statement regarding the controversy, Hill argued that the measure of a good society could be gauged by its "treatment of minorities," which, he made certain to emphasize, might include "the Jewish people, the Polish people, the Catholics or the Protestants." But he clearly understood that African Americans might especially benefit from the ideological opportunity offered by a war against fascism and totalitarianism. As he went on to note in his "Statement," "there is little appreciable difference between the economic and social treatment of Negroes in many places in America and the treatment of the Jewish and Polish people" in Nazi-occupied Europe.[56]

Sadly, the mini-riot surrounding the Sojourner Truth homes proved but a prelude to the much more serious violence that erupted in June 1943. According to the governor's committee that investigated the riot, tensions between black and ethnic (likely Catholic) youth sparked the violent eruption. Trouble started, the report concluded, days before the riot began, when African American boys were pelted with stones at an amusement center and decided to retaliate by "[taking] care of the Hunkies." This retaliation began on Belle Isle, an island park in the middle of the Detroit River. Hot, irritable, and overcrowded, whites and blacks in the park engaged in scuffles that eventually swept the city and produced a wave of racial violence that went virtually uncontrolled until federal troops arrived two days later. Thirty-four people, 20 of them African American, lay dead after three days of fighting.[57]

The rhetorical response to the race riot perfectly captures the politicized shape of Christian discourse heading toward the postwar period. For Gerald L. K. Smith, the riot was a textbook example of the failure of interracialism, the fruits of moral dissolution, and the mendacity of communists. Northern "screwballs and sentimentalists," according to Smith, encouraged black politicization, upset the "natural" order of racial separation, and hastened the disintegration of traditional sexual mores. Once in the North, African Americans were "actually encouraged by politicians and Communists to make dates with white girls and to flirt with white girls on the street." Communists employed white women to bait gullible black men, thus artificially fomenting black discontent. "What can some of the white girls expect," Smith asked. "They parade half-nude . . . they tempt morons and undisciplined men beyond the borders of self-control." The only solution, Smith averred, was "Christian statesmanship," which might preserve the hierarchies of race and gender, oppose communism, and in the process save "traditional" American democracy.[58]

Louis Martin of the *Michigan Chronicle*, meanwhile, invoked Christian rhetoric to draw diametrically opposite political conclusions. After a special governor's committee claimed that the African American bid for equality helped spark the riot, Martin angrily compared the governor's blame-the-victim language to Nazi pogroms against Jews. "By a similar procedure," Martin observed, "passages could be taken out of the Holy Bible which would make the Scriptures equally inflammatory." Had the committee read the Bible,

Martin stated, its report would have "repudiated the principle of brotherhood of man as an incitement for oppressed Negroes to riot." Martin, like Claude Williams and other religious leftists, linked "true" religion to both political democracy and racial equality; "false" religion, or simple godlessness, produced both racial oppression and fascism.[59]

Conclusion

The Second World War pushed the imaginative linkages between class, religion, and politics into uncharted directions. At a historical moment in which democracy seemed genuinely imperiled, Americans were forced to think closely about just what their political creeds meant, and how they might be improved. The religious cultures of the city's vast working classes were closely implicated in this process. Modernists and progressives in Detroit had, since the early twentieth century, disdained the supposedly overemotional, authoritarian, and antisocial tenor of working-class religion. The war, however, pushed many progressives to even more dramatic conclusions: that working-class religion offered a uniquely American opening for fascism, totalitarianism, and the collapse of liberal society.

The idioms, practices, and organizations of worker religion had first emerged in the late 1930s to reconcile the creative tensions between class identity and religious tradition. In the war years, worker religion expanded its ambition and imaginative scope, placing working-class religion not only within the orbit of the organized labor movement, but at the very heart of the democratic experiment. Catholics in the ACTU and Catholic Worker movement, white Protestants associated with Claude Williams and the PIAR, and African Americans inspired by preachers like Horace White and Charles Hill all promoted a vision of religion serving as a tolerant framework for a free society of worker-citizens.

With the war won, any fears about an American Hitler emerging through working-class churches had been resolved; Charles Coughlin was officially "silenced" by the Catholic Church in 1941, Gerald L. K. Smith moved to Arkansas after the war, and Frank Norris receded into the background. Indeed, in their efforts to thwart the anti-Semitic and racist nostrums of Charles Coughlin and Gerald L. K. Smith, the reframers of worker religion raised a potent issue that had been temporarily subsumed in the 1930s by debates over the labor question: racial inequality. Having raised new issues, the postwar years also produced a new cultural and political context that would challenge the resonance of worker religion.

THE MASS OF SAINT JOSEPH THE WORKMAN

we pray

The prayers at the foot of the altar

▦ PRIEST. In the name of the Father, and of the Son, and of the Holy Ghost. Amen. I will go up to the altar of God.

PEOPLE. To God, the giver of youth and happiness.

PR. O God, sustain my cause; give me redress against a race that knows no piety; save me from a treacherous foe and cruel.

P. Thou, O God, art all my strength, why hast Thou cast me off? Why do I go mourning, with enemies pressing me hard?

PR. The light of Thy presence, the fulfillment of Thy promise, let these be my escort, bringing me safe to Thy holy mountain, to the tabernacle where Thou dwellest.

P. There I will go up to the altar of God, the giver of youth and happiness.

PR. Thou art my God, with the harp I hymn Thy praise. Soul, why art thou downcast, why art thou all lament?

P. Wait for God's help; I will not cease to cry out in thankfulness: My champion and my God!

1

FIGURE 9. This Catholic prayer to St. Joseph the Workman epitomizes the effort to place worker religion within the liturgical calendar. Copy in Association of Catholic Trade Unionists Collection, Box 4, Folder "Labor Day Mass 1956," Walter P. Reuther Library, Archives of Labor and Urban Affairs, Wayne State University.

FIGURE 10. Clement Kern, the "saint of the slums," was one of Detroit's most vibrant and active labor priests. Courtesy of Walter P. Reuther Library, Archives of Labor and Urban Affairs, Wayne State University.

5. The Decline of Worker Religion, 1946–1963

In 1954, the *Michigan Catholic* applauded the "widespread religious observance of Labor Day." The newspaper's claim—that a civil holiday for working people had acquired the spiritual power of a religious feast—may seem startling, but was quite common in the 1950s. George Higgins, one of the nation's most famous labor priests, similarly noted that, "Labor day has almost come to be regarded as an unofficial holy day in the United States." In 1955, 1,400 people attended Higgins's Labor Day Mass, prominently celebrated at Detroit's Blessed Sacrament Cathedral. The following year witnessed even greater fanfare as, for the first time, Pope Pius XII officially established the feast of St. Joseph the Workman as a universal feast day within the Catholic Church. In his sermon to Detroit Catholics commemorating the occasion, Rt. Rev. Arthur F. Bukowski explicitly connected the political surge of the labor movement in the 1930s to the idioms of worker religion, observing that, "The rise of popular devotion to St. Joseph roughly parallels the rise of unionism." Indeed, when Bukowski argued that "St. Joseph . . . took his rightful place in the hearts of Catholics" at the same time that working people rose from historical "obscurity," the parallel seemed to imply a causal connection. The separate threads of faith, unionism, and democracy—first stitched together in the 1930s—seemed to mature richly in the 1950s.[1]

Yet, just a few years after Bukowski's stirring sermon, a writer for Detroit's ACTU newspaper, the *Wage Earner*, made an ominous observation. Despite the liturgical innovation of labor priests, the incorporation of the Feast of St. Joseph the Workman into the formal devotional calendar, the social involvement and religious internalization of the laity spurred by Catholic Action, and the working-class origins of so many Catholics, the character of

Christ the Worker "does not seem to have gotten a foothold" among Detroit's Catholic workers. The newspaper was frustrated and a little perplexed. True, the paper admitted, new devotions—such as those to St. Joseph or Christ the Worker—take time to develop. But, with automation transforming the workplace, unemployment swelling across the city, and the most ambitious goals of New Deal–era social unionism in retreat, the *Wage Earner* was worried: "The need for this devotion exists in our country today." This hope went largely unfulfilled. In 1964, the *Wage Earner* published its last issue.[2]

How do we explain the seeming contradiction between the rise of St. Joseph the Workman and the collapse of the *Wage Earner* just a few years later? Further, how do we explain the erosion of the once-vibrant idioms of worker religion, as a cultural movement, all across Detroit's working class: African American and white-evangelical, as well as Catholic? And, what is the larger significance of this disappearance to working-class history? Answering these questions compels a reexamination of Detroit's shifting social and economic context during the postwar years and the ambivalent valences of religious consciousness among working people themselves.

Worker Religion and Cold War Culture

Worker religion emerged as a strain within the broader culture of the 1930s, an era shaped by narratives of "forgotten men," migrant mothers, and plain-folk communities. After the Second World War, however, the United States stood as the world's wealthiest and most powerful nation, locked into conflict with a totalitarian communist adversary. Religion became a powerful component of Cold War anticommunism and a bulwark for patriotic nationalism. From the anticommunist harangues of Billy Graham, to the inclusion of "under God" in the pledge of allegiance, to the sober neorealist theology of anticommunist Reinhold Niebuhr, religious culture was widely viewed as a key national resource in a conflict that was perceived as spiritual and metaphysical as much as geopolitical. This religious turn against communism was, as historian Jason Stevens suggests, perhaps most painful for precisely those American leftists who had supported the radical dreams of the thirties, only to repudiate their seemingly naive idealism in the fifties. The CIO's traumatic 1949 expulsion of eleven unions with alleged communist leadership crystalized this cultural shift, symbolizing both American labor's rejection of '30s-era politics and its movement into the anticommunist mainstream of American life. Therefore, as anticommunism remade Americans' attitudes toward capitalism, freedom, and liberalism, the religious idioms and political assumptions undergirding worker religion were likewise reexamined.[3]

For working-class Catholics, the staunch anticommunism of the early Cold War was perfectly consistent with Church teachings stretching back decades. Still, the conjunction of Catholic devotional culture and anticommunism was especially robust and vigorous in the postwar years. Catholic rituals of anticommunism nearly always involved the Virgin Mary, who literally embodied the divine struggle against atheistic materialism. In October of 1948, a statue of Our Lady of Fatima (a Marian apparition that Catholics believed had appeared to Portuguese children in 1917, urging them to pray the rosary for the destruction of communism) arrived at Detroit's Assumption Grotto parish while touring the country. During a single day, over 40,000 Catholics flooded through the church to pray with the image. Again in October of 1950, the exquisitely named parish priest, Fr. Marx, urged the Young Ladies Sodality to pray the rosary to "stop the spread of communism"; this practice quickly grew into a parishwide block rosary movement, wherein small groups, arranged on a block-by-block basis, met in homes to pray the rosary together.[4]

These activities were ubiquitous throughout the Archdiocese. Beginning in 1946, and continuing throughout the 1950s, the Archdiocese broadcast a "Radio Rosary Crusade" every May. Coinciding with the radio programs, thousands of Catholics converged at St. Aloysius in downtown Detroit to take part in massive programs. In 1950, for instance, up to 10,000 Catholics attended services, spilling out of the church and across Washington Boulevard, many holding banners reading "Pray for Russia." "If Josef Stalin saw Detroiters praying he would smile scornfully," the presiding priest intoned triumphantly, before reciting examples of Christian armies subduing non-Christian enemies due to Mary's intercession. On May Day during Mary's "glory year" of 1954, 100,000 Catholics filled the University of Detroit stadium to witness Archbishop Mooney celebrate mass and repudiate communism. Meanwhile, at St. Ladislaus parish, the 1954 Marian day celebration produced the largest religious gathering in the history of Hamtramck. Throughout the year, twenty-eight different parishes erected Marian shrines to encourage cross-city pilgrimages and additional devotional worship. Of course, as with so much in Catholic culture, the images of peace, purity, and motherly love invoked by anticommunist representations of Mary were also highly ambivalent, linked to darker warnings of sin, torment, and lurid destruction. As the Korean War erupted, the *Michigan Catholic* advised, "We should get down on our knees and beg Mary, our Mother, to save us from death and destruction, from the forces of Communism."[5]

As a symbol of both virginal purity and motherly love, Mary presented a stark contrast to the rugged, masculine characters of St. Joseph the Workman or Christ the Worker so central to worker religion. The feverish Catholic hostility to communism thus eroded the resonance of these cultural symbols, but it also attenuated political alliances formed during the Depression. By the mid-1950s, cracks began appearing in the pro-union consensus among Detroit's most prominent Catholic clergy. Fr. John Coogan, a professor of sociology at the University of Detroit, offers the most illustrative example. Over the course of the 1940s, Coogan built a reputation as one of Detroit's most liberal priests, especially on matters of racial equality; indeed, Coogan chaired the city of Detroit's "racial" agency, the Coordinating Council on Human Relations, in the late 1950s. But in 1955, Coogan wrote an inflammatory article in the *American Ecclesiastical Review* favoring right-to-work legislation that most unionists felt was blatantly antilabor. George Higgins, the country's preeminent labor priest and a staunch supporter of Reuther's UAW, responded angrily to Coogan's piece, writing to Detroit Archbishop Mooney that Coogan showed "a disgraceful exhibition of ignorance, prejudice and bad taste." The American labor movement, Higgins assured Mooney, "is still the best labor movement in the world from the point of view of Catholic social teaching." But Coogan, while cordial to Higgins, remained unbowed, and insisted that it was Higgins's view—not his own—that was the minority in Catholic circles. "[O]ne pastor has told me, 'We all feel as you do. But we are too afraid of the unions in our parishes to say so,'" Coogan responded. Unions *were* under an increasingly skeptical public scrutiny in the 1950s. Brooklyn-based labor priest William Smith, for instance, reported hearing so many priests express a vague disdain for Reuther and the UAW that "it amounts to a minor scandal." Some priests likely felt that the idealism of the 1930s-era unions had been lost; others were probably never converted to labor's cause in the first place, and found greater safety expressing this view in the anticommunist environment of the 1950s.[6]

A number of ordinary Catholics seemed to feel the same way, to the frustration of worker-religion advocates. One anonymous writer to the *Michigan Catholic* complained in 1954 that too many of his coreligionists were antiunion, duped into the false belief that "all unions are Communistic." "Frankly," another Detroit union member wrote to the *Michigan Catholic*, "I am tired [of] being considered a radical" simply for citing papal encyclicals or position papers by the National Catholic Welfare Conference. Laity such as these struggled to convince fellow Catholics that continued involvement in the labor movement was a moral duty. Morosely, ACTU chaplain Karl Hubble guessed that, of the 200,000 unionized Detroit-area Catholics in 1958, less than 1 percent had been exposed to the fundamental convictions of Catholic social justice. By that time, the labor schools were virtually defunct, and Detroit's ACTU even broke from the national organization in 1956 (it reestablished itself as the Detroit Catholic Labor Conference and functioned much the same as earlier but failed to recruit many members). As one especially keen observer noted, "Some ACTU leaders, hardened by nearly two decades of battle—against Communists, against racketeers, against hostile employers, against even some fellow-Catholics—have a hard time growing out of attitudes and answers patented in the '30s."[7]

If the liberals of the DCLC floundered, the more radical Catholic Worker drew sharp suspicion. In 1948, Michael Rawlins, a former seminarian who spent time at the Catholic Workers' Detroit area farm for health reasons, became so alarmed at what he perceived as the group's subversive nature that he composed a detailed complaint for submission to the FBI. Perusing the published material so avidly consumed by Catholic Workers, Rawlins discerned a lack of respect for the hierarchy, priesthood, and sacraments of the Church. One magazine, according to Rawlins, condemned "what it calls the 'Bourgeois Spirit,' and then subtly identifies the Catholic Church of today with this bourgeois spirit." Another publication, called "A Hymn to Work," presented "a text that glorifies and deifies work as an end in itself, as a reason for being," with little regard for the traditional sacraments or the priesthood. Rawlins puzzled over the group's lack of record keeping and transparency, its resistance to clerical oversight, and its constant ability to locate financing. The most likely conclusion, Rawlins asserted, was that "The Catholic Worker is Communistic, propagandizing under the mantle of Catholicism. . . . What is more likely than that Communists should burrow from within the Church, masking their undercover and real work with a cloak of Catholicism, under the form of devotional atmosphere and objects, charitable activity in the form of soup lines for down and outs?" Rawlins was wrong in his suspicions; the lay activists of the Catholic Worker were spiritually devout and deeply Catholic. But Rawlins's disavowal of the ideas and idioms of the Catholic Worker—indeed, his linkage of those idioms to a dangerous and subversive ideology—suggests the cultural weakness for worker religion in the early Cold War.[8]

If the Cold War narrowed the scope of Catholic worker religion, the postwar movement toward an anticommunist consensus carried disastrous implications for Claude Williams. Williams had long been accused of communist affiliation, and he never stifled rumors of political unorthodoxy. In fact, his defiance regarding the issue only heightened emotions. According to one credible report, Williams often made allusions to communist rhetoric, referring to himself as a "fellow-traveler with the Man Who Went to the Cross." In a letter to Henry Jones of the Dodge Community House, Williams angrily dismissed the Communist charge as "irrelevant and untenable both from a civic and a religious viewpoint. This is America." Rather than refute the accusation, Williams simply changed the subject. "The issue is not the 'evil' of Communism vs the 'purity' of the church," Williams declared, but the church's painful awareness that communists confronted evils with which the church was itself complicit. Later, under duress, Williams admitted that he did indeed pay dues to the Communist Party for a few months in 1937.[9]

By 1945, Williams's unorthodoxy jeopardized the future of his mission in Detroit. Still, his key supporters, Henry Jones and John Forsyth, argued strenuously that Williams was reaching people "whom none of the rest of us have been able to reach. To them he represents the Gospel of Christ in action." Labor leaders, "long alienated from the Church,—in some instances bitter toward it,—are becoming warm and receptive to its message." In fact, Jones and Forsyth argued that Williams had built relationships with at least twenty labor leaders of Presbyterian backgrounds who had been outside the church orbit. Some union leaders had even been married by a minister, who, without Williams's influence, "would never have thought of having a Christian marriage."[10]

Perhaps the most visible of these labor converts was Shelton Tappes, a militant African American activist and influential figure at Ford Local 600. After Williams founded the Detroit Council of Applied Religion, Tappes agreed to serve as cochairman. According to Williams, Tappes's commitment to the Detroit Council proved that labor leaders were "interested in religion if it effectively deals in that matters of brotherhood and human betterment." Tappes himself expressed these sentiments when he wrote to protest the Presbyterian Church's temporary suspension of Williams in February 1945. Only months before Williams's arrival, Tappes claimed, "an easily recognizable condition in this area was the growing apathy toward the established Church." But Williams changed that. "We, Detroit need Claude Williams," Tappes pleaded. Cecil Galey, president of UAW Local 351, also protested Williams's suspension: "I have attended his church services," Galey wrote, and "his work is more paralleled to the life of Jesus, preached since the Churches have been established, but not accepted by any of the major powers in religion."[11]

Nevertheless, Williams was let go. For a while, the Peoples' Institute of Applied Religion forged on bravely under the leadership of Williams's protégé John Miles. In August of 1946, PIAR members held open-air mass meetings in African American and southern white neighborhoods in Detroit, denouncing southern lynchings. Later that year, PIAR members marched with striking workers seeking unionization at the Frigid Foods Co; Rev. Miles even convinced eight scabs to join the picket line after speaking from the union sound truck. "Interest in our church service is very good, and so is attendance," Miles claimed in 1947, noting that fifty people had recently attended a meeting on "Religion in the Soviet Union" (a topic that suggests the provocative, leftist internationalism of the group, which was so suspect in the early Cold War). But the organization was difficult to maintain and abruptly disappears from the records by the end of the decade. Williams, meanwhile, exiled to farm life in the South, found himself convicted of heresy by his own church in 1952. The charge was communism.[12]

Finally, anticommunism played a significant role in shaping and narrowing the public religion within African American churches. As early as the 1930s, critics on the far right had conflated the growing African American civil rights movement with communist subversion. Black ministers who had supported the UAW, promoted the unionization of black workers, and fought for economic and housing equality during the war thus needed to promote racial liberalism while avoiding Red-Baiters. Charles Hill offers the most important and revealing example from the period. Entering the postwar period, Hill believed, as he explained to the *Michigan Chronicle* in 1947, "The plight of the Negro today is a challenge to the church, to lead and function in all phases of his life—civic, social, economic, and political." By the middle of the decade, he was elected president of Detroit's NAACP (he lost reelection in 1947 to another minister, the son of his mentor, Robert Bradby). In 1945, he launched the first of six campaigns for election to Detroit's Common Council. Hill garnered 142,000 votes in his first campaign, although he never won the seat he sought. However, he did successfully politicize the consciousness of previously apathetic black churches. With every campaign, Hill claimed, the numbers of registered black voters kept increasing. "At one time some of the churches said, 'We don't bother that way—we leave to the Lord,'" Hill told an interviewer. "I said, 'The Lord isn't coming down here to vote for you; you've got to vote for yourself.' Now, I don't know of a single church that is not willing to play its part in these elections." While Hill never attained the political success he hoped for, his "mentorship" of the activist Coleman Young bore fruit when Young became Detroit's first black mayor in the 1970s.[13]

But Hill also ran up against a wall of anticommunism. Through his close association with activists at Ford Local 600 and other radical organizations like the National Negro Congress, Hill had befriended Detroit-area communists, and he saw no reason to condemn them. When Hill launched his first campaign for the Common Council in 1945, communists and radicals were quick to support him—a fact that Hill's opponents adroitly exploited. In 1948, Hill lobbied for presidential candidate Henry Wallace and his Progressive Party rather than support the Democratic incumbent, Harry Truman (despite the fact that other left-liberals in Detroit—most notably the UAW—publicly backed Truman). Although Hill's political unorthodoxy never undercut his effectiveness as a pastor at Hartford Baptist, it likely did ensure the defeat of his political aspirations. When the House Un-American Activities Committee (HUAC) held hearings in Detroit in 1952, Hill was called to testify and refused to impugn communism.[14]

Hill's former allies in the black church, Horace White and Malcolm Dade, both testified to HUAC as well—and, revealingly, both condemned Hill's stances. White was particularly sharp in his remarks, characterizing Hill as a well-meaning communist "dupe." This denunciation was especially revealing, considering that, in 1947, White was unrelenting in his indictment of the Red Scare, believing it a way of forestalling action on issues like housing and fair employment. Nevertheless, White—like almost all other black ministers—condemned communism, and in the process he limited legitimate civil rights activity to the approved channels of liberal society.[15]

The campaign for the FEPC in Detroit perfectly captures the dynamics and divisions of the liberal, religious anticommunist coalition. The basic idea was simple: to prohibit, in law, race-based job discrimination. The momentum for an FEPC had been building ever since President Franklin Roosevelt issued an Executive Order in 1942 creating a Fair Employment Practices Committee for the war industries. Yet, in the early 1950s, two distinct groups of FEPC supporters emerged to lobby for a city-level law: The Detroit Citizens Committee for Equal Employment Opportunities (DCCEEO) and the Detroit Negro Labor Council (DNLC). The DCCEEO represented what had become the norm among liberal civil rights groups: a broad coalition with "representatives of civic, labor, religious, trade, political, fraternal and veterans' organizations," under the leadership of Fr. John F. Finnegan, moderator of the Catholic Interracial Council. The authority of pluralistic civil religion was integral to the DCCEEO. When the group wrote to members of Detroit's Common Council in July of 1951, it argued that the "American Christian tradition tolerates no restriction based on irrelevant factors such as race, color, creed, nationality or ancestry." At a pro-FEPC rally held a month later, Fr. Finnegan presided, the Rev. Fred Porter of the Interdenominational Ministerial Alliance provided the invocation, and a welcome was offered by Rev. Sheldon Rahn of the Detroit Council of Churches' Social Services Department (Rahn was also chairman of the group's executive committee).[16]

The DCCEEO wanted Detroit's Common Council to enact an FEPC, while the DNLC lobbied for a public referendum, which it believed would carry. The difference between the two organizations, however, was not strategic. Instead, the DCCEEO opposed the DNLC solely out of the belief that the latter organization was a communist front composed of members expelled from the CIO. Marie Oresti, president of the Catholic Interracial Council and supporter of FEPC, wrote to members that blocking the DNLC and boosting the DCCEEO represented "your chance to do something against Communism." The Michigan State Committee of the Communist Party, meanwhile, slyly offered to unite with the Detroit Council of Churches, perhaps in an effort to demonstrate what it felt was the emptiness of Christian rhetoric. "Would you consider your Council a 'communist front' just because your Council and the Communist Party oppose the suppression of the Protestant Churches by the Franco Regime in Spain?" the CP asked. "Your argument against the petition is shallow indeed. . . . All we want is a City FEPC." In the end, neither group succeeded in 1951; in fact, Michigan would not have a fair employment practices law until 1955.[17]

By the late 1940s, the general political parameters for civil rights and working-class activism in the postwar period had formed, with religion occupying a central role and anticommunism serving as a cultural lynchpin. The *Michigan Chronicle* expressed this position well. Despite all its abuses, democracy offered a better way of solving the problems of racial inequality than communism. Communists had a history of lobbying for minority rights, the *Chronicle* acknowledged, but the philosophy (and those espousing it) needed to be condemned principally because it threatened religion. "The Communist attitude toward the church and Christianity is absolutely unacceptable to us," the paper opined. "We are a God-fearing people, and we base our fight for full citizenship" on Christian morals. Detroit needed the combined forces of Christian morality and political action, the paper averred—not communism.[18]

The Church in the Changing City

While the culture of the early Cold War helped to undermine the idioms of worker religion, an even more profound challenge emerged from the shifting economic and demographic nature of the city itself. Already by the early 1950s, Detroit was enduring the first major pangs of an urban crisis rooted in the technological transformation of automation within area auto plants and the social dilemmas associated with race, segregation, poverty, and housing. Over the course of the 1950s, both Ford and General Motors committed to automating the labor process with enthusiasm. Although the new machinery spared workers some dangerous tasks, it also thoroughly undermined Detroit's economy. In 1947, Detroit firms employed 338,400 manufacturing workers, a number that had dropped to 209,700 by 1967. Already by 1953, over

4,000 jobs had been eliminated from Ford factories because of automation. Overall, employment at the River Rouge plant fell from 85,000 jobs in 1945 to only 30,000 in 1960; between 1954 and 1961, Chrysler's workforce dropped from 130,000 to 50,000 (African Americans were twice as likely as whites to lose their Chrysler jobs). Many of Detroit's smaller auto-supply shops failed completely—for instance, when Murray Auto Body was subsumed by Ford, the new owner slashed an additional 11,000 jobs. For workers who kept their jobs, both overtime and the "speed-up" became regular aspects of labor, and—though workers routinely expressed grievances over these issues—the UAW proved unable to reverse the trend. Moreover, auto-work remained unstable and cyclical; over the decade of the affluent 1950s, Detroit suffered four recessions, throwing hundreds of thousands of autoworkers in and out of the labor market.[19]

Detroit suffered from a loss of people, as well as jobs and capital. The city's population declined 10 percent between 1950 and 1960, but the *white* population of Detroit declined a dramatic 23.5 percent. Religiously, at midpoint in the decade, Detroit was still 66 percent Catholic, 28 percent Protestant (mostly African American) and 6 percent Jewish, but this was a heavily working-class population becoming blacker and poorer. In 1959, Mel Ravitz investigated the urban effects of these economic transformations on white Protestant churches. He found that half of the sixty white Protestant churches in downtown Detroit had moved since 1940. Some had opened a satellite church in the suburbs and kept the old church running, often utilizing a "Negro assistant minister" to "help serve the inner city church." Unfortunately, this usually led to the creation of two separate and segregated churches, with poor blacks often subsidizing the white suburban church. Other congregations turned their old churches into settlement homes to provide neighborhood services, although settlement work itself had become increasingly difficult. A study of the neighborhood center in Brightmoor found that Detroit's settlement workers "are in the thick of the cross currents of a bewildering city.... There does not seem to be that ebullience of feeling shown by adolescent youth at the advent of World War II" but instead "an unsettled, nervous tension which affects behavior." The Franklin Settlement—Detroit's oldest and most prestigious—saw the African American proportion in its neighborhood grow from 31 percent in 1940 to 67 percent in 1950. The urban problems associated with racism, segregation, and poverty, concluded a 1951 Franklin Settlement report, were "different and delicate, to put it mildly."[20]

These demographic shifts sharply focused the attention of Detroiters on the racial makeup of their own neighborhoods. And Detroit was, as the historian Thomas Sugrue has noted, a "city of homes." Among major cities, only

Philadelphia had a higher rate of home-ownership. By the late 1950s, therefore, the intersection of an increasing black population and a segregated housing market formed the city's most explosive and pressing political issue. A major study of religious beliefs and behaviors in Detroit found that whites were far more worried about integrated neighborhoods than either schools or workplaces, believing that the presence of African Americans inevitably resulted in lower property values. One Lutheran factory worker told researchers, "It's all right to work with 'em [African Americans], but I don't believe in living with 'em." In fact, even as whites abandoned the city for the suburbs, housing remained "a foremost problem" for black Detroiters because of persistent patterns of segregation, as the Urban League concluded in 1967.[21]

As historian John McGreevy has documented, the strong correlation between religion, residence, ethnicity, and class created especially tense relationships between urban Catholics and incoming African Americans. According to one major study from the early 1960s, roughly 60 percent of Detroit's Catholics were characterized as working-class, and the blue-collar neighborhoods these people had built at considerable personal sacrifice deeply shaped the Catholic consciousness of community and religious peoplehood. Indeed, Catholic religiosity was physically defined by the territorial boundaries of the city parish; Catholics thus preferred, and had generally been able to build, religiously homogenous neighborhoods. Ethnic chauvinism and fears of declining property values could complicate an already difficult problem. As early as 1951, Msgr. John O'Grady, president of the National Conference of Catholic Charities, began holding a forum on the changing city in Detroit to confront the issue. "The changing parish of today," O'Grady solemnly intoned, "presents a greater challenge to the church than any of the changes that have taken place during the past half century." O'Grady acknowledged that, when most people used the euphemism "conservation . . . they are talking about keeping out Negroes." While he urged Catholics to "conserve their own neighborhoods," O'Grady also condemned segregation, arguing that racial integration on a Christian basis would advance "the work of the lay apostolate" of the Mystical Body of Christ.[22]

Some Detroit Catholics certainly rose to O'Grady's moral challenge. As we have seen, the Catholic Interracial Council was founded in the early 1940s, and Catholics, both lay and clerical, advocated for fair employment laws and served on civic "human relations" boards. Four Detroit parishes served African American Catholics, and some Catholic settlement homes served large African American populations. More significantly, there is suggestive evidence that a good number of white Catholics were moving beyond a "separate but equal" mentality, and were attempting to actually *live* as equals. After the

Brown v. Board of Education decision in 1954, St. Leo's parish, near Detroit's downtown, became the Archdiocese's first self-consciously integrated parish; in 1956, St. Leo—spurred by a group of "public-spirited Catholics"—observed National Negro History Week, during which the parish priest castigated segregation. Meanwhile, social workers at the Sophie Wright settlement in the mid-1950s noted that African Americans had started attending the Old Neighbor Progressive Club with Polish Americans. Meetings of the group had once ended with the singing of Polish folk songs, but now African Americans "join in with the music they know—usually Hymns with a definite beat. . . . Singing has now become an important part of their meetings as each group encourages the other having found a liking and appreciation for their different type of song." In fact, mixed black-Polish neighborhoods were quite common through the 1960s. One young Polish priest captured the reality of residence patterns (and the race politics of the 1960s) when he told urban demographers in 1971, "It really annoys me to hear White liberals who have fled to the suburbs accuse my mother of being racist when she has lived next door to the Blacks in the inner city for years." Paul Clemens, born into a devoutly Catholic family in the 1970s, likewise observed that the city's demographic changes from white to black "were less lamentable" to his parents and grandparents "than were the changes in the Church after the Second Vatican Council."[23]

Still, if racial tensions between Catholics and African Americas were sometimes muted, the era of the insulated, working-class, immigrant parish was nevertheless quickly closing. The fate of Detroit's urban Catholic schools—the greatest source of pride in many parishes, built with the laity's money at the strong urging of clerics—epitomized this transition. St. Josaphat school enrolled over 500 students (and often over 700 students) every year between 1906 and 1928, but by 1960, its enrollment had shriveled to 78; it was closed in 1961. Sweetest Heart of Mary's elementary and high school together educated around 300 children a year in the 1960s, but this was down from over 800 per year throughout the 1930s. Our Lady Queen of Apostles maintained impressive numbers in the 1960s—over 800 students a year from 1960 to 1965—but these were still modest compared to enrollments that topped 1,000 every year between 1922 and 1938. Likewise, from 1916 to 1941, St. Florian's school never enrolled fewer than 1,000 students (between 1919 and 1930, never fewer than 2,000), but by 1966, the number fell permanently below 500.[24]

The remaking of the urban parish played a significant role in reducing the resonance and relevance of worker religion. The life and career of Fr. Clement Kern, one of Detroit's most notable "labor priests" and a former chaplain of the ACTU, illustrates how the city's transformations shifted religious consciousness away from Christ the Worker and toward a focus on racial identity and urban poverty. Born into a typically working-class Catholic family in Adrian, Michigan, in 1907 (his father became one of the first stewards of the UAW), Kern was ordained a priest in 1933. After serving in two blue-collar Detroit parishes, Kern was appointed, in 1943, as pastor of Most Holy Trinity in the inner city, near-west-side neighborhood colloquially known to Detroiters as Corktown. By the time Kern took over pastoral duties, however, the Irish who had founded the parish and named the neighborhood had long since escaped to better areas. Sandwiched between massive urban renewal projects in the early 1960s, Most Holy Trinity survived as one of the most polyglot parishes in postwar Detroit, dominated by Mexican and Puerto Rican immigrants but also servicing an additional 22 nationalities (plus African Americans and the southern "hillbillies" who crowded into the neighborhood).[25]

Kern responded to the poverty surrounding his parish with a seemingly endless series of charitable endeavors. According to street lore, Most Holy Trinity always seemed to have extra coats and clothes in the rectory, which Kern freely gave to anybody in need. Cash, too, always seemed to materialize whenever it was sought, and was always given without questions asked. Kern even kept bottles of liquor handy, although he personally never drank. More systemically, he established the Mother Cabrini free clinic (and encouraged other inner-city churches to establish clinics of their own), a reading room for rest and relaxation, Alexandrine House for parolees (essentially committed by the city court to Kern's care), and Corktown College, a free night school to provide job training and language skills to the many Latino parishioners.[26]

For many members of the laity, service to Kern epitomized their own commitment to the lay apostolate. In the late 1950s, for instance, Ed Starr founded the Corktown Coop, a band of thirty-five "lay monks" who went door to door soliciting for Corktown's poor; it was, the *Wage Earner* noted, "the poor man's way of working for the poor." The men of the Coop lived communally and used their four vans (bearing the Corktown Coop logo) to accumulate, rehabilitate, and sell clothes, furniture, or any other items of value. Profits went to Kern to provide lunches, medical care, and other services to poor children, but the purpose of the Coop was basically spiritual, intending "to make apostles out of the men who do this soliciting." Likewise, newsmen and local politicians, while congregating at a local pub in the late 1950s, heard of Most Holy Trinity's financial woes and formed a group they playfully named the Ecclesiastical Shakedown Society; for well over a decade, the volunteers of the Shakedown Society twisted the arms of Detroit's most prominent citizens every Christmas, ensuring a flow of resources into Kern's numerous charitable ventures.[27]

Commentators commonly referred to Kern as the "conscience of the community," a "Roman-collared version of Robin Hood," and the "Saint of the Slums." Abraham Citron, organizer of an equal housing conference, credited Kern with developing the spirit of interfaith fellowship and commitment to direct action that made the conference work. African Americans, too, hailed Kern. UAW activist Horace Sheffield described an evening with Kern as "One of the great experiences of my life"; through Kern's charity, Sheffield saw, "the church took on a new and meaningful dimension for this suffering and dispossessed humanity" (Sheffield's celebration of Kern's work for the "here and now" may have also been a veiled critique of the "other-worldly" orientation of some of Detroit's black churches). Detroit's African American congressman, Charles C. Diggs, even took the extraordinary step of placing a celebratory newspaper profile of Kern into the proceedings of the Congressional Record in order to memorialize the priest's service. And, in 1971, a panel of Detroit civic leaders voted Kern one of the ten most influential people in the city (Cardinal Dearden joined Kern on a list otherwise composed of financiers, businessmen, and UAW president Leonard Woodcock).[28]

Kern's deeply generous spirit and utterly unassuming demeanor explain much of his popularity, but people who were inspired by Kern were also responding to specific religious themes of "personalism" and "authenticity" made acute in the 1950s and 1960s. In the 1930s, by contrast, Kern was known as a quintessential labor priest. He was actively involved in the formation of the ACTU and the Archdiocesan Labor Institute. At St. Leo's and St. Edward's parishes in the 1930s, Kern allowed union leaders to hold meetings and plot strategy during the UAW's formative years. Throughout the 1940s, Kern hosted numerous labor schools sponsored by the ALI. Likewise, he served as ACTU chaplain from 1941 to 1949 and often officiated at Labor Mass services. But Kern's connection to the labor movement seems to have had little connection to his popularity and influence in the 1950s and 1960s. When commentators acknowledged Kern's labor connections, they generally pointed not to his decades of work with the UAW but to his characteristically iconoclastic decision in 1963 to picket Detroit's Playboy Club with the underpaid "bunnies."[29]

Kern's ministry increasingly focused on the dark-skinned, foreign-born, "undeserving" poor, not the "working man" of Depression-era popular culture. Well before the civil rights movement racialized religious consciousness, Kern had committed himself to the temporal and spiritual well-being of Michigan's Mexican immigrants. Beginning in the early 1950s, Kern conducted yearly trips to Mexico, absorbing the culture, commiserating with Latin American priests, and becoming fluent in Spanish. Indeed, Kern became one of the foremost North American authorities on both Catholicism and labor conditions throughout Latin America, and he often found himself recruited by Latin American Catholic authorities to survey labor conditions in their own countries, while testifying before similar labor commissions in the United States. In 1958, Kern advised the Archdiocesan Migrant Program for Mexican workers in Michigan, providing 48,500 pounds of clothing, 450 religious articles, and 84 cases of canned food. Kern's experiences with the lowly farm worker even caused him to challenge his traditional allies in the unions. In his 1958 Labor Mass sermon, for instance, Kern chastised the "selfishness" of organized labor for leaving Mexican migrants unorganized. The priest's endorsement of Cesar Chavez and the United Farm Workers in the early 1970s infuriated Detroit's powerful Teamsters' union, which opposed the UFW and was financially pinched by the Chavez-led produce boycotts. The Teamsters responded by abruptly cutting its considerable financial support of Most Holy Trinity's charities—only a timely donation by the UAW averted disaster for Kern and those that depended upon him. The conflict was telling: by the early 1960s, Detroit's premier labor priest was more closely associated with the dark-skinned poor of his parish than the white working class of the Depression era.[30]

While Catholic worker religion eroded during Detroit's urban remapping, southern evangelicalism flourished. When *Wage Earner* reporter Kenan Heise headed down 3rd Avenue in 1958, three institutions pointed toward the cultural presence of a southern colony. First was the large number of secondhand stores. Browsing these shops, Heise found many books on personal finance and childcare, which he claimed offered proof that southerners were responsible and sensible, not the feckless "hill-billies" of caricature. Next were the many honky-tonk bars. But the "clearest indication" of a southern colony was "the large number of store-front, Pentecostal churches that can be seen along the street." Indeed, hundreds of storefront churches were documented throughout Detroit in the early 1960s. In a single neighborhood—the lower east side surrounding the Franklin settlement—42 of the district's 55 churches were in storefronts. As white mainline Protestant churches—defenders of the social gospel and theological modernism—fled the urban core, working-class southern whites flooded in.[31]

Northern Protestants had long puzzled over southern evangelicalism in Detroit, and they remain mystified in the postwar years. What had become clear was that southern evangelicals were not fulfilling the self-confident prediction of many northern ministers that they would "naturally" gravitate toward northern congregations as they "matured" in the city. To the contrary, as a sociological set of interviews with people from eastern Tennessee demonstrated, experiences in the north only reinforced southern migrants' "surprising contempt for material things, strong family and community ties, and deep Fundamentalist religious beliefs. . . . The church is the principal community institution in the Southern Appalachians and it commands very strong year-long allegiance." Few southerners wanted to make Detroit a permanent home; many were "dissatisfied with the churches ('card playing and drinking beer')" in Detroit. As one woman remarked, "The farther North you go, the wickeder they seem to get." In the postwar period, with no Claude Williams present to promote a more activist evangelical vernacular, southern religion nurtured traditional theological concerns.[32]

One northern minister, Cleo Boyd, unsuccessfully struggled to lure migrants into his mainline church. Finally, in 1958, Boyd decided to visit one of the storefronts to see why southern migrants were so resistant to the religious culture of the North. While framed through the lens of Protestant liberalism, Boyd's uniquely detailed description of religious services in the working-class storefront offers a rare eyewitness account of southern religiosity in the city:

> The one-room store-front church is nicely decorated. The pulpit stands on a platform at the front. The tile floor, knotty pine walls and second-hand theater seats make the meeting house very attractive. . . . It was a Sunday night when most of the "old line" churches have no services. . . . I was impressed immediately with the large number of children and babies present. . . . The pastor called on one of the brethren to lead the singing. . . . A woman came forward to play the piano. The singing was spontaneous, sincere and uninhibited. . . . An invitation was then extended for all who wished to join them in "handshaking" and in the "altar prayer." About ten or twenty persons got up and went to the front and began milling around shaking hands with each other. . . . Announcing that he was preaching on the subject, "How Can I Win Lost Souls?" the minister took his text from Psalm 126 and "started out in all directions at one" to preach the 'Gospel. He was soon off to a high pitch with a cadence not unlike that of a tobacco salesman, in which it was very difficult to understand his words. I wondered afterward if this is what they would call "speaking in tongues."

According to "urban standards," Boyd concluded, "such behavior is abnormal." He reasoned that the exuberant religion of the storefronts was "a release . . . for these repressed and maladjusted people."[33]

Boyd promoted a religion that was emotionally demure, more oriented toward social issues, less explicit about God's direct action in human lives, and much less willing to accept the entire Bible as a literal reality. From the perspectives of southerners, it was also simply less vital as a community. And, however "universal" the northern churches claimed they were, blue-collar southerners fully understood that the prosperous mainline churches of Detroit were theaters for the performance of middle-class identity. Storefront churches, on the other hand, were the genuine provinces of the working class and emerging underclasses. Both men and women were successful storefront preachers; in either case, the preacher was "generally an unskilled laborer having little formal education," according to a report from the Mayor's Commission for Community Action. As the Mayor's Commission condescendingly described it in language echoing Boyd, "Here the poor, beleaguered lower classes, both Southern white and Negro, may retreat to primitive and infantile forms of behavior without fear of censure." It was true that the religion performed in storefronts was understood, both by participants and observers, as communicating a working-class identity; but the storefronts could hardly be dismissed as "retreats" from the world. Rather, even as the storefront theology emphasized other-worldly considerations, the congregations themselves served as vital centers of community, identity, and orientation for *engaging* the world.[34]

Finally, the congregational life of Detroit's African American churches was also transformed by urban change, discrimination in housing and education, and swelling commitment to a national civil rights movement. In particular, Detroit's African American churches were deeply impacted by the policies of "urban renewal." By March 1963, efforts at redesigning the city had led to the demolition of more than 10,000 buildings; 43,000 people were either relocated or threatened with relocation. Even rumors of renewal projects sparked anxiety in most neighborhoods, for residents of targeted areas understood that such projects represented "a continued and deliberate uprooting of low-income communities. . . . They see ethnicity as a major factor in the process," one study revealed. Freeway construction bisected once-integrated neighborhoods: the Jeffries Freeway split across a downtown Mexican community, while the Ford and Davison Freeways carved up Hamtramck. Over 70 percent of Detroiters uprooted by urban renewal were African Americans. At a public hearing in 1965, one angry resident shouted that the only way for African Americans to move back to the Black Bottom after urban renewal "is to go back as maids and butlers." Another resident, who had moved to Detroit from the South, told an interviewer that his neighborhood had been protesting removal plans since 1956, and declared "we will fight every way possible to preserve our way of living."[35]

Given the massive dislocation of African American people that urban renewal entailed, African American churches shouldered a disproportionate burden in relocating or persisting. Fortunate congregations, like Our

Father Baptist Church or C. L. Franklin's New Bethel Baptist, turned the relocation process itself into a religious ritual of sorts. The 93-car procession leading to Our Father Baptist's new location one Sunday morning in 1963 represented the solidarity of the congregation, but also symbolized a type of intraurban exile; similar pageants of displacement became a regular sight in inner-city neighborhoods as urban renewal projects advanced. As early as 1960, Rev. Louis Johnson of Friendship Missionary Baptist, Rev. Nicholas Hood of Plymouth Congregational, and James Chambers of St. John's Presbyterian (all of whom had been compelled to relocate their own congregations) realized that urban planners had "left the church out of the planning." In June of 1963, they founded the Detroit Fellowship of Urban Renewal Churches—a support-and-advice organization that included the "better established" churches as well as storefronts. By 1965, the ministers felt they had established a small "beach-head" in city hall.[36]

But by that date, many predominately black neighborhoods had already been demolished—indeed, Rev. Chambers claimed that 490 churches in the Boulevard redevelopment zone had been impacted by urban renewal. The social effects of this transformation on church life were already detectable. In 1964, Wayne State graduate students interviewed 77 relocated residents of Elmwood Park #1, a project that had been torn down in 1962. Two years after their relocation, half of these people had experienced a disturbance in church participation. The cost and difficulty of commuting to the old church, combined with concerns about crime and safety, disrupted the churchgoing life of older people, poorer people, and children (30 percent fewer children participated in Sunday school lessons after relocation). Only young families with more education and more money were likely to seek new affiliations with nearby churches. These church-switchers were the only group not experiencing a disruption in patterns of participation, although even these switchers likely faced challenges integrating themselves into established congregations, especially given the centrality of the concept of the "church home" in African American culture.[37]

But God had not forgotten his people. In 1960, Detroiters were amazed at the appearance of a large, mysteriously glowing cross on the door of a black family's unit in the Jeffries housing project. Although the Page family had recently converted to Catholicism, the cross was apparently prophesied by radio preacher Charles Beck, an Elder at the Way of the Cross Pentecostal Church in Buffalo. According to Beck, God had designated the Page home as a holy shrine. "The cross has been viewed and rubbed by the hands of hundreds of persons of both races who have marched up the narrow stairway to see with their own eyes," including *Michigan Chronicle* religion reporter Isaac Jones. After visiting the shrine, Jones "agreed that it is something strange—that it must be the work of God." The miraculous appearance of a religious symbol might be dismissed as ephemeral to the larger story of Detroit's urban transformation in the postwar period. To the working-class faithful, however, it would hardly be surprising that God chose a poor but devout family in a housing project, a family perhaps facing removal themselves, to provide a sign of divine favor. The glowing cross reinforced the beliefs of African American Detroiters that God directly intervened in human affairs, that his will was communicated to the world, and that the socially marginal were the true heirs to righteousness. In an era of increasing consciousness of racial inequality, such beliefs would carry profound political impact.[38]

Gender Ideology in Transition

In 1956, the Reverend Hugh White, an Episcopal priest at St. Martin's parish in Detroit, established the Detroit Industrial Mission (DIM), an ecumenical organization that intended to conjoin the burgeoning ethos of "Christian existentialism" with the working lives of people in the plants. White recruited Scott Paradise, a minister from the Sheffield Industrial Mission in England, in 1957; meanwhile, the group absorbed and incorporated similar industrial missionary efforts by other mainline bodies, notably the Presbyterian Industrial Project (PIP). PIP originated with George Coleman, David Lowry, and Orrie Hopper, students at Princeton Theological Seminary who decided to form a triple pastorate in an industrial, blue-collar community. They eventually established their experiment in Ecorse, a southwestern suburb of Detroit, and began work at Ecorse Presbyterian Church in the fall of 1956. But, while Colman, Lowry, and Hopper worked out of the church, two other Princeton Seminary graduates—Jesse Christman and Jim Campbell—took jobs on assembly lines at the nearby Cadillac plant to directly share the world of auto-work with other workers. PIP also maintained contact with the Methodist Phil Doster, who began his own plant job in 1957; all three soon reported to DIM. In effect, half of DIM's ministers assumed a life of industrial labor, while half ministered from a declining urban church; collectively, they hoped to build cultural and spiritual bridges between the two worlds.[39]

In the fall of 1960, after three years of experience working in Detroit's factories, DIM's shop-floor ministers dramatically concluded that the "GREATEST PROBLEM IN THE LIFE OF THE ASSEMBLY LINE WORKER IS TO BE A MAN." They described what this meant in some detail:

Neither the elements of [the assembler's] job nor his relationships therein afford him much opportunity to be a man whom others respect and who respects and esteems himself. And so he attempts to prove his manhood by other means; by drinking the other fellow under the table, by philandering, by success in petty arguments, by violence, by cleverness in gambling. He pathetically tries to prove it by building up his chest and arm muscles, and then by wearing tight T-shirts. . . . When he returns home his wife is reading romance stories concerning actors or statesmen or business and professional men, or watching TV on which a factory worker never appears as hero and rarely as an extra. . . . He is nothing—He is not even a man. He is a machine and the more machinelike he is the better the corporation likes it. At the plant basically he is a statistic, at home a shadowy figure in the chair watching TV with his beer bottle beside him. . . . But Father and Man he is not.

While working-class masculinity appeared in a state of near-crisis, DIM lamented that religion, which should be providing inspiration and meaning, was instead dismissed by many male industrial workers as the realm of women and children. They reported overhearing an evangelizing effort by one of the shop-floor "sect" preachers rebuffed by another worker, who responded: "'I make sure the kids go (to R.C. Church) but not me. . . . I know a woman who goes to Church every morning and prays all the time. . . . But she is a widow and all alone with nothing else in her life. She needs this.'" When Scott Paradise spoke at a union local meeting, he found it necessary to argue that "Christianity is not just for children, but has vital importance for grown men and adult society."[40]

Although they were not responsible for developing the idioms of worker religion in the 1930s and 1940s, DIM's ministers were fully invested in the gendered assumptions and legacies of this earlier formulation. Worker religion was articulated almost entirely by men, targeted almost entirely at men, and imagined religion in entirely masculine terms. Clergy and lay leaders hoped that by offering a muscular religion, one that was relevant for a life in the shop and the union hall, they could reinforce the spiritual commitment of working-class men. "The religion of Jesus," Claude Williams claimed with typically stark language in one of his Sunday school lessons, "is a man's religion. It is too severe for timid souls and weaklings." Of course, this rhetoric masked the reality of women's crucial importance in both the workplace as well as within religious bodies. Indeed, one would be hard-pressed to describe Williams's wife, Joyce—who voluntarily endured near-poverty as a partner in her husband's mission—as a weakling. But the idioms and rituals of worker religion simply didn't create imaginative space for the possibility that women were also workers who, like men, sought to reconcile their classed, gendered, and religious identities.[41]

Catholic formulations of class and gender were especially rich and complicated. Charles Coughlin, for instance, blended his support of unions and a living wage with a defense of Christian masculinity. Jesus himself, Coughlin claimed, declared the gospel in a "manly voice." Chief among the manly Christian duties were a defense of the home and resistance to communism. The Jesus that emerged from the working class, according to Coughlin, was also "the Protector of homes and womanhood." As such, Jesus "asks you to have courage and fight the battle manfully in your struggle to protect the roof that shelters your little ones." Furthermore, Coughlin reminded his listeners that the bedrock of the State was the family; thus, the State's first duty should be protecting the "rights of families to own and possess their homes." By allowing men to defend domesticity, the government might fulfill natural law and offer a strong check against communism.[42]

Like Coughlin, labor priests during the Depression sought to reinforce the link between class, masculinity, and religion. Fr. Clare Murphy, hoping to spread the Church's prolabor message throughout the unions, sought to enlist "men who are above all thorough Christians, profoundly in love with God, . . . men who have zeal, courage and real attack like the great St. Paul." The ACTU certainly couched its definition of working-class religion within a context of masculinity. When the ACTU convened a rally on May Day, 1940, the group's attempt at conjoining "manly" work with "feminine" religion could not have been more explicit. Addressing a May Day crowd at Holy Rosary auditorium, Archbishop Mooney counterpoised the "delicate and refined manifestation of Catholic faith in devotion to the Blessed Mother of Christ Our Lord" with "one of the most sturdy and dynamic movements of American industrial life today in modern Unionism." His language evoked ideal images of pliant womanhood in the home and active manhood in the shops. To many secular observers, the Archbishop admitted, such forces "are ill-mated partners."[43] But the real contest, according to Mooney, raged not between male labor and female religion but between "Marxian chaos or Christian social order." When viewed through a Catholic prism, the real test of manliness was a resistance to godless radicalism, a preservation of democracy, a support of honest unionism, and a defense of the home that only religion made possible. These principles, Mooney assured his listeners, "will win the assent of the essentially fair-minded, peace-loving, home-making men who make up the vast majority of American unionists." Through the threat of communism, religion was made masculine, even as it retained its roots in family life.[44]

Devotional culture—in which the performance of religion gave expressive shape to personal identities—offered similar idioms. Catholic men were encouraged to seek the assistance of St. Joseph, father of Christ and the "patron of workers." Joseph witnessed a profusion of novenas and honorariums every March, the month set aside for his special reverence. The *Michigan Catholic* explained Joseph's significance:

> He knows from personal experience the trials of the worker and the worries of the head of a household. He had to toil daily in his carpenter shop. He can and does sympathize with the toiler and the unemployed. Neither will seek in vain his prompt and powerful intercession.

Joseph fulfilled his manly duties through honest work and devotion to his family; it was a model Catholic men were expected to emulate.[45]

In fact, despite religious rhetoric to the contrary, Catholic women had long been an important presence in Detroit's workplaces. The first successful slowdown in UAW history depended upon the discipline and class loyalty of the nearly 20,000 Polish and Hungarian women workers at General Motor's Ternstedt plant, on Detroit's west side. A similar spirit motivated Polish American female cigar rollers, who launched an impromptu sit-down strike after the success at Ternstedt. The women demanded the assistance of the UAW's Polish American liaison, Stanley Nowak, in organizing their factory. According to Nowak's wife, Margaret, women developed a routine whereby "each striker went home every third day to bathe and change clothes, do the family laundry, prepare food for her family, get medical aid for herself or family members, and perhaps go to mass." Indeed, 75 percent of all female cigar workers in Hamtramck were not only Catholic, but belonged to the same Polish-dominated parish, St. Florian. These women remained deeply shaped by traditional Catholic definitions of womanhood and motherhood, as evidenced by their continuing commitment to cooking, cleaning, and attending church in the middle of a major strike. But the bonds of friendship they had developed in the parish made working-class solidarity a very palpable and realistic concept—one that became incorporated into their religious consciousness.[46]

Catholic women were also leaders in the civic sphere on a number of key social justice issues that paralleled the political direction of postwar liberal culture. The Archdiocesan Council of Catholic Women, for instance, was Michigan's most vocal and active advocate for Mexican migrant workers, incessantly publicizing the miserable living conditions of migrants and providing the bulk of social services. In the late 1950s, Catholic laywomen remained among the most prominent civil rights leaders. In 1959 alone, Hope Brophy, chair of the Race Relations Committee of the Archdiocesan Council of Catholic Women, spoke to 1,900 people living in integrated or changing neighborhoods. Brophy insisted that Catholics needed to examine themselves and see that "discrimination is a part of their lives and that they are unwittingly, perhaps, tolerating and even fostering it." Marie Oresi, a long-time activist in the Catholic Interracial Council, even attained a position of formal power beyond her involvement in the CIC; in 1961, Oresi was elected vice chairperson of the Coordinating Council on Human Relations, the city of Detroit's "official" mechanism for monitoring and defusing racial conflicts. Even the ACTU, the institutional embodiment of masculine worker religion, was led by a woman, Marguerite Gahagan, between 1949 and 1952.[47]

The widespread obsession with traditional gender roles in worker religion therefore suggests the depth of anxiety over the demographic and economic changes in women's lives unleashed by World War II. On the eve of American entry into the war, 202,960 Detroit-area women worked for wages; by 1955, that number had leaped to 383,900. While the majority of women in the mid-1950s worked retail jobs, 98,100 held manufacturing jobs: 15 percent of Detroit's manufacturing workforce. Certainly, Catholic workers at the Dodge Main plant in Hamtramck would have been aware of women's presence on the shop floor; nearly eight hundred women assembled electrical systems in Dodge Main's wire room. Moreover, there is evidence that some of these female Dodge workers explicitly brought their Catholicism into the workplace. In January of 1954, wire room worker Helene Barwick stopped work to listen to Bishop Fulton Sheen's radio program. "Good as usual," she noted in the Dodge Main newspaper. "Next week his talk is to be about 'Workers.' Musn't miss this broadcast." Barwick seemed every bit as interested in combining her class identity and religious identity as men. Yet, as increasing numbers of working-class women encountered the "masculine" culture of the shop floor, they also often retained primary responsibility for child-rearing, homemaking, and religious instruction. These demanding circumstances obviously affected women workers' quality of life. In a survey of UAW members in the late 1950s, very few women described themselves as "highly satisfied"; more typical were responses showing 62 percent of women (versus 26 percent of men) claiming that they worried "a lot." Asked about their chances "to enjoy life," women dissented twice as often as men. In religion as in work, women remained on the margins of 1950s-era society.[48]

Gender conflicts also created significant tensions in Detroit's African American churches. Many black ministers—including those instrumental in shepherding black workers into unions and political activism—continued to view religious authority as a male prerogative; revealingly, Charles Hill's seminary thesis was entitled "Religion, A Man's Work." Radical enough to share his pulpit with Paul Robeson, Hill remained traditional in his attitudes toward gender—possibly because, like Claude Williams and the ACTU, he feared that the large number of women in the churches would drive black men away from religion. But ministers like Hill could not easily minimize the importance of black women to church life, for their involvement often extended well beyond membership and attendance. Frequently, women were responsible for the all-important choir, and leadership options often exceeded choir work. Georgia Jackson presided over the Missionary Society at St. James Baptist Church. Willie B. Wall, known to many in her church as "Mother Wall," was married to a deacon at New Grace Baptist, served as one-time president of the Missionary Society at Mt. Olivet Baptist Church, and later moved on to the National Foreign Missions Committee of the National Baptist Convention. Likewise, Martha Lee served as the Traveling Missionary at Everybody's Universal Tabernacle.[49]

More notably, black women preached and led services as well. Mary Watson Stewart, for instance, led an "overflowing congregation" at Ebenezer AME church in 1946, with a sermon "God Made Visible in Christ." In September 1946, a female evangelist, EJ Tyree, traveling with her small daughter, concluded two weeks of successful revivals at the Church of the Living God. A woman known as "Mother Williams" preached, and even "demonstrated the power of God in a great healing service" at Truth Temple. Metropolitan AME church hosted a group of women evangelists, with Catherine Harris of Ebenezer AME reading scripture and Elizabeth Crews preaching the traditional jeremiad that "only a few" in the church "have felt the spirit."[50]

Ministers' wives typically accentuated their husbands' work, contributing vitally to the success of any pastorate. Gertrude M. Williams, married to the Rev. David Rhonee, recommended that a woman should "search her own conscience and seek God for her companion, especially if she is choosing a minister as her husband." Williams, for her part, was an active volunteer and headed the Missionary Department of Western Michigan AME. Occasionally, ministers' wives could be as renowned as their husbands. E. G. Hickman, wife of Rev. Paul Hickman, earned fame in her youth as a popular "girl preacher"; by virtue of scholarship support, she became the only girl in her class at Wilberforce University in the early 1940s. In Detroit, Hickman organized the Consecrated Goodwill Society—a provider of social services—and also evangelized around the country, receiving "many into the fold of Christianity." Even among the public prophets, wives proved vital to maintaining both ministry and political advocacy. Charles Hill's wife worked for sixteen years with the local YWCA, while she was raising eight children and attending to necessary church business. Malcolm Dade similarly thanked God for the "helpmate" he found in his wife.[51]

Like Catholic women involved with Mexican migrant work or civil rights activism, African American churchwomen were visibly "public" actors, typically as social workers or members of citizens' committees. In 1946, black churchwomen led the effort to integrate Detroit's YWCA. "The women are trying to live up to the Christian principle of the 'fatherhood of God and the brotherhood of man,'" the *Michigan Chronicle* commended. Moreover, the paper argued, women's activism "will not surprise students of American history. The women of the republic have always been in the forefront of our democratic battles." Of his own congregation, Malcolm Dade recalled, "docile women they were not, and although they supported me, they were always there to also give me my come uppance"; in particular, Dade commended the social worker and "staunch Episcopalian" Beulah Carter, who led one of the city's most popular Sunday schools and also participated in numerous civic committees. Willa Grimes, president of the Women's Auxiliary of the National Baptist Convention and member of Mt. Olivet Baptist Church, exemplified this spirit when she declared it the "duty of the church" to help solve "social problems."[52]

And then there were women like the pastor of Everybody's Universal Tabernacle in Paradise Valley, a "slight, strident-voiced housewife who deserted the ranks of choir singers to 'answer the call to preach,'" known to all as "Mother Hooks." Following a divine revelation in 1940, Hooks entered what the *Michigan Chronicle* wryly called the "increasingly competitive profession of religion" over the objections of her husband (although she remained a "housewife and home maker" when out of the pulpit). Launching her ministry in a storefront with three members, by the early 1950s she had attained a large building with a capacity for 1,000. Hooks, who described herself as a spiritualist, understood the class dimension of her religious culture:

> I know I am not educated as well as other ministers. . . . But the Lord never said anything about schooling being necessary to spread His word. It has to come from the soul. . . . Some people don't understand what happens when others get the spirit of the Holy Ghost. . . . It takes all shame out of you. That's why we clap our hands, sing and dance. It's our way of expressing our love for our Savior.

Hooks was expressing a populism and antielitism deeply embedded in evangelical Christianity, black as well as white. Her church created an acceptable social space in which other working-class people could embody religion on their own terms in a meaningful fashion. Yet, Hooks's experience was also ambivalent; while she defended religious practices that some observers scorned for its emotional excesses, she was also careful to maintain her "respectability" as a wife and mother.[53]

Charleszetta Waddles was perhaps the most celebrated black woman evangelist of the era, and her approach to religion suggests a potent counterweight to the more overtly political appeals of social gospel ministers like Hill or White. Born in St. Louis in 1912, Waddles's personal life was often tumultuous. Married at age 13, she was widowed five years later. After another marriage, to Le Roy Walsh, Waddles moved with her husband to Detroit in 1936, where the couple lived on Hastings Street in the heart of the Black Bottom. However, after Walsh lost his job, the couple divorced. Waddles cohabited with another man before ultimately marrying Payton Waddles, a Ford employee, in 1957 (this union lasted until Payton's death in 1980). These relationships produced ten children, all of whom were raised by Waddles. Throughout these years, she often survived on welfare and Aid to Dependent Children, and even picked up extra money running numbers. Mother Waddles, as she came to be known, wasn't posturing when she told an interviewer, "I can certainly understand the pregnant girl. I can understand the widowed woman. I can understand the separated woman. I can understand the common law woman."[54]

In 1956, Waddles became an ordained minister in a nondenominational church. Dissatisfied with this affiliation, she was reordained in 1961 in the Pentecostal organization, International Association of Universal Truth. More significantly, in September 1957, she began organizing prayer groups with other poor women, and together the women established a clothes mission to help others. "I felt that you are never too poor to help someone," she explained. Her prayer group became a storefront church dedicated to the service of others, and from this storefront grew the Perpetual Mission for Saving Souls of All Nations, a nondenominational charitable endeavor that served 100,000 mostly inner-city Detroiters per year by 1980. Besides a thrift store, her ministry grew to include a medical clinic, free legal service, a low-cost restaurant, and HUD-sponsored housing.[55]

If her race, gender, and denominational adherence made Waddles appear the opposite of Fr. Clem Kern, Detroiters revered the Pentecostal minister for many of the same personal and spiritual qualities they found in the Catholic priest. Like Kern, Waddles exuded a serene and unassuming demeanor; she was born with a "kind heart," Waddles explained, which she later understood to be the presence of God. Like Kern, she expressed no interest in attempting to discern the "deserving" from the "undeserving" poor—indeed, both indicated a special sympathy for the "undeserving." Waddles's charity, like Kern's, was unattached to any larger government program and remained "flexible enough to help anyone." In other words, both Kern and Waddles preached a spiritual gospel of love and service, not a political gospel of liberal progress. This distinction proved critical in remaking the religious as well as the political imagination in the 1960s.[56]

Working-Class Religion in Practice

By the end of the 1950s, the combined pressures of anticommunism, urban change, shifting gender ideologies, and generational transitions had steadily eroded the resonance of the worker-religion idioms forged during the 1930s and early 1940s. Yet, many of the key issues that worker religion addressed—the challenge of reconciling class identities with distinctive religious lifeworlds, the promise of a moral economy premised on the dignity of common people, the struggle to create meaning from the grind of daily labor—remained urgent. In some ways, these questions were even *more* compelling at the end of the 1950s, as automation transformed the workplace and the high tide of industrial capitalism receded. But, of course, no single answer sufficed. The nature and consequences of working-class religion remained ambivalent and contested, braided within larger cultural power struggles.

This ambivalence can perhaps be seen most acutely in the struggle to define the relationship between religious culture and working life. Worker religion praised work, dignified workers, and hoped to diffuse a sense of pride, self-respect, and empowerment throughout the workplace and union hall. This is not what the shop-floor–based ministers of the Detroit Industrial Mission witnessed. In June of 1957, Methodist minister Phil Doster started work at McLouth Steel, while his Presbyterian colleagues Jim Campbell and Jesse Christman took jobs at Cadillac in October. Putting their Bibles aside, Doster, Campbell, and Christman sought to share the experiences and partake of life with autoworkers; but they also closely observed religious life in the plants, and, by 1960, they had reached a startling conclusion about the relationship between working-class religion and working-class labor: "THE MORALIST GOD AND THE FACTORY SYSTEM," DIM declared, were "ONE AND THE SAME":

> The religious background of most of the men around us is that of the southern sect groups. A few have behind them old world Catholicism. Most are

estranged in one way or another from this background. . . . They have good reason for leaving it. . . . The religion with which [many workers] are deeply imbued and from which they have fled but not escaped is the religion of merit, of holiness in moralistic terms, of earned righteousness, of do's and don'ts, mostly the latter. . . . The workingman faces the same thing in the work and the religion available to him. God and the factory are one and the same. The man is dominated by them and coerced by them, but he hates them both, because they have refused him his manhood.

From DIM's perspective, religion had not only failed to minimize the human costs of industrial capitalism: it had actually aggravated them.[57]

There can be little doubt that, underneath the organizational triumph of the UAW and the rising financial security of senior autoworkers, alienation and even a sense of dehumanization was pervasive. "There is nothing more discouraging than having a barrel beside you with 10,000 bolts and using them all up," one worker told two sociologists. "Then you get another barrel with another 10,000," and the Sisyphean task begins anew. Only camaraderie and the chance to talk with others significantly enhanced the experience of work—yet, as studies showed, many workers labored in isolation or only in loose proximity to others. In 1957, when Ford worker Pat Hamilton was asked to reflect on the intersection between his life as an industrial worker and his faith as a Catholic, he began by acknowledging the frank reality of his day-to-day existence: "Factory work can be very dull and monotonous." Hamilton lamented auto work's impersonalism, the limited opportunities it offered for interaction, and the lack of mental stimulation. "It doesn't take much imagination," Hamilton concluded, "to see that life in a factory, despite all the modernization, can be very depressing."[58]

Hamilton's response to this challenge was clear, and diametrically opposite to DIM: "This is where one's Faith comes in." In "lift[ing] our hearts," faith instructed Hamilton to give his employer an honest day's work. Without faith, Hamilton implied, people could bear the drudgery of auto work only by chiseling extra time out of a lunch break, slowing the pace of production, or lashing out in acts of petty theft and sabotage. Hamilton especially stressed the strength his faith gave him in providing a witness of moral behavior for other workers. Catholicism, with its emphasis on self-discipline and self-denial, and its glorification of sacrifice, suffering, and duty, convinced Hamilton to avoid "the use of so-called 'shop-language'" and discouraged him from the "telling of lewd stories." The insight is telling. DIM's ministers wanted religion to serve as a tool to reinvent the experience of industrial work, to prophetically critique the whole system as unethical and dehumanizing. Hamilton entertained no such illusions. Rather, he recommended receiving the sacraments often and praying daily. Religion was meaningful to Hamilton because it allowed him to endure ongoing struggles with dignity and purpose. It promised comfort and continuity, not a new and challenging paradigm or any type of social or political redress. Whereas DIM's religion offered spiritual reinvention and social renewal, working-class believers like Hamilton experienced religion as solace and inspiration in the hard struggle to make meaning out of the realities of laboring lives.[59]

Meanwhile, across town at the Dodge Main Body Shop, workers boasted of "being the only automobile manufacturing plant in the world, where Bible classes are held at noon daily." Frank Favor, a Dodge welder, had launched the program, and had brought a minister into the plant to provide "some spirited and instructive advice, pertaining to ways and means, of efficiently serving 'The Good Lord,' here in this vale of tears, so that we may be happy with Him in the next." From DIM's point of view, the Dodge workers' close attention to Bible study and their otherworldly focus on the afterlife, would have been proof of the debilitating literalism and moralism that crippled the working-class soul. But the workers themselves clearly felt differently. As Favor pointed out, workers who heard the shop preacher "came away with a spiritual uplift, that mere words fail to properly describe." Again, like the Catholic Ford worker Pat Hamilton, these Dodge workers saw religion as a source of inspiration, uplift, and meaning. That DIM's view differed so strongly illustrates the ambivalent meanings underlying the interpretive relationships between religion and labor.[60]

African American churches, filled with working-class congregants, evoked many of the same qualities emphasized by Pat Hamilton and Frank Favor. For the average black churchgoer, preaching defined the everyday culture of religion; most churches floundered without the oratorical talent of a strong preacher. The content of sermons was usually evangelical and moralistic in tone, and the measure of a good preacher was his ability to provoke a powerful response from the congregation. As described in the *Michigan Chronicle*'s "Church Pages," sermons were typically "uplifting," "stirring," or "dynamic"—in other words, they provided an emotional punch. Sunday crowds were routinely reported as "overflowing," especially at churches known for their strong preachers: Ebenezer AME, St. Stephen AME, Bethel AME, Second Baptist, and New Bethel Baptist were especially popular. St. Stephen, for instance, swelled to 5,000 members in 1947 largely because people flocked "from all parts of the city to hear the great teachings of our pastor." Periodically, churches would host popular traveling evangelists or stage revivals, or combine with other churches to host "preaching missions" that might stretch on nightly for two or more weeks.[61]

Music shared the center of African American religious culture with preaching. Sallie Green, minister of music at Christ Temple, spoke for most black churchgoers when she claimed, "The role of music in the church is as important as the sermon preached by the minister." The larger churches often hosted multiple choirs, and, as one observer of Good Friday services noted in 1947, "Every modern church prides itself on having outstanding singers among its membership." Occasionally, entire services would revolve around music. Moreover, as one musicologist from the late 1950s demonstrated, African American "religious songs of the folk tradition flourish in comparison to the secular songs" because spirituals were passed orally, binding family to family and generation to generation. Frances Carter, an organist at Detroit's John Wesley AMEZ Church, similarly stressed the role of orally transmitted gospel songs. Much of the typical AMEZ church service was predictable, with distinct genres of religious music for each part of the service: anthems, taken from the words of the Bible, were always the first choir songs; spirituals were sung during the offering; congregational hymns preceded the sermon. All of these songs could be found in the traditional Methodist hymnal or the AMEZ hymnal. But, according to Carter, the "old hymns of zion and folksongs" transformed the service: "they produce such a release of emotions . . . that it looks as if some people have lost their minds. . . . It seems as if the building itself has come alive." Tellingly, Carter observed that, throughout the 1950s, her church viewed these songs as "the lowest form of church music," thus betraying the ambivalence at the heart of the struggle between respectability and emotional release that troubled many black churches—and yet, the folk songs remained a persistent and joyous aspect of worship. As Joseph Washington put in his study of African American religiosity, the "combination of suffering and music" bound black churches together.[62]

Beyond prayer, sermon, and song, many workers of all faiths embraced the idea of personal, pragmatic relationships with supernatural figures. At the heart of this supernatural relationship was a conviction that seemingly defied modernity: the belief in miracles. Among southern-white evangelicals, three-fourths interviewed for one study believed in faith healing. Jessie Blankenship, for instance, was born in West Virginia. Her husband, a one-time coal miner, worked in a Detroit steel plant, while she worked at a dairy freeze. According to Blankenship, her father was healed of a terrible illness after her mother wrote to radio preacher and "laid hands" on her father while the preacher preached. Although she had not personally been to a faith healer, she "would go to one" if she was sick. Likewise, Laverne Highsby worked in a Tennessee shirt factory and a tool company in Indiana before finally settling in Detroit. She, too, "definitely believes in [faith healers]." One of her relatives prayed to Billy Graham on the radio after doctors gave up on him, and prayer saved a leg and hip; the doctors declared "it was a miracle."[63]

Miracle stories similarly abounded in Catholic culture. Edward Reilly, for instance, became deaf after an accident in a Detroit war-industries plant during the 1940s. But in 1954, Reilly traveled to the basilica of St. Anne de Beaupre in Quebec and was miraculously healed after the priest touched his head with a relic of St. Anne. One Catholic woman, asked about beliefs she learned in Catholic school during this period, recalled a "slew" of stories about sacred articles. In one such account, a soldier in World War II was hit by an enemy bullet, but escaped with only bruises thanks to a scapular he wore under his dogtags. As this source recalled with wry humor, "It's peculiar, but I also heard almost the exact same story about the Miraculous Medal, a prayerbook, and a Bible. They can't all be true!"[64]

Catholic enthusiasm for miracles might be seen as entirely traditional and orthodox; miracles were, after all, foundational to Christianity. But ordinary working-class Catholics also knew that miracles provided a means to direct divine contact and facilitated a personal spiritual autonomy that escaped clerical supervision. Indeed, clergy and members of the church hierarchy insisted upon their authority in judging the veracity of miracles with a defensiveness that hints at the ubiquity and variety of miraculous belief among the laity. In Edward Reilly's case, his healing came at a designated place of Catholic worship, was administered by a representative of the church, and proceeded via the divine powers of a Church-sanctioned relic. Contrasting this ideal, church-legitimated miracle, the *Michigan Catholic* cautioned in 1954 that "There are many self made faith healers," especially Protestant healers, that bore a superficial resemblance to traditional Catholic beliefs about the nature of miracles. "Of course," the newspaper continued dismissively, "such pretensions are false." In 1957, the newspaper again pointed out that the Catholic Church maintained an exacting standard in ascertaining miracles, and that few Protestant healings "would stand the searching test that the Catholic Church applies" to miraculous claims. Almost as an afterthought, but with a clear sense of authority, the newspaper reminded Catholics that they "may never attend non-sectarian or non-religious healing services." But beyond miraculous healing, laity adhered to a variety of folk beliefs that blended Catholic orthodoxy with supernatural appeals. Some Catholics apparently believed they needed to walk three circles around a church before entering to pray a novena. Others were convinced that they were required to mail a chain letter to nine friends (reflecting the nine days which a novena lasted) to make prayer more effective. While the Church certainly encouraged the offering of novenas, "if a Catholic were [to] attach such undue importance to the number nine as to believe that the same prayers offered for a shorter or longer period would not possess proportionate value, he would be guilty of superstition." Power was at the heart of these denunciations: namely, the Church's power to shape orthodoxy and draw boundaries between the sacred and profane, the holy and the taboo. In practice, however, working-class religion was syncretic, creating meaning in the ambivalent spaces where boundaries met and identities blurred.[65]

Similar cultural tensions between official church "beliefs" and unofficial lay "superstitions" deeply affected African American religion. Horace White was especially outspoken on the matter. At the same time that he supported the UAW, promoted movements for black politicization, and championed racial equality, White bitterly denounced religious "racketeers," whom he charged with exploiting the gullible masses. "Most Negro adults have not improved their religious concepts beyond the necessary escapisms of slavery," White boldly charged, "and are thus preyed upon by peddlers of superstition and witchery." In particular, White was thinking of James Jones, known to his thousands of followers as "Prophet Jones." Born in a Birmingham slum, Jones arrived in Detroit in 1938 as missionary for the sect Triumph the Church and Kingdom of God in Christ and emerged into Motown's version of Father Divine or Big Daddy Grace. Shortly after his arrival, Jones began receiving divine messages and established his own denomination, Church of Universal Triumph, the Dominion of God. Jones, now claiming to be the reincarnation of the savior, took the title Dominion Ruler. By the mid-1950s, Jones commanded 50,000 followers. He had converted an abandoned movie theater into his temple, where he staged nightly, televised services that could stretch well past midnight; boasted an elaborate, extravagantly expensive wardrobe; offered faith healing and prophecy (for a $10 fee); lived in a regal chateau among Detroit's African American elite; and, in 1951, even delivered the invocation at the opening session of the Michigan State Legislature.[66]

For White, Jones was just the most egregious example of a cultural epidemic that crippled the African American intellect and undermined claims to racial equality. Listening in on nine different religious radio shows, White complained that none offered any "constructive religious thought" while five "moaned, groaned, and intoned. . . . The music is presented in the same key, jazzed up, loud. . . . In other words, it was low-brow, in the name of the highest thing we know, religion." According to White, these religious programs not only warped the practice of Christianity; they also created a dangerous public image by convincing whites that "religion among Negroes is purely emotionalism, noise and ignorance" with a "great reliance on magic, superstition, and mouthing of the same phrases." The "clowning" of "so-called preachers," therefore, perpetuated white perceptions of black fecklessness and proved "detrimental to increased job opportunities" and "the progress of democracy." White seamlessly blended the culture of "respectable," orthodox Christianity with liberal progress and working-class empowerment. At the same time that White championed the political equality of the black masses, he claimed the authority to judge the expression of their beliefs.[67]

In fact, the dynamic between formal church life and informal networks of folk belief deeply marked the experiences of African Americans. The *Michigan Chronicle* continued to feature advertisements for urbanized hoodoo doctors throughout the 1940s and 1950s. "If you need help," the Rev. Mme. Parker advised, "see the woman of God who knows that prayer is the key TO SUCCESS!" "Bishop" A. Ewell, DD, implored, "COME AND SEE A WOMAN THAT GOD HAS SPOKEN TO," and promised solicitors "Blessed Articles direct from Jerusalem." Particularly popular in the 1940s was a medium named Prince Herman, who claimed that "so-called sickness, lack of money, strained conditions, jealousy, infatuations, crosses, home conditions, bad luck, and so forth are all overcome by the application of the mysterious element or principle that overcomes all obstacles." Prince Herman even broadcast nightly, half-hour nostrums through a local radio channel. By the early 1950s, "Prof. Herman" (who can tell whether this was a promotion or demotion from the rank of "Prince"?) was also writing a newspaper advice column.[68]

When Richard Dorson visited African American communities throughout Michigan in the 1950s, tales of hoodoo remained vibrant. One of Dorson's informants, a woman named Lulu Powell, claimed she "never believed in this hoodooism business," but after becoming sick with cramps and heavy sweating, her husband called in a hoodoo doctor, a woman named Young. After communicating with a spirit named "Dr. McCoy," Young told Powell she had been poisoned at a church fish fry by another woman jealous for her husband's affections. For a cure, Powell was bathed in her own urine, after which the hoodoo doctor whipped the remaining urine in a bowl with seven thorns and buried the concoction in the ground. "But she cured me," Powell claimed, "and I never went to the hospital."[69]

One visitor to Quinn, a black township north of Detroit populated mainly with people displaced by the city's mid-1950s urban renewal projects, found a dynamic mix of formal religion and informal folklore. Many African Americans were Baptists and Methodists, and "a number belong to a religion called the 'Sanctifed Holy,' which . . . bears a resemblance to the 'holy-rollers'" (generally, a reference to Pentecostal denominations). While most people maintained formal affiliation with a church, traditional folk beliefs with origins in the rural South remained vibrant. An expectant mother, for instance, was forbidden from having her photograph taken, for fear that the baby would have a weakness and "the mother's picture will not appear as a true image." Two ministers declared that they would not eat possum, because possums were believed to live inside dead horses. One of these ministers explained the persistence of African Americans' belief in ghosts by pointing to the context of slavery, when white masters warned slaves of "haunts" if they went out after dark—consequently, many southern-born blacks in Quinn refused to take out their trash after dark. Many traditional songs circulated as well, including "I'm Working on the Building": "When you hear me singing / When you here me praying / When you hear me preaching / When you here me moaning, [Chorus] I'm working on the building / It's a true foundation / I'm holding up the blood stained banner for me Lord." Specific themes and images from this folksong—working, moaning, holding a blood-stained banner—both informed and reflected the religious consciousness of these black workers.[70]

The Bible stories related by an African American factory worker who migrated to Detroit from the South in the 1940s or 1950s are especially rare and interesting because they reveal the ways in which formal religious narratives were adapted and revised by ordinary working-class African Americans. Asked to explain how God created humanity, "Joe" sardonically related that woman was made from Adam's rib, and "that's why man is supposed to be boss over his woman although it don't always work out that way." Describing the aftermath of a flood that drowned the world, Joe claimed that Noah "throws a big party but not too many people came because they all been destroyed in the flood but Noah have a good time anyway." Joe told an especially rich version of "Jonah and the Whale." Jonah tried to avoid his duty to God, but "God didn't go for no bullshit from Jonah," and so God made a storm upon the water. After being thrown overboard, swallowed by a whale, and resting in the whale's belly for three days, the whale spit Jonah onto the beach. "And the Lord have another talk with Jonah and He say you better stop fucking up. Then Jonah say yeah and he finally do like the Lord say. See the Lord always give you another chance no matter how many times you all don't do like he say because He be like that." These irreverent interpretations of biblical accounts speak to basic issues of human frailty, conflict, and in some cases, fatalism not uncommon within folk cultures. But most especially, they indicate that the sacred narratives of Christianity could be deeply embraced among the working class, even as they were revised and reinterpreted to resemble traditional Afro-American folklore. These religious narratives vividly reflected the lived experience of class, without translating that experience into the worker-religion idioms of political engagement or social consciousness.[71]

Collectively, the prevalence of folk traditions and miraculous beliefs suggests that many workers maintained a syncretic religious lifeworld, partly shaped by the theologies and rituals of their church and partly shaped by a nondoctrinal collection of stories, traditions, beliefs, and practices that they deemed personally significant. As we have seen, this blending was hardly uncontested. While workers usually respected clerical prerogatives, they were nevertheless jealous of their own spiritual autonomy and were fully aware that, whenever their beliefs were condemned, priests and preachers were claiming authority over them. The role of the minister in working-class culture, then, was ambivalent. When coworkers learned of the ministerial background of DIM's minister-workers, for instance, the social dynamic immediately shifted. Scott Paradise sensed an "intense discomfort" in his visits to the shop floor, which he related to workers' "underlying sense of guilt," based on their perceptions of him as the "minister-judge." Relating an anecdote in one of his reports, DIM minister Jesse Christman agreed that workers had definite ideas of what a "preacher" represented:

> Phil and I were discussing Bible reading, someone else having brought it up. [Another worker] made several extremely crude remarks about this practice and also about those who engage in it. I asked him why he felt this way and pushed him a little about why he should be so hostile to the idea that some might find bible reading helpful. Before I knew it he was accusing me of trying to get him to go to Church and telling others, "HEY, HE'S TRYING TO GET ME TO GO TO CHURCH." It was almost as if he were saying "now, I've finally found him out."

Workers' definitions of a preacher, as Christman recorded them, focused on behavior and social utilitarianism: "Well, he don't go in bars, and he don't swear. . . . he's a leader, and sets an example to others." Preachers, in other words, were in a world apart: occasionally a source for good, but often unwelcome, burdensome, mettlesome, or a killjoy.[72]

This cultural tension was especially acute in African American churches. Marvin Arnett grew up in the church in the 1930s and never rejected Christianity; but she approvingly noted that, as her God-fearing mother grew older, she "listened to the minister less but read her Bible more. She appeared altogether better for it." Folklore collected among African American Detroiters (including one source who served as deacon in a Baptist Church) indicates an abiding suspicion of black ministers. Many sources repeated the conviction that, as one put it, "Black ministers . . . are just in the ministry for money." Another source agreed, stating "They are more interested in money and big cars than saving souls." Other sources accused black ministers of sexual licentiousness (both hetero- and homosexual), engaging in witchcraft and voodoo, and promoting gambling. Ministers "harm the people more than they do good," one subject concluded. Church reporter Isaac Jones certainly heard the gossip, which he paraphrased: "These old preachers ain't after nothing but money. God didn't say anything about money. He said go into the highways and hedges and preach his gospel." Jones thought these grumblings unfair, and sought to dismiss them. "Without regard to the ministers' families and themselves, these critics seem to feel that a preacher can live alone on the promises of the Bible," Jones complained. He advised churchgoers to ignore the "rascals," quiet down, and focus on the preaching, prayers, and choir.[73]

These discursive struggles within black culture led a growing generation of secularized African Americans—usually associated with organizations like the UAW, the National Negro Congress, or the NAACP—to become critical of specific ministers and often suspicious of religion in general. For these secular-leaning activists, religion simply remained too supernatural, too escapist, too individualistic, and too ensnared in the old system of hierarchy, obedience, and racial deference. Gloster Current perhaps best represents the secularized black intellectual in postwar Detroit. Current's grandfather was a church-building reverend who, according to Current, left the church "in revolt against dictatorship." The experience of his grandfather, Current explained, "deterred me from my original ambition to preach." Nevertheless, his life remained closely linked with church-based institutions. As a young man, he worked for the YMCA; later, Current earned an Interchurch scholarship, went to law school, and got a job with the NAACP.[74]

Although Current maintained close ties with leading clerics like Dade, Peck, Hill, and White, the anticlerical impulse inherited from his grandfather remained just below the surface. When the African American William Banks of the Civic Brotherhood Association admitted to an audience of white business people that "many of us are often embarrassed by the boisterous conduct and other displays of ignorance of some of my race," Current was thoroughly disgusted. Banks had argued that only the church could solve the problems of black dissolution and irresponsibility, which, he implied, were largely self-imposed. Current provided a revealing retort:

> The churches in Detroit don't need Banks to help them raise the cultural level of their members. Already our most cultured people are in the

churches. . . . The people Banks obviously wants to reach don't go to the church. . . . Give us complete social and economic equality. The "culture" will then take care of itself.

Current's stark and unambiguous demand—immediate social and economic equality—would not recede. It would swell, grow, and produce one of the most important social movements in American history. For Dade, White, Hill, and their white allies in the worker-religion generation, an urgent question loomed: would the religious formulations of the New Deal era provide the cultural ground upon which this movement would be based? If not, what would take its place?[75]

Conclusion

Worker religion had always straddled a somewhat uncomfortable boundary between political activism, class identity, and traditional faith. Absent the urgent, crisis-driven atmosphere of the 1930s and early 1940s, and challenged by the shifting urban and political context of the postwar city, the creative pressures that drove the explicit commingling of class and religious identities abated. Worker religion, in retrospect, represented a rare cultural moment, emergent at a unique time: with capitalism in crisis, the labor movement ascendant, and the generational maturation of working-class religious leaders (both clergy and lay) providing a grass-roots impetus within local communities and congregations.[76]

As the 1950s waned, that moment was passing. The idealized images of Jesus as an archetypal working man, or what the *Wage Earner* piece had called Christ the Worker, no longer served the same cultural need. Raced as white, gendered as aggressively masculine, and invoked as a symbol of universalistic, democratic virtues, Christ the Worker was born in an era of economic depression and ideologically driven wars between nation-states. Contrarily, the postwar years enjoyed unparalleled affluence, not depression. Public culture idealized mass consumption and excoriated radicalism, while confidently announcing the end of the labor question. Yet, even as its potency faded, worker religion had created an important social and political precedent for a new generation of activists who were themselves operating within the cultural web of religious ideas and norms. During the 1960s, deeply rooted conflicts over racial equality and a war on poverty galvanized Detroit; in its new context, worker religion was remade.

FIGURE 11. Fire threatens a church during the 1967 Detroit riot. Courtesy of Walter P. Reuther Library, Archives of Labor and Urban Affairs, Wayne State University.

FIGURE 12. Churches played a vital role in urban and working-class life. Here, a storefront church distributes aid during the 1967 riot. Courtesy of Walter P. Reuther Library, Archives of Labor and Urban Affairs, Wayne State University.

6. Race and the Remaking of Religious Consciousness

On the hot night of July 23, 1967, a police raid on a "blind pig" (an illegal after-hours saloon) frequented by African American Vietnam War veterans erupted into five days of looting, rampaging, and armed violence. Angry over the disappearance of good jobs, the blight menacing their neighborhoods, the slow impact of civil rights reforms, and the perceived harassment of a nearly all-white police department, black (and some white) Detroiters exploded in what they termed "rebellion"; most white observers called it a "riot." Ultimately, 17,000 law enforcement personnel, including National Guard troops with fixed bayonets marching alongside military tanks, ended the "uprising." Forty-three people, mostly rioters, lay dead; over 7,000 people had been arrested, and more than $36 million in insured property was lost.[1]

At some point during the uprising, the large, white statue of Jesus standing on the grounds of the Catholic Sacred Heart seminary (located on the northern boundary of the rebellion before violence spilled across the city) was painted black. A more literal embodiment of the racialization of religious consciousness could scarcely be imagined. Participants in the uprising were clearly expressing their awareness that racial power in Detroit was not only political or economic: it was cultural—and, specially, religious—as well. A "white" Jesus, they seemed to say, reflected oppression; Jesus must be made "black" in order for African Americans to harness his cultural power and take ownership of their religious identities. Remarkably, the white editorialists of the *Michigan Catholic* seemed to agree. The statue was "not defaced," the newspaper averred, "but very carefully and deliberately painted. It should have been done long ago."[2]

The "black Jesus" that emerged in the wake of Detroit's 1967 rebellion illustrates the extent to which race displaced class in the religious consciousness of the 1960s-era generation. The culture of worker religion formed in the 1930s in tandem with the labor question, a moment when the rights of workers, the social role of labor unions, and the expansion of a social safety net dominated political discourse. By the early 1960s, the labor question no longer commanded the same urgency; indeed, for many Americans, the issue had largely been settled since the mid-1940s. Moreover, questions about the rights of workers or the role of unions were waning precisely at the moment that the quest for African American equality emerged as the defining domestic political question of the day. Consequently, the idioms of Christ the Worker, so central to worker religion, steadily retreated in the minds of many religious activists; in the place of *the worker* emerged a new obsession with *the poor*. This rhetorical "poor" (obviously reflecting a good measure of reality) was almost always imagined as black, was female as well as male, and was sometimes used to legitimize (even romanticize) particularistic, as opposed to universalistic, identities. The main setting for socially activist religious dramas was no longer the factory floor or the union hall but the inner city slum. "Authentic" religion was acquired through solidarity with unemployed black youth, not through collusion with blue-collar workingmen paying dues to a bureaucratic and indifferent union. African Americans increasingly reimaged Jesus as black and poor, and sometimes as a black revolutionary. Albert Cleage, Detroit's most influential black minister in the 1960s, rechristened his church the "Shrine of the Black Madonna" and launched an unapologetic call for "black Christian nationalism." The 1960s, in short, witnessed the unmaking of worker religion, and the making of religious "race consciousness."[3]

These changes, however, occurred gradually, subtly, and incompletely. Superficially, the sociopolitical culture of the New Deal coalition appeared stronger than ever in the early 1960s, especially in Detroit. The city's young, liberal, Irish Catholic Mayor Jerome Cavanaugh, emerged as one of the most widely regarded big-city mayors, deeply committed to urban renewal and to President Lyndon Johnson's War on Poverty. The UAW also appeared strong, both in terms of sheer size and in moral credibility, as its highly visible support of Martin Luther King's 1963 Detroit rally indicated. And many churches appeared to be on the vanguard of political and cultural change, energetically marshaling considerable organizational resources on behalf of urban renewal, the civil rights movements, and the War on Poverty. In fact, rather than viewing the tumult of the 1960s as evidence of a wrenching change, these examples suggest connections and continuities between the worker religion of the 1930s/1940s and the new race-conscious religion of the 1960s. Worker religion had provided a rich template of religious idioms for a rising generation of socially oriented activists, who proceeded to mediate political, class, and religious identities through the prism of their faith. Indeed, since the early 1940s, racial equality had been a key tenet of worker religion, a commitment that gained institutional expression in numerous interracial commissions, civil rights committees, and union-affiliated groups. The emerging 1960s generation faced a distinct set of problems—urban decline, automation, and poverty in the midst of affluence—and sought its own identity; but it did so from a cultural scaffolding that worker religion built. Race-conscious religion transformed worker religion, but it did not emerge sui generis.[4]

Race, Civil Rights, and the Remaking of Religious Consciousness

Racial equality had been part of the discourse of worker religion since World War II. Civil rights protests in the 1940s and 1950s were closely joined to the culture of New Deal–era liberalism—a culture that had been fundamentally shaped by labor struggles that continued to view industrial unions as essential social agents of democratization, and that viewed all discrimination as essentially the same. However, the specific history or grievances of African Americans were often subsumed under a universalistic condemnation of all discrimination. A Catholic pro-FEPC pamphlet from the 1940s, for instance, surreptitiously condemned racism along with broader discrimination against "Catholics, Jews, Irish, Negroes, Italians, Poles [and] foreign born." Likewise, any type of race relations civic panel or pro-FEPC political campaign led by black ministers was bound to prominently feature UAW activists, and quite possibly to rely upon UAW financial support. Although some black workers certainly struggled with insensitivity and even outright discrimination in their union locals, as a rule, black workers and community leaders alike supported the UAW as a powerful and necessary agent for social change.[5]

By the early 1960s, the direction of political and imaginative energies was clearly moving toward a specific reckoning with the American legacy of anti-black racism. 1963 emerged as a watershed year. In 1957, Edward Cardinal Mooney of the Catholic Archdiocese, G. Merrill Lenox of the Metropolitan Detroit Council of Churches (MDCC), and Rabbi Morris Adler offered the first major multireligious statement urging an end to segregated housing. The language of the statement was modest and timid, merely urging churchgoers "to follow the teachings of their respective faiths by judging new neighbors in terms of their respectability, decency and individual merit and not on terms of color or creed." But by 1963, when Detroit hosted a major conference on open housing, participants "were often shocked to realize," as the organizers wrote in a published account of the conference, "that we felt more in common with those of other faiths who were dedicated and working on this problem, than we did with members of our own faith who were apathetic or negative." Abraham Citron, one of the Conference organizers, wrote a detailed letter to Gene Wesley Marshall of the National Conference on Religion and Race (an organization inspired by the Detroit group) in which this theme was considerably elaborated.[6]

According to Citron, Protestant and Jewish groups had produced much discussion but little action until August 1962, when Archbishop Dearden announced that he would attend and that the Archdiocese would serve as cosponsor. At that point, "everything began to hum." The "personal contact and mutual respect and trust" among black and white, Protestant and Catholic, Christian and Jew, produced a "loose fellowship" among organizers. "When Catholic laymen would contact Protestant clergy and laymen in a tension area, ask their cooperation, arrange meetings in Protestant churches, bring out members of Catholic parishes to these meetings; when they would furnish organizational time and know-how, indicate no interest in control or in obtaining or holding leadership, but only in getting a community job done, many Protestants and Jews began to rethink their own roles and responsibilities." As Citron indicated, the political rhetoric of equality and integration promoted by civil rights activists began effecting practical changes to the ways in which religiously different people responded to each other. This change, in turn, produced tremors within religious culture and stimulated the creation of a new set of moral idioms. Yet, at the same time that civil rights eroded some *religious* boundaries, it also significantly highlighted the *political* divisions between liberal, conservative, and, somewhat later, radical religious elements.[7]

As with politics, racial idioms also would break to the surface of religious cultures in 1963. Detroit's "A Challenge to Conscience" conference from that year, for instance, clearly indicates the increasing purchase of race on the religious imagination. Most obviously, the organization formed in the conference's wake explicitly described its mission as focusing on "Religion and Race," eschewing the usual euphemisms of brotherhood or charity. The conference itself also directly engaged ideologies of race. "The religious and creative way to think and act toward men," participants concluded, "is as if there is one race, the human race." Racial injustice was clearly understood as distinct from working-class struggles (although city councilman Mel Ravitz did note that, without secure employment and income, the opportunity to buy a house in a nicer neighborhood meant little). Conference members debunked the charge that "many Negroes have not absorbed middle class cultural values" and that this deficiency led to neighborhood deterioration. Many whites, the report argued, were not middle-class either, but nobody protested when a working-class white family moved into a new neighborhood—clearly, then, *racial ideology*, not class prejudice, was the real problem they addressed.[8]

By late in 1963, the religious consciousness that once focused with such precision on workingmen and the related struggles of unionization was clearly being remade with a new, equally precise focus on un- or underemployed African Americans, especially young men, locked in both an economic and cultural cycle of inner-city poverty. A conference on disadvantaged youth, sponsored by the National Council of Churches and held in Detroit in November of 1963, explicitly articulated these new issues. Delegates were challenged to "look at the issues of life in the inner city and what they were doing about these issues in relation to the Gospel's demand"; some openly bemoaned ministers' "inability" to "come to grips with" the culture of poverty. Ministers and lay social workers sensed the class boundaries of their own sensibilities. Kenneth Wells, representing the YMCA, noted that Protestant social workers were "'value-laden' groups," and argued that "for the most part we are only flexible around the edges." John Wagner, of the NCC's Department of the Urban Church, cautioned against the potential for class imperialism in "servicing" the poor. He pointed to one NCC study that found many inner city ministers "orbiting around a pole of personal martyrdom." Such a "sentimentalized" approach was dangerous, for youth in the inner city "hate phonies" and knew when churchmen were using them to serve their own psychological needs. He urged ministers to become prophetically oriented toward the community, not preoccupied with the professional duties of the church itself. Indeed, "advocates of the disadvantaged" must openly conflict with power-holders of the status quo—an engagement that was certain to highlight the "limitations of congregational polity." Wagner seemed to place greater faith in the "small action group," largely led by laity, as having a quicker and more direct impact than the institutional church.[9]

The symbolic gravitas of the centennial of the Emancipation Proclamation in 1963 also seemed deeply striking—even chastening. Black churches throughout the city held Emancipation services, while white religious leaders moved by the civil rights movement publicly rent garments. Episcopal Bishop Richard Emrich declared his church "repentant for its failures," while G. Merrill Lenox lamented that the white churches had "unhappily faltered at many points and in many situations." These religious leaders were determined to rectify past sins, and many became increasingly consumed by the gathering force of the civil rights movement. That year, many observers began referring to the emergence of the "civil rights revolution" or the "Negro revolution." While this language may sound hyperbolic, many participants at the time accepted the term as a legitimate description of massive social change. Indeed, as Detroit Mayor Jerome Cavanaugh observed, the campaigns for civil rights represented not only a political revolution, but a religious and moral revolution as well. "Among the first to respond" to the revolution, Cavanaugh told members of the Holy Name Society, "were clergymen." Priests and nuns who believed in the doctrine of the Mystical Body of Christ saw "a need to take up picket signs." Protestants, once consumed with issues of domestic morality, were "running for public office, organizing the poor, starting ambitious housing programs." The revolution was so powerful, the mayor averred, that it forced all Detroiters to reimagine the ideals of "brotherhood, love, and compassion."[10]

Unlike the South, where "civil rights" generally focused on voter registration drives or integrating public spaces like restaurants, schools, and buses, "civil rights" in the North—certainly in Detroit—referred first and foremost to the battle against residential segregation. Thus, in January of 1963, Catholic, Jewish, and Protestant organizations (both black and white) hosted A Challenge to Conscience, mentioned earlier, that intended to "*emancipate the housing market*." Participants in this conference concluded that racial injustice was not merely wrongheaded; it was in fact a *sinful* denial of moral law. "We express our deep sadness that for the most part the churches and synagogues have failed to assume their role of leadership in awakening the conscience of the people . . . and have acquiesced to its existence," the final report stated. "We can call this no less than sin and disobedience to the will of God." Ironically, this moral certitude eventually led many socially involved lay people (and some ministers) to question the very necessity of institutional religion, which so often fell short of these ideal principles.[11]

In 1963, Detroit also marked a year of struggle within its black churches and especially among Detroit's traditional black leadership. Albert Cleage, the child of a middle-class doctor, was at one time something of an establishment product himself. As a high-school student, Cleage lead the youth group at Malcolm Dade's St. Cyprian's Church. Similarly, he became youth pastor at Horace White's Plymouth Congregational Church, hoping one day to succeed White. After a peripatetic young manhood, Cleage obtained a divinity degree from Oberlin in 1943 and returned to Detroit as pastor of the Central United Church of Christ on Linwood, just west of Twelfth Street (the area that erupted as the epicenter of the 1967 riot). Ironically, the light-skinned

Cleage, who led what had apparently been considered a "white church" for light-skinned blacks, emerged as the most important and vocal articulator of a theology of "black Christian nationalism."[12]

By the 1960s, Cleage was making a bid for leadership among the radical vanguard of black Detroit. Early in 1963, Cleage argued strenuously for black voters to reject an upcoming referendum that would provide a tax boost to city schools. To most black leaders, this position seemed virtually suicidal, but Cleage argued that he was the leader most in line with the "national freedom struggle against second-class citizenship." He pointed out that, even with votes at stake in an important election, Detroit's school board was dragging its feet on integration and was providing a substandard education to black children—*after* the election, he reasoned, schools would have little motivation to improve. Cleage wanted to issue a protest vote and paralyze the school system. In the end, the school millage vote failed at the polls, but this was likely due more to Detroit homeowners' general hostility toward taxation than black political discontent.[13]

Cleage had his finger on an undercurrent of restiveness that became explicit during Martin Luther King's protest marches in Birmingham, Alabama, in April and May of 1963. Detroit's black churches were jolted from what a *Michigan Chronicle* editorial referred to as a "second-class slumber" by the drama of Birmingham. As television broadcast images of black schoolchildren assaulted with fire hoses and attacked by police dogs, impromptu drives for food and funds to support the Birmingham marchers sprang up in black churches across Detroit. Broadus Butler, writing in the *Michigan Chronicle*, made explicit the prophetic religious cosmology underlying King's movement: "God is walking this nation" through the Birmingham crisis. As Butler made plain, he believed that God was literally intervening in human history, anointing the black community with divinely inspired leaders and providing otherwise-ordinary blacks the courage to endure suffering and struggle. If white Americans rejected this divine intervention, Butler intoned, then, in prophetic fashion, God would destroy America as a great nation. The thinking of African American civil rights leaders like King and Butler "stood out for their rejection of this world and its natural tendencies," historian David Chappell has noted. Liberal education and economic-development programs were not sufficient to dismantle American racism, they believed; the sinfulness of humanity itself demanded a reckoning. Civil rights leaders in the black churches, Chappell concludes, "were more akin to the Hebrew Prophets . . . than they were to mainstream liberals."[14]

C. L. Franklin, minister of New Bethel Baptist Church and King's personal friend, took the Birmingham crisis one step further. At his church in May

1963, Franklin was elected chair of a new organization, the Detroit Council for Human Rights. Franklin planned to use the DCHR not only to support King in Alabama but to raise funds for a major, King-led march in Detroit, planned for June 23. Between Cleage and Franklin, the older generation of black church leaders sensed their authority dissipating. The Baptist Ministerial Alliance, which initially supported the Detroit march, reversed itself in early June, largely because many ministers resented Franklin's flamboyant personal success and his previous aloofness to social activism. Disputes between Franklin and other Baptist ministers would continue up to the march's eve. James Guinan, a white minister affiliated with the Congress of Racial Equality (CORE), was a gadfly in the civil-rights community. As such, Guinan became aware of the "real power struggle for Negro leadership," as he noted in his journal. After a speech by Mayor Cavanaugh at Calvary Presbyterian Church, Guinan observed Harold Hunt, a young black organizer on Detroit's east side, instruct city councilman Mel Ravitz on this power struggle. "Hunt reminded him . . . he better know what this new movement was really saying about the old leadership."[15]

Nevertheless, despite these personal conflicts, King's march proved to be a tremendous public success, drawing over 100,000 into the streets, and thence into Cobo Hall to hear an early version of King's "I Have A Dream" speech made famous in the March on Washington later that summer. "What had happened," according to radical organizer James Boggs, was that "the blacks had organized all over the city and the churches. Reverend Cleage did lots of organizing. All of the preachers agreed that they would have a rally, and every one of their churches had a premarch rally. That's what got out so many people." Richard V. Marks, director of the Mayor's Interracial Committee in 1963, agreed that the balance of power in the country was shifting toward civil rights. "You had all the religious denominations that up to that point had never really joined the battle. They joined with King. You had major Catholic, Protestant, Jewish, the labor movement just involved up to its ears with money and personnel."[16]

Consequently, the meaning of "ministry" itself was shifting. Mainline Protestants, in particular, were no longer encouraged to exhort Gospel for the sake of conversion, but to "witness" their religion through "servanthood." The Protestant retreat center Parishfield, located in rural Brighton, Michigan, offers a telling example. In the 1950s, Parishfield had served as a key supporter of the Detroit Industrial Mission, believing (along with the Catholics in the ACTU) that the "workingman" should be a main focus for ministry. But by the early 1960s, Parishfield staff became increasingly self-conscious of their own removal from the pressing urban needs of Detroit and of the possibilities urban ministry held. The city, not the factory, became, in the words of one report, "the main battleground in the fight to expand the possibilities for human life in our society." In 1962, two Parishfield ministers—James Guinan and Roger Barney—opened an office in downtown Detroit and jumped into the crosscurrents of a city humming with civil rights and antipoverty initiatives. Guinan and Barney, like the DIM ministers who immersed themselves in the lives of assembly workers, acknowledged that mainline Christianity did not provide a center for urban culture. Indeed, the group hoped "to discover those who were discernibly working for a more human environment and life in the metropolis, to get next to them in order to share their perspective, and to *see what they could teach us* about ministry" (italics added).[17]

Guinan quickly became involved with CORE and volunteered to serve as crowd marshall for Martin Luther King's historic 1963 march down Woodward Avenue. Hinting at the shifting religious consciousness that the civil rights movement was effecting on its participants, Guinan later admitted that he first needed to learn "that the place of whites in the Negro revolution was a subordinate one, and this lesson was not easy to accept." However, his personal experience with the King demonstration epitomized the evolving religious consciousness of other white mainliners suddenly exposed to the religious and material worlds of African Americans. Meeting with other marshals at C. L. Franklin's New Bethel Baptist Church the night before the march, Guinan was skeptical, jittery, and unimpressed, feeling the whole affair was poorly organized. Nevertheless, on the morning of June 23, Guinan took his post along the march's route—ironically, he stood in the shadow of St. John's Episcopal Church, once one of Detroit's grandest and most influential mainline churches, celebrated for its civic activism by H. Paul Douglass in the late 1920s. "The whole air seems to be that of a Sunday School picnic," Guinan noted "and yet there is a tenseness about it all."[18]

As the march began in the afternoon, Guinan looked on in disbelief: he had "never seen so many people converging on one spot in my whole life" (estimates place the number of marchers at around 150,000). His first reaction, as a marshall, was panic. But, "In spite of the possibilities of riot, in spite of the fear of the white people of Detroit, many of whom fled the city for the day. . . . In spite of all these anxieties . . . this was undoubtedly the most orderly demonstration that the country has every known." The "joyous spirit" that pervaded the march gave him a feeling of "deep humility and a sense of gratitude to have been a part of this momentous occasion." The power of the march was reinforced by its almost poetic timing, which Guinan noted: "The

Negro revolution had made its impact in Detroit exactly twenty years to the day since the bloodiest riot that this city has ever known between the races."[19]

In its first year, Parishfield-Detroit coordinated with teachers and social workers involved in the Great Cities School Improvement Project. By late 1964, Parishfield workers were "coming face to face, through legitimate and constructive means, with some of the poor in our midst." Finally, in 1965, Parishfield formally closed its Brighton retreat and moved its entire operation into Detroit. "We did not decide this lightly or suddenly," its newsletter explained, but community members had simply become too self-conscious of urban needs. Maintaining the Brighton center, they concluded, implied "that middle-class, agrarian life is the good life" and highlighted the separateness of suburban life.[20]

Just as the experience of industrial labor transformed DIM ministers, the immersion in urban problems wrought a similar transformation in Guinan and his colleague, Roger Barney. In November of 1965, Barney and his wife attended a speech by William Strickland of the Northern Student Movement and concluded, "[I]t was a definitely 'radicalizing' experience; after that day, we could never feel the same about American racism—it was an undoubted fact." The day after the speech, Barney was already struggling to make sense of his new reality. While attending a baptism ceremony for black children at the "proudly integrated congregation" of St. Joseph's Episcopal Church in Detroit, Barney couldn't help but wonder at the integrity of the institution these children were being baptized into—it was, he admitted, "as thoroughly middle class a church" as any Protestant establishment. To be middle-class and orthodox in the mid-1960s, without an appropriately radical commitment to racial and economic justice, was to court spiritual fraudulence in the eyes of "service"-minded young people. For both black and white Detroiters, religion had become enveloped with race.[21]

The Spirit of the War on Poverty

At the end of the 1960s, 45 percent of Detroit's population was African American. Yet, as a result of jobs lost to automation and opportunities stunted because of educational and housing segregation, African Americans consistently comprised 75 percent or more of the city's welfare cases throughout the 1960s, even as the city's overall unemployment rate declined from 15 percent in 1961 to below 5 percent in 1963. Religious communities were intimately familiar with these dire circumstances. Fr. Raymond Maiberger, pastor of the all-black Our Lady of Victory Catholic parish, claimed unemployment in the area surrounding his church neared 80 percent in early 1960s. Cass Community Center, originally a Methodist Church in Detroit's "Cass Corridor," had become "a Port of Entry for a lot of people"—especially African Americans and southern whites—with high rates of transience and overcrowded housing. The neighborhood was, one report concluded, a "sick community from a sociological standpoint" with high rates of alcoholism and preventable disease, although it was also drawing 500 people per month for religious services. Social workers at the Franklin Settlement, a member of Protestant Community Services, faced essentially Third World conditions on Detroit's lower east side. In 1965, the neighborhood surrounding the settlement was 98 percent African American. Infant mortality rates were the highest in the city. Twenty-two percent of area residents were unemployed. When employed, most residents were service workers, craftsmen, or laborers, but the median family income was half of the Detroit average. Fifty-nine percent of residents had completed eight or fewer years of schooling, while one in twenty over the age of 25 had no formal education at all.[22]

By the middle of the decade, then, most civil rights activists realized that they were combating not just racism, but poverty as well. Culturally and ideologically, Protestants and Catholics in Detroit were primed for President Lyndon Johnson's declaration of a "war on poverty" in early 1964, to be waged through the Office of Economic Opportunity (OEO). They were fortunate that Mayor Cavanaugh was equally excited by the prospect and emerged as one of the nation's most effective mayors in securing OEO money for his city. In June 1964, Detroit's poverty program, targeting geographically zoned areas within the city, was christened the Total Action against Poverty (TAP) program; by the time of the 1967 riot, Detroit had received $47,725,000 from the OEO and the Department of Labor for programs to combat poverty, a sum surpassed by only Chicago and New York.[23]

Of course, the moniker "Total Action" was a misnomer. The root cause of Detroit's swelling urban misery was the transformation of its single great industry. The automation of auto plants and flight of capital into cheaper labor markets devastated Detroit's manufacturing economy. The historian Jacqueline Jones has well-described the dilemma for churches concerned with the War on Poverty: "no amount of faith . . . could create economic opportunity out of whole cloth." Nevertheless, many churches urgently and genuinely wanted to combat poverty, and many believed in the potential of the Great Society. Moreover, the religious consciousness of many religious communities had been thoroughly remade around morally compelling narratives of service to the "black poor"; this culture insisted on some type of action. Thus, as money for antipoverty initiatives came rushing into the city's coffers, church organizations wasted no time lobbying for their fair share. In January 1966, the MDCC's Merrill Lenox wrote Cavanaugh for clarification on how "the churches fit into this." Lenox argued that churches were already doing many of the things—providing recreation centers, health clinics, neighborhood work, and so forth—into which the mayor presumably intended to invest the city's money. Churches, in Lenox's phrase, presented a "ready-made structure," and that—more to the point—"churches are profoundly concerned about the future of our city."[24]

Lenox had a point. The Reverend Richard Venus, for instance, led the West Central Organization (WCO), the city's most effective community-action group, which at its peak represented some 60,000 Detroiters. "Our job," Venus explained, "is to build power. It is to channel the discontent that exists in slums into constructive change." Catching the temper of the times, the WCO wanted to be "a little nasty" and to use "unacceptable tactics" in its critiques of urban renewal and housing policies. Similarly, the Reverend David Eberhardt, pastor of the inner-city Riverside Lutheran Church, worked with African Americans, Puerto Ricans, and "orientals" in the neighborhood surrounding his church. By 1967, he had built a staff of twenty working for community development, including four college students who lived at the church residence and were paid to serve almost any need. In addition, he had founded an Inner-City Community Clinic staffed with volunteer professionals, a co-op food center, and a day-care center. "Reverend Eberhart is a phenomenal man," an admirer wrote to Mayor Cavanaugh. "The City of Detroit is lucky to have him. He demonstrates what total commitment to the Christian ideal 'Love Thy Neighbor' means in action." The Rev. Arlie Porter headed the Ad Hoc Clergy, the "employment task force" of the MDCC. Porter persistently encouraged Cavanaugh to pursue more aggressive fair housing and employment initiatives. He remained cordial toward Cavanaugh throughout the early 1960s, and seemed to accept that the mayor's efforts at bettering the city were sincere. By later in the decade, however, Porter was accusing Cavanaugh's urban renewal policies of destroying existing neighborhoods while completely failing to provide low-income housing to its most needy citizens. Therefore, he encouraged clergy "to dramatize the moral issue in this housing need" and *force* action "compatible with the Christian concern for persons." The moral law—clear and unambiguous—had grown more powerful than the promise of liberal policies, and Porter openly supported "lay and clergy alike, who have been willing to accept even arrest and imprisonment for the sake of securing decent housing for their neighbors."[25]

Cavanaugh acknowledged and encouraged the participation of churches in the war on poverty. Early in 1965, the mayor appointed the Reverend E. M. Wahlberg of St. Mark's Methodist Church as the "general" in Detroit's War on Poverty (an appointment reminiscent of the clerical leadership on Frank Murphy's Mayor's Unemployment Commission). In a speech at Central Methodist Church, Cavanaugh suggested that church bodies might provide "seed money" for public housing units to assist those displaced by urban renewal, indicating that such efforts could later receive federal support. In fact, church-led housing projects became common endeavors: the Rev. Nicholas Hood, Horace White's heir at Plymouth Congregational Church, led one in 1965, and the MDCC followed suit in 1966. The Catholic Archdiocese was most ambitious in this regard, turning a $203,000 federal grant into a partnership with the UAW, with the goal of building 500 low-cost homes in 1967.[26]

The experience of Detroit's oldest settlement house, the Franklin Settlement—incorporated into Protestant Community Services when that group formed in 1959—offers a microscopic portrait of Christian social workers in the trenches of the war on poverty. The Franklin neighborhood, on Detroit's lower east side downtown, had been designated Target Area 1 of TAP. The advent of a concerted war on poverty produced two important changes for Franklin, as documented in a report from December 1965. First, settlement workers were brought closer to poverty's roots: it became "more neighborhood-oriented because of the great many home visits made by staff." Likewise, the Neighborhood Institutional Advisory Council, composed of "clergy, educators, [and] social workers" met monthly and helped coordinate services. The second and perhaps more notable change was the collapse of public and private welfare into multiservice centers: "the boundaries of institutionalism break down and . . . agencies work cooperatively in a 'concerted services' approach to solve the problems in a given neighborhood." For instance, a TAP Sub-Center and a health clinic were founded by Franklin but funded and operated by the Public Health Department. Nevertheless, Franklin workers maintained a cautious approach to the government's new interest in poverty. "Even though there are federal funds available for practically everything being done by private agencies," noted the 1965 report, Franklin workers remained concerned about the quality and quantity of these agencies. They were especially hopeful that the "supermarket" approach to services, which had "proven particularly effective in poor neighborhoods where the social worker has to wear many hats and serve many different roles," might be further studied and financed.[27]

On a macroscopic level, the most important religious institution involved in the war on poverty was clearly the Catholic Archdiocese—not because the Catholic effort differed substantially from Protestant ones, but simply because of the size, scope, and organized nature of Detroit Catholicism. In 1965, Archbishop Dearden launched Project Equality, a prototypical form of "affirmative action" declaring that the Archdiocese would reward future building and servicing contracts only to firms that met equal-hiring requirements. Considering that the Catholic Church was estimated as the second-largest purchaser of goods and services in the city (after the federal government), this put substantial pressure on companies that continued to discriminate against black workers. The Michigan Catholic Conference, representing the six dioceses in Michigan, similarly embraced the fair-hiring measure and established a job-training center for minority workers in Lansing.[28]

As important as these independent efforts were, the Archdiocese also became formally involved in the government's "war on poverty" to a significant extent. Indeed, although the majority of federal antipoverty dollars funneled into the Detroit Board of Education, the Archdiocese was the second-largest recipient of federal funds in the city. The major conduit for this funding was a unit called the Archdiocesan Opportunity Program (AOP). In its first year of operation, the AOP received $191,572 (90 percent of its operating budget) in federal money; eventually, the AOP's budget would reach $3 million. Led by auxiliary bishop Thomas Gumbleton, the AOP debuted at a public meeting in St. Edward's parish in January of 1965. By the end of 1965, 46 inner-city parishes were involved in the antipoverty effort, with 450 nuns teaching job-training and Head-Start programs for marginalized Detroiters, who were overwhelmingly African American.[29]

In a bitter irony, the chickens of the grass roots came home to roost in the heart of the Catholic war on poverty. During the summer of 1968, personnel disputes within the AOP led to "acrimonious reflections on the quality of administration," according to a major report commissioned by Mayor Cavanaugh. On August 28th, with a divided vote, the Policy Advisory Committee (PAC) of the OEO responded to these concerns by suspending the AOP as a delegate agency. Two weeks later, on September 12, 1968, some 35 to 50 AOP employees, frustrated in their efforts to meet with Dearden, launched a strike against the Archdiocese. Protesting unfair seniority policies and alleging financial mismanagement and impropriety, "the walkout," according to the mayor's report, "was an act of frustration by people who were committed to an effective program." Many of the strikers told the *Michigan Catholic* that they believed the Archdiocese was endeavoring to evade the "war on poverty at its present level in the Detroit ghettos," and they were committed to keeping poverty services alive.[30]

The Archdiocese—once the great ally of the UAW, sponsor of the ACTU, the Archdiocesan Labor Institute, and the Labor Mass—responded by summarily firing the striking workers. Although generally sympathetic to the work of the Archdiocese, the mayor's investigatory committee was stunned by this move; if such power was granted an employer, the report noted, "it would mean that Detroit has without due consideration turned its back on a labor principle established over thirty years ago after an acrimonious struggle"—a struggle consistently endorsed by the Archdiocese! Ultimately, while admitting that the AOP's record keeping and personnel management was sloppy, the mayor's report concluded that the AOP's programs were "generally considered to be among the best poverty programs in the country" and that the Archdiocese provided "badly needed physical facilities." It argued that the Catholic Church was qualified to receive OEO funds because of its facilities and social service staff and advised that the AOP be reinstated as a delegate agency.[31]

In fact, the most revealing and vociferous criticism of the AOP came not from secular outsiders, but from clergy and laity *within* the church—precisely those "people of God" granted newfound status by the liturgical innovations of the Second Vatican Council. In October of 1968, 25 protestors—including Sheila Murphy, the daughter of the founding family of the Catholic Worker movement in 1930s-era Detroit—crowded outside Cavanaugh's office demanding that the AOP be held accountable for "gross mismanagement." In an indignant open letter directed at the Archdiocese and the city of Detroit, the protestors lambasted the perceived hypocrisy of the AOP:

> Where is honesty in Our Church? . . . Is there a double standard? Perhaps one for the administration of "Christianity" and one taught to people? We, as members of the Church and people of Detroit will not allow this "rape of the poor" to continue. . . . There can be no tolerance for actions that maintain the poor must suffer. It is our concern that THE POOR MUST BE SERVED.

The solution these protestors proposed echoed the reform-minded themes of the Detroit Archdiocesan Synod, convened in conjunction with the Second Vatican Council: the administration of these programs should be turned over "to those in the poor community on a grass-roots level."[32]

St. Agnes, on the corner of 12th and Bethuns (later the epicenter of the 1967 riot), was one of these churches. It had long been "a mystery" to non-Catholics in the overwhelming black neighborhood, according to the *Michigan Chronicle*. But in 1965, it became a center of the antipoverty effort, led by its new pastor, Fr. Francis Granger, and his assistants, Frs. Arnold Brouillard and John Markham. At Granger's appointment, Protestant ministers and the surrounding neighborhood were invited to a welcoming service to learn about the new preschool the parish was operating for the community. Three months later, during the crisis surrounding Martin Luther King's 1965 Selma to Montgomery march, St. Agnes parishioners loaded a truck with $2,000 worth of supplies, held a "songfest, farewell send-off," blessed the truck, and sent it south (several other priests, nuns, and laity from Detroit personally journeyed to Selma).[33]

The Catholic Church had long mythologized itself as a church of "the poor." As long is it remained a church composed predominately of working-class immigrants, this identification with the poor was easily reinforced among parishioners. In this sense, Catholic enthusiasm for the war on poverty was continuous with its broader traditions. By the late 1960s, however, "the poor" of Catholic discourse referred to Protestant African Americans, not immigrant Catholics. No ceremony better catches this transition than the visit of Martin Luther King's Poor Peoples' Campaign in the summer of 1968. When a caravan of 4,000 marchers, en route to the national Poor Peoples' rally in Washington, arrived in Detroit on May 13, they were symbolically welcomed into the city by Bishop Walter J. Schoenherr and Mayor Jerome Cavanaugh at the Catholic Blessed Sacrament Cathedral (the event nearly sparked a riot when belligerent police forced one of the protestors' cars away from a no-parking zone in front of the Cathedral).[34]

Moreover, this embrace of the "Poor People" even provoked a reevaluation of the Catholic theology of poverty. Generally, church leaders viewed poverty as either a spiritual discipline or a benign social necessity. But in light of King's movement, a *Michigan Catholic* editorial declared that, although Jesus admitted that poverty would always exist, he did not "urge its enforcement and absolve the rich from alleviating it by sharing what they have with the poor." In 1968, the spiritual impact of poverty was not meant to prompt Christian reflection or personal asceticism but direct action. The Poor Peoples' Campaign, observed the Catholic newspapers, was peaceful—if it was rejected by whites and replaced by violence, "the comfortable society will have no one to blame but itself."[35]

As a handful of studies from the early 1970s make clear, the Catholic laity had undergone profound changes over the course of the 1960s. In 1958, only 117 out of 226 Detroit Catholics questioned for one study believed they had the right to question their church's teaching on religious matters; by 1971, in contrast, 561 out of 659 Catholics believed in the right to question religious authority. More importantly, disciplined Catholics who attended mass two or three times per month were *more* likely to espouse this view than periodic churchgoers. Social mobility also produced a very different Detroit Catholic than earlier generations: only 40 percent of Catholics in 1971 earned less than $10,000 a year, compared to 70 percent of the general Detroit population. Catholics had also surpassed the general population in terms of educational attainment. This relative affluence and independence produced deep disagreements between the clergy and laity. Two-thirds of lay adults reported that they did not want "politics" in the pulpit, while three-fourths of Detroit clergy disagreed. As one major Archdiocesan investigation found, only 30 percent of lay members approved of church involvement in social issues—consequently, "Clergy are more committed to Black people and their problems than the laity." Catholic religion, this report concluded, "continues to be other-worldly," with most people viewing religion as personal and private. By the early 1970s, the institutional church felt it had lost the "moral force" necessary to compel what it deemed to be right action by the laity. As the Second Vatican Council and Detroit's own Archdiocesan Synod had intended, Catholic religious consciousness was remade in the cultural context of the 1960s—but the consequences of an empowered grassroots were often unforeseen and beyond the church's formal control.[36]

The New Idioms of Race-Conscious Religion

Preoccupied with the problems of racism and poverty, and committed to local involvement, religiously minded Detroiters crafted narratives which, in the 1930s, might have focused on workers in the factory, but in the 1960s increasingly told stories about the unemployed in the city. Even the "Labor Sunday" messages of 1963 and 1964, written by the National Council of Churches and distributed through the MDCC to local pulpits, skirted the usual conflation of ethical unionism with Christian democracy. Instead, sermons focused on the "tragic" circumstances of ill-educated and unemployed youth, bemoaning especially "the lot of countless Negroes and other non-white minorities." Protestant Community Services (PCS), an agency formed through the merging of four previously independent settlement homes in 1959 (including the Dodge Community House, once Claude Williams's base of operations), published the booklet *Limbo* in 1965.[37]

"Limbo," it explained to a presumably white, suburban audience, "isn't just a place between Heaven and Hell. It's right here in Detroit." Although most Detroiters avoided this theological no-man's-land by "sticking to the expressways," it was there "if you have guts enough to see." Limbo contained kids like Jimmy, who played in a "park" made of rubble; Jimmy's mother, Mary, lived on ADC checks that got eaten up by rent. Across the street lived Bob. "He used to be on the assembly line at one of the auto plants. He was proud of his skill. He was a man." But Bob lost his job and was floundering in Limbo. The point of the booklet, of course, was to explain and legitimize the business of PCS social workers in "attacking neighborhood problems at many levels simultaneously." Bob, for instance, was successfully retrained as an office machine repairman, while his wife got into a free clinic and had a dangerous lump removed. But Limbo also indicates the remaking of religious consciousness. In an earlier era, Bob's identity—that of a skilled autoworker, and "a man"—would likely have been understood via the prism of worker religion. But in a community remade by automation and suburban sprawl, PCS found a new way of narrating the role of religion in urban life.[38]

The urban realism characteristic of Limbo extended even into pedagogical religious stories of the era. In 1964, the Detroit Lutheran Urban Study Committee produced a six-week lesson plan for inner-city Sunday Schools entitled "R is for Religion." Although basic Christian themes—sin, redemption, God's love—remained at the core of the lessons, these themes were framed within a narrative context acutely aware of race and poverty in the modern city. Photographs of Detroit, placed throughout the booklets, depicted trash-strewn urban alleyways with church spires peeking through in the background; of black men sitting on stoops and black children climbing fences; of street corners, traffic signs, and pawn shops. Specific lessons examined issues like "revolt" and "rebellion"—theologically, of course, this referred to human rebellion against God's will, but textual references to the Vietnam War and cartoon drawings of raised fists (likely a reference to the symbol for Black Power), urban alleyways, and even a black Jesus hanging on the cross wound traditional biblical stories around a profound awareness of the racial contours of inner-city Detroit in the 1960s.[39]

White Catholics shared similar experiences. In 1965, Fr. Jerome Fraser of Sacred Heart Seminary joined seven other priests and two laypeople who participated in Martin Luther King's planned march from Selma to Montgomery, Alabama. "There is real tension here," Fraser reported. White onlookers "took on an expression of awe" at the march—they had clearly never seen anything like it—but hostility was prevalent. One onlooker shouted to a marching priest, "just wait until you try to get out of Alabama." Still, Fr. Joseph Tracy of St. Dominic parish returned to Detroit with "a deeper love for my brothers and sisters." He was particularly affected by the charity and courage of a black family that offered him shelter when it became unsafe for him to return to his hotel. Adele Saunders, a lay marcher, declared, "here was a chance to step out and be counted a human being devoted to freedom and rights for all people." Lori McNay seemingly went to Alabama as an act of penance for growing up in a prejudiced home; after becoming involved in the lay apostolate, McNay's consciousness was awakened to the fact that "Negroes are human, real people." The *Michigan Catholic*'s editorialist perfectly captured the intermixture of racial consciousness and religious symbolism by comparing the Selma march with Jesus's march to the crucifixion. "Who is this man who walks with death?" the paper asked. "His name is Martin Luther King. . . . He is black and he is white. And he is Jesus Christ."[40]

Many African Americans were similarly intent not only on countering white racism, but in proudly and self-consciously asserting their own racial identity as black people. However, just as the civil rights movement and the war on poverty produced conflicting religious responses within white communities, so, too, black religious communities wrestled over the implications of a racialized religious consciousness. In 1964, after Malcolm X appeared in Detroit at the behest of the Group on Advanced Leadership (GOAL) and the Michigan Freedom Now Party, the city's Baptist Ministers Conference denounced what it called "race hatred" acting under the guise of civil rights. "Extremism is neither God's way nor the American way," declared Charles Williams, president of the 200-minister-strong conference. "I want you to make this clear to your people from your pulpits," he instructed the ministers. Charles Hill, no stranger to radicalism, agreed with his fellow Baptists on this issue. "I'm opposed to this Black Power they talk about," Hill told an interviewer; "you don't need black power," he continued, "you need human power."[41]

But throughout the 1960s, young people especially became more attentive to the decolonization movements in Africa and promoted a pan-black identity that critiqued racism, capitalism, and white nationalism in equal measure. Religion, so much a part of African American culture, was inevitably implicated in this shifting consciousness. Charles Hill himself, however unwilling to endorse black liberationists, nevertheless opened his church to the black Marxist Claude Lightfoot after Lightfoot's tour of Africa in 1965. Even more telling was a speech by John Felix Koli in January of 1965. Koli, president of the African Union at Wayne State University, praised the ongoing Congolese rebellion before a tense crowd at Scott Methodist Church. This "powder-keg type situation" exploded when a white minister rose and shouted, "The only answer will come when HE comes!" Black militants, there to support Koli, hooted the minister down and shouted back, "Preach Christianity to whitey." This racialized, anti-Christian response, shouted in a black Methodist church, indicates the unstable relationship between religious culture and racial identity at a time when religious consciousness itself was being remade.[42]

The racialization of religious consciousness also undermined traditional *ethnic* identities; changing, for instance, what it meant to be "Polish" and "Catholic." A 1970 self-study by the Priests Conference for Polish Affairs (PCPA) in the Archdiocese of Detroit, representing 190 priests, starkly revealed this split between younger and older Polish priests. The PCPA was, revealingly, itself predominately "an organization of older priests." Younger priests—more individualistic, less ethnic or group-minded—questioned the PCPA's very relevance, "especially in terms of inner city problems." Younger priests were more than twice as likely to believe that "white racism was a problem in their communities." Conversely, older priests felt *ethnic* discrimination (against Poles) was real and increasing. Most telling, older priests "felt that being Polish meant, most of all, being a pillar of Roman Catholicism." Not one younger priest made the connection. The young people who carried the banner of the Polish-founded St. Ladislaus parish (dressed in full parochial school uniforms) in Martin Luther King's Poor Peoples' march in Detroit hinted at the emerging generational rifts within Catholic communities, and the eroding potency of ethnic—as opposed to racial—identities.[43]

Some whites responded to the new emphasis on racial justice by becoming increasingly possessive of the privileges accorded their own racial status and consequently much more hostile toward African Americans in particular and 1960s-style liberalism in general. No document quite captures the passions unleashed by the racialization of religious consciousness like the typed, single-spaced, twelve-page letter sent by a group of "irate [white] residents" to Charles Hill in 1964. After Hill led a civil rights march and spoke in a white church, the writers of this letter (many of whom were obviously members of the church Hill had addressed) urged Hill to leave town. Clearly, these white residents felt deeply imperiled. Hill, they charged, sought to destroy "THEIR HOMES, THEIR WHITE COMMUNITIES, THEIR VERY LIVES, *ALL* THEY HAVE WORKED DECADES FOR." It was hardly uncommon for white anti–civil-rights protestors to accuse integrationists of destroying property values. More revealingly, however, the authors of this letter also clearly conflated their whiteness with their religion and explicitly described integration as ungodly. The letter took special offense at the white ministers who had supported the recent civil rights march:

TO THOSE POOR MISGUIDED MINISTERS, SO *GROSSLY* IGNORANT OF THE TRUE FACTS . . . WHO SO GROSSLY *DEFY* THE *WILL* OF GOD, WHO MADE THE RACES *SEPARATE* & DISTINCT, WE SUGGEST THEY GO TO . . . BLACKEST AFRICA, FIND SOME "NIGGER" COMMUNITY THAT WANTS THEIR SERVICES, WE DO *NOT*!!! . . . IT IS NAESOUS [*sic*] ENOUGH TO SEE [white ministers] BECOME TRAITORS TO THEIR RACE, LET ALONE ATTEND A CHURCH SERVICE WHEREIN THEY CONTINUE FROM THE PULPIT TO *DEFY* GOD HIMSELF. AND TO "PLANT" A "NIGGER" IN THE CHOIR IS THE

LAST STRAW! OUR CHURCH WAS A PLACE OF WORSHIP UNTIL A
MINISTER SO *PROFANED IT, DESECRATED IT, VIOLATED IT!*

For these white Christians, integration threatened to destroy "EVEN *OUR*
VERY CHURCH." As contentious a religious issue as class was in the 1930s,
race penetrated far deeper and hit far rawer nerves in the 1960s.[44]

Race, Religion, and Rebellion: 1967 and After

In 1967, the Detroit Industrial Mission published a small booklet by the noted
theologian Gibson Winter, one of the original cofounders of Parishfield and
longtime DIM board member. In his work, Winter lamented the inadequacy
of old models of Protestant culture for comprehending the anger of the urban
poor in an affluent society. He pointed to Billy Graham's response to the 1965
Watts riot in Los Angeles as an example. After being flown over the ensuing
mayhem in a bulletproof helicopter, Graham declared that Watts was an area
of homes and businesses and, as such, was not really a ghetto; therefore, he
attributed the riot to morally derelict hoodlums. Graham's reaction, according
to Winter, was "typical of the way in which the churches have dealt with the
ghetto poor—hovering 800 feet over them with a bullet-proof seat." Winter
saw this reaction as not merely ineffectual, but irrelevant. "This day is past for
the churches. We can no longer see our task as cultivating the piety of deserving and undeserving people." Churches, he declared, must "find themselves
participants in the slums and the suburbs" to create "human community."[45]

Sadly, Winter's friends in Detroit would be put to the same test as Graham
the very year his booklet was published. Almost inevitably, the riot produced
starkly polarized responses within religious communities. A large number of
white Protestants and Catholics reacted with tremendous sympathy. Clergy
in the riot's vicinity quickly formed an Interfaith Emergency Center, which
arranged for twenty-five food collection centers and twenty-one distribution
centers across the city. When it ceased operations on August 4th, the IEF "had
served 28,610 persons through July 28th, a figure that excludes the almost
sixty thousand persons served by agencies like the Community Development Centers, whose food distribution the IEC coordinated," according to
Sidney Fine. Beyond the matter of practical, emergency aid, the riot further
sharpened developing contours of the religious consciousness of the era. A
pamphlet written by the Interfaith Emergency Council and issued July 27th,
for instance, asked, "Does God Use the 'Riot' to Speak to Us?" Referring to
the violence as "rebellion" (rather than "riot"), the writers invoked prophetic
thinking and argued for the "need to see the hand of judgment" at work.

The major failures were those of the white-led war on poverty: "Our welfare programs have been paternalistic and demeaning, and inadequate. . . . We have perpetuated a system of paternalism." The solution called for greater empowerment of the grass roots in all institutions, so that "those previously excluded from decision making will now be involved in determining what we do and how we do it."[46]

While the IEC reiterated the importance of the grassroots, religious consciousness in the wake of the riot followed the course of secular black politics to emphasize the particularistic influence of black power. Cameron Wells Byrd of the United Church of Christ in Detroit urged the white church to adopt the three main tactics of black power. First, the church should exude "impoliteness," or the willingness to "tell it like it is." Second, the church must exhort "imposition," and "reclaim" its identity as a social "misfit." "It is very difficult for anyone to be totally unaffected by authenticity," Byrd noted, implying that the "well-adjusted" church was inauthentic. Finally, the church must embody a "Christian conspiracy," it must be "gutsy" and teach kids how to influence the world. "If the church cannot get with it and involve itself in these strategies, then it should stop bothering people, especially black people; it should stop tampering and meddling just to sooth its own ego." Nevertheless, despite building a religious consciousness marked by a racialized and democratized vision of servanthood, the peak of mainline influence over these issues seems to have passed by the late 1960s. In a postriot conversation with G. Merrill Lenox, Cavanaugh complained that "too many people . . . don't really recognize some of the policies and the leadership that's been developed" and that most Protestant churches "are really in the dark" regarding the MDCC's civil rights and antipoverty measures. Unable to impact congregational culture, the MDCC was also less able to financially support social programs; after raising a record $221,500 in revenue for 1964, its income had plummeted to $121,000 by 1970.[47]

Inner-city Catholic parishes, like St. Agnes and Visitation, "were witnesses to the first scenes of violence," as their pastors reported to the Archdiocesan newspaper. Visitation's basement became one of the first of three Red Cross centers organized, while Fr. Thomas Cullen of St. Catherine's parish reported that his rectory was "jammed" with people seeking shelter. The editorialist for the *Michigan Catholic*, like many white mainline Protestants, cast blame on structural economic inequality, not the personal anger of African American rioters: the riot was "poverty's convulsive shudder." For Archbishop Dearden, who had invested a great deal of the Catholic Church's resources and moral authority into fighting racism and poverty, the rebellion made him "Sick at heart." He urged Catholics to respond "with the heart of Christ." Many did.

In November of 1967, for instance, the Interested Citizens of the Blessed Sacrament Cathedral Community Affairs Council passed a resolution with 3,000 signatures, which they forwarded to President Lyndon Johnson and Mayor Cavanaugh. "The riots in our cities have pointed up the urgency for immediate attention to the poor's needs for human dignity, job security, quality education and fair and adequate housing," the petition announced. The group urged Cavanaugh to back the resolution, and, in an emerging critique of American involvement in Vietnam, argued that "human dignity" should override defense spending as "the primary concern of government."[48]

This argument, however, proved unconvincing to many white Catholics, who may have once been tolerant or even supportive of civil rights and antipoverty initiatives. Fr. Stanley Borucki quickly wrote back to criticize the "barbaric inclinations" in painting the Sacred Heart statue. How would African Americans respond, Borucki wondered, if "some 'whitey'" whitewashed a picture of Martin Luther King? Over the course of the next year, tensions and animosity further polarized Catholic opinion. When a group of black Detroit priests—who held monthly "soul" masses, yet another transformation of the earlier tradition of "labor" and "interracial" masses—apparently declared in a 1968 meeting that the "Catholic Church is a white, racist institution" and "the policy of non-violence is dead," the layman Leo Kelly responded that Catholics were providing $1.5 million from their development fund to enable free education for poor, inner-city black children. Attempting to subtly link white Christianity with the concept of "civilization," Kelly argued that so-called "racist" Catholics willingly provided missionaries to Africa, and yet "we read of virgin nuns being raped in the Congo." R. Frank was considerably less nuanced but made the same point. Through the intervention of "slavery and the white man," he wrote, American blacks had been given the gift of Christian civilization while their African cohorts remained primitive savages. American blacks, he decided, were "'cry-babies' of the human race." From the opposite perspective, Mrs. Claude Jackson, a former social worker, flatly declared that Catholics who withheld charitable funds for fear of the money's use in inner-city neighborhoods had renounced any right to be called Christian. Keep complaining, Jackson taunted her fellow Catholics, "because I, personally, like to know just who the enemy is. We have at last come to the day when we must stand up and be counted."[49]

Finally, of course, African American culture was itself drastically shaken by the rebellion. On Easter Sunday, 1967, some three months before the uprising, Albert Cleage unveiled a dramatic mural of a black Madonna with a black Christ child at his Congregational church, which he then renamed the "Shrine of the Black Madonna" (the mural's model was reportedly a neighborhood woman living on ADC). Cleage, perhaps cannily, refused to urge calm in the midst of the riot. The Rev. Nicholas Hood of Plymouth Congregational, the only black city councilman and pastor of the church that Cleage once pined after, did attempt to calm rioters and (according to Coleman Young) was greeted with death threats. Instead of calm, Cleage announced a call for "black Christian nationalism," and his church saw "phenomenal" growth in the riot's aftermath.[50]

Cleage's Black Madonna and Sacred Heart Seminary's Black Jesus were not the only artful conflations of race and religion in the 1960s. A team of artists took to a wall on a building on Mack Avenue to paint a "Wall of Dignity": black glory in ancient Egypt continuing through the freedom struggle waged by ordinary blacks in America. Interestingly, across the street from the wall, the façade of St. Bernard's Church was decorated with similar work. Like the stained-glass windows inside Catholic churches, the mural on St. Bernard's exterior depicted a historical narrative in pictures. "The huge center façade depicted a black Pharaoh, while side panels emphasized mass struggle and contemporary leaders such as Martin Luther King, Elijah Muhammad, Adam Clayton Powell, and Malcolm X."[51]

The most dramatic signal of change within black churches was revealed by the proceedings of the Black Economic Development Conference, held in Detroit on April 26–29, 1969. Financed—ironically, it would turn out—by the Interreligious Foundation for Community Organizations (IFCO), a nonprofit foundation involving nine Protestant, Catholic, and Jewish agencies, the BEDC brought many local black activists under the influence of James Forman, the former SNCC leader. A year removed from the murder of Martin Luther King, Forman and his cohorts in BEDC were no longer moral universalists seeking a common center. As the BEDC's "Black Manifesto" declared, "We are tall, black and proud." Addressing the "White Christian Churches and the Synagogues" and other "Racist Institutions," the Manifesto demanded a payment of $500 million in reparations ("$15 a nigger") by these churches distributed through a southern land bank, four northern publishing centers, a labor defense fund, and an educational body, the International Black Appeal.[52]

The most remarkable aspect of the Manifesto might seem the most obvious, but it should not be overlooked: the central place of religion and religious culture as the document's target. Indeed, although the Manifesto criticized the U.S. government and global capitalism, churches stood at the head of the firing line. This emphasis suggests the centrality of religion to the historical experience of Africa's descendants in America. The Manifesto's authors realized, after all, that they must respect the religion of black Americans if their pronouncement was to have any chance of appearing as a truly representative plan. "We do not intend to abuse our black brothers and sisters in black churches who have uncritically accepted Christianity," the Manifesto insisted. Rather, it wanted to highlight the "hypocritical declarations and doctrines of brotherhood" that white churches had allegedly used to delay the justice due to African Americans. "Brotherhood" had, of course, been a central tenant of worker religion: the hope that the "universal" interests of working people might be joined into a shared moral and political coalition. For BEDC, this promise was hollow, and the basic premise of shared interests was false. Like many shaped by the experiences of the 1960s, BEDC interpreted the world—religion especially—through the lens of race. The class-based identities of worker religion had withered.[53]

Epilogue

In the 1930s, working people laid claim to a language and symbol system that allowed them to mediate their spiritual identities and class experiences. The process—as with so much in religious history—was fraught with ambivalence, never uniform, and often contentious. Sometimes, the varied elements of religion, race, gender, and class clashed or conflicted. Often, the attempt to fuse these identities with the liberal political culture of the New Deal was vigorously combated by countervailing religious visions, both apolitical and conservative. Still, worker religion, for a time, provided a powerful cultural template that rooted workers within traditional ideas of community, history, and morality, while also encouraging social action, political change, and new conceptions of freedom and pluralism.

Over the course of the 1960s, worker religion seemed increasingly incapable of addressing the problems of racism, sexism, poverty, and urban decline that marked the era. Although worker religion in many ways facilitated the emergence of the new religious and political imaginaries of the 1960s, it was soon forgotten, effaced from the memories of unionists, ministers, and working people alike. By the 1970s, stories of progressivism, equal rights, and the labor movement became tales of secular activism; accounts of religion became a narrative of conservative captivity or (once again) otherworldly escape. Worker religion receded silently into the past.

Why remember it? For starters, we should want an accurate and empathetic historical record. Minimizing, or even deleting, the role of religion in working-class cultural and political movements of the twentieth century probably says more about modern intellectuals' assumptions about religion (and politics, and the working class) than it does about the world of the past.

To be sure, working-class religions were messy, complicated, and sometimes paradoxical creations. It can be difficult to discern precisely how religion influenced society, particularly when religious communities themselves often divided bitterly over political and social questions. Nevertheless, religion clearly mattered to many working people, and the very fact of this "mattering" to the people of the past demands historical attention. Religion, after all, helped shape what it meant to *be* working class: the way a person performed religion, and the religious communities that one joined, defined—for oneself and others—so much else about that person's social and economic status. Religion also shaped political consciousness, impelling some workers to organize unions, participate in political campaigns, and demand racial equality, while spurring others to denounce communism, excoriate liberalism, and defend traditional hierarchies. Moreover, cultural debates about the political meaning of working-class religions were instrumental in developing broader categories of social discourse: on modernity, rationality, morality, and democracy. These divisions and complexities only reemphasize the importance of analyzing religion—workers, along with their champions and their critics, would hardly disagree so vehemently over something of little consequence. Working-class religion, then, is a precious historical commodity: a valuable prism, a rare window into the worldview of ordinary men and women and the ways they made meaning out of their lives and labors.

Notes

Introduction

1. "Work: Curse or Joy?" *Life and Work*, September 1961, PR, 1948–1971, Box 2, Folder "Detroit Industrial Mission, 1958–1967," Bentley Historical Library (hereafter BHL), University of Michigan, Ann Arbor.

2. See, for instance, Peter Linebaugh and Marcus Rediker, *The Many-Headed Hydra: Sailors, Slaves, Commoners, and the Hidden History of the Revolutionary Atlantic* (Boston: Beacon Press, 2000), 36–49.

3. Bill Goode, "The Skilled Trades: Reflections," in *Auto Work and Its Discontents*, ed. B. J. Widick (Baltimore: Johns Hopkins University Press, 1976), 43.

4. The notion of "webs of culture" is a paraphrase of Clifford Geertz, *The Interpretation of Cultures* (New York: Basic Books, 1973), 5.

5. Karl Marx, "Contribution to the Critique of Hegel's Philosophy of Right," in Robert C. Tucker, ed., *The Marx-Engels Reader*, 2nd edition (New York: W. W. Norton and Company, 1978), 54.

6. For two excellent summaries, see Sean McCloud, "The Ghost of Marx and the Stench of Deprivation: Cutting the Ties that Bind in the Study of Religion and Class," in *Religion and Class in America: Culture, History, and Politics*, ed. Sean McCloud and William A. Mirola (Leiden: Brill, 2009), 91–107, and Christopher D. Cantwell, Heath W. Carter, and Janine Giordano Drake, "Accommodation, Resistance, and the World In Between," in *The Pew and the Picket Line: Christianity and the Working Classes in Industrial America* (Urbana: University of Illinois Press, 2016). Works referenced include E. P. Thompson, *The Making of the English Working Class* (New York: Vintage Books, 1966); E. J. Hobsbawm, *Primitive Rebels: Studies in Archaic Forms of Social Movement in the 19th and 20th Centuries* (New York: W. W. Norton, 1965); Paul E. Johnson, *A Shopkeeper's Millennium: Society and Revivals in Rochester, New York, 1815–1837* (New York: Hill and Wang, 1978), 138; Robert Mapes Anderson, *Vision of the Disinherited: The Making of American Pentecostalism* (Peabody, Mass.: Hendrickson,

1979); Lizabeth Cohen, *Making a New Deal: Industrial Workers in Chicago, 1919–1939* (New York: Oxford University Press, 1990).

7. Herbert Gutman, "Protestantism and the American Labor Movement: The Christian Spirit in the Gilded Age," *American Historical Review* 72 (October 1966): 83; Ken Fones-Wolf, *Trade Union Gospel: Christianity and Labor in Industrial Philadelphia, 1865–1915* (Philadelphia: Temple University Press, 1989); Jama Lazerow, *Religion and the Working Class in Antebellum America* (Washington, D.C.: Smithsonian Institution Press, 1995); William R. Sutton, *Journeymen for Jesus: Evangelical Artisans Confront Capitalism in Jacksonian Baltimore* (University Park: Pennsylvania State University Press, 1998); Jarod Roll, *Spirit of Rebellion: Labor and Religion in the New Cotton South* (Urbana: University of Illinois Press, 2010); Erik Gellman and Jarod Roll, *Gospel of the Working Class: Southern Prophets in New Deal America* (Urbana: University of Illinois Press, 2011); Joe Creech, *Righteous Indignation: Religion and the Populist Revolution* (Urbana: University of Illinois Press, 2006); Michael Kazin, *A Godly Hero: The Life of William Jennings Bryan* (New York: Knopf, 2006); Leslie Woodcock Tentler, "Present at the Creation: Working-Class Catholics in the United States," in *American Exceptionalism? U.S. Working-Class Formation in an International Context*, ed. Rick Halpern and Jonathan Morris (New York: St. Martin's Press, 1997); Evelyn Savidge Sterne, *Ballots and Bibles: Ethnic Politics and the Catholic Church in Providence* (Ithaca: Cornell University Press, 2003); Kenneth J. Heineman, *A Catholic New Deal: Religion and Reform in Depression Pittsburgh* (University Park: Pennsylvania State University Press, 1999); William Issel, 'A Stern Struggle': Catholic Activism and San Francisco Labor, 1934–1958," in *American Labor and the Cold War: Grassroots Politics and Postwar Political Culture* (New Brunswick: Rutgers University Press, 2004); James Terence Fisher, *On the Irish Waterfront: The Crusader, the Movie, and the Soul of the Port of New York* (Ithaca: Cornell University Press, 2009); Nick Salvatore, *Singing in a Strange Land: C. L. Franklin, the Black Church, and the Transformation of America* (New York: Little, Brown, 2005); Kimberly Phillips, *AlabamaNorth: African-American Migrants, Community, and Working Class Activism in Cleveland* (Urbana: University of Illinois Press, 1999); Angela D. Dillard, *Faith in the City: Preaching Radical Social Change in Detroit* (Ann Arbor: University of Michigan Press, 2006); David L. Chappell, *A Stone of Hope: Prophetic Religion and the Death of Jim Crow* (Chapel Hill: University of North Carolina Press, 2004).

8. This interpretation is not directly based on psychological theories. However, Freud's broad-ranging notion of "ambivalence" as a simultaneously personal, social, and historical dynamic nicely captures the complexity of the term. See Sigmund Freud, *Civilization and Its Discontents* (1930; New York: W. W. Norton, 1961).

9. For two influential works that argue against "secularization" in the 1920s, see Joel A. Carpenter, *Revive Us Again: The Reawakening of American Fundamentalism* (New York: Oxford University Press, 1997), and Darren Dochuck, *From Bible Belt to Sun Belt: Plain-Folk Religion, Grassroots Politics, and the Rise of Evangelical Conservatism* (New York: Norton, 2011). For a recent "Forum" on the idea of a 1930s-era "religious Depression," see *Church History* 80 (September 2011).

10. Jon Butler, "Jack-in-the-Box Faith: The Religion Problem in Modern American History," *Journal of American History* 90 (March 2004). On this theme, see also Richard Wightman Fox, "Experience and Explanation in Twentieth-Century American Religious History," in *New Directions in American Religious History*, ed. Harry S. Stout and D. G. Hart (New York: Oxford University Press, 1997); John T. McGreevy, "Faith and Morals in the Modern United States, 1865–Present," *Reviews in American History* 26 (March 1998).

11. Liston Pope, "Religion and the Class Structure," *Annals of the American Academy of Political and Social Science* 256 (March 1948): 84–91; N. J. Demereth, *Social Class in American Protestantism* (Chicago: Rand McNally, 1965). Many of these patterns were reconfirmed by Christian Smith and Robert Faris, "Socioeconomic Inequality in the American Religious System: An Update and Assessment," *Journal for the Scientific Study of Religion* 44 (2005): 95–104.

12. Thompson, *Making of the English Working Class*, 6; Robert Orsi, "Everyday Miracles: The Study of Lived Religion," in *Lived Religion in America: Toward a History of Practice* (Princeton: Princeton University Press, 1997), 9–10.

13. James P. McCartin and Joseph A. McCartin, "Working-Class Catholicism: A Call for New Investigations, Dialogue, and Reappraisal," *Labor: Studies in Working-Class History of the Americas* 4 (2007): 99–110; Laurie Maffly-Kipp, David G. Hackett, R. Laurence Moore, Leslie Woodcock Tentler, "Forum: American Religion and Class," *Religion and American Culture* 15, no. 1 (Winter 2005); *Radical History Review* 99 (Fall 2007); *Labor: Studies in Working-Class History of the Americas* 6 (Spring 2009); Robert Anthony Bruno, *Justified by Work: Identity and the Meaning of Faith in Chicago's Working-Class Churches* (Columbus: Ohio State University Press, 2008); Richard J. Callahan Jr., *Work and Faith in the Kentucky Coal Fields: Subject to Dust* (Bloomington: Indiana University Press, 2009).

14. Nelson Lichtenstein, *The Most Dangerous Man in Detroit: Walter Reuther and the Fate of American Labor* (New York: Basic Books, 1995); Thomas J. Sugrue, *The Origins of the Urban Crisis: Race and Inequality in Postwar Detroit* (Princeton: Princeton University Press, 1996). See also Victoria W. Wolcott, *Remaking Respectability: African-American Women in Interwar Detroit* (Chapel Hill: University of North Carolina Press, 2001); David M. Lewis-Colman, *Race against Liberalism: Black Workers and the U.A.W. in Detroit* (Urbana: University of Illinois Press, 2008), and Heather Ann Thompson, *Whose Detroit? Politics, Labor, and Race in a Modern American City* (Ithaca: Cornell University Press, 2001).

15. Three essential works are Leslie Woodcock Tentler, *Seasons of Grace: A History of the Catholic Archdiocese of Detroit* (Detroit: Wayne State University Press, 1990); Salvatore, *Singing in a Strange Land*, and Dillard, *Faith in the City*.

Chapter 1. The Contours of Religious Consciousness in Working-Class Detroit, 1910–1935

1. Florence B. Seymour, "Immigrant Welfare Work," in *Eighth National Conference of Catholic Charities* (Washington, D.C.: Catholic University of America Press,

1922), 238; "Detroit Is the City of Young Men" (n.d., 1924?), in United Community Services of Metropolitan Detroit, Records (hereafter UCS), Box 68, Folder 13, Walter P. Reuther Library of Labor and Urban Affairs, Wayne State University, Detroit, Mich. (hereafter ALUA); Thomas Klug, "Employers' Strategies in the Detroit Labor Market, 1900–1929," in *On the Line: Essays in the History of Auto Work,* ed. Nelson Lichtenstein and Stephen Meyer (Urbana: University of Illinois Press, 1989), 53.

2. *1926 Census of Religious Bodies* (Washington, D.C.: Government Printing Office, 1926); Tentler, *Seasons of Grace*, 422–426; "Report of the Industrial Committee of the National Council of Catholic Women" (Washington, D.C.: September 1929), 5–6.

3. *1926 Census of Religious Bodies*; John Dancy to National Urban League, TL, November 24, 1930, Records of the Detroit Urban League, microfilm edition (hereafter DUL), reel 4; "Questionnaire" by Associated Negro Press, TMs (n.d., 1929?), in DUL, reel 3; Joseph Nicholson and Benjamin Mays, *The Negro's Church* (New York: Institute of Social and Religious Research, 1933), 218–222; Ulysses S. Boykin, "A Handbook of the Detroit Negro" (Detroit, 1948), microfilm edition, 31.

4. For the sake of chronological clarity, the experience of southern-born white evangelicals is picked up in Chapter 3 and continued throughout.

5. *1926 Census of Religious Bodies*; Oliver Zunz, *The Changing Face of Inequality: Urbanization, Industrial Development, and Immigrants in Detroit, 1880–1920* (Chicago: University of Chicago Press, 1982).

6. Lois Rankin, "Detroit Nationality Groups," *Michigan History Magazine* 23 (Spring 1939): 179–180. See also Jeanie Wylie, *Poletown: Community Betrayed* (Urbana: University of Illinois Press, 1989), and Arthur Evan Woods, *Hamtramck, Then and Now: A Sociological Study of a Polish-American Community* (New York: Bookman, 1955).

7. Klug, "Employers' Strategies," 43.

8. Rankin, "Detroit Nationality Groups," 148, 156; see also Michael and Martha Wichorek, *Ukrainians in Detroit* (1968, n.p.), 7, copy at Immigration History Research Center (hereafter IHRC), University of Minnesota, Minneapolis; Zaragosa Vargas, *Proletarians of the North: A History of Mexican Industrial Workers in Detroit and the Midwest, 1917–1933* (Berkeley: University of California Press, 1993).

9. John Dancy, "Unemployment," TMs (n.d., 1920?), in DUL, reel 2; "Questionnaire" by Associated Negro Press, TMs (n.d., 1929?), in DUL, reel 3. For context, see Wolcott, *Remaking Respectability*; Richard Walter Thomas, *Life for Us Is What We Make It: Building Black Community in Detroit, 1915–1945* (Bloomington: Indiana University Press, 1992).

10. "For Negro Working Men," TMs, September 1927; "Report," TMs, November 21, 1925; "Facts Concerning Negroes in Detroit," TMs, October 25, 1925, all in DUL, reel 3.

11. "Working Conditions among Negroes in Detroit" (n.d., 1924), in DUL, reel 2.

12. National Industrial Conference Board, "The Cost of Living among Wage Earners" (October 1921), 6–7; For living conditions, see also Marcella MacHale in *Twelfth National Conference of Catholic Charities* (Washington, D.C.: Catholic University of America Press, 1926), 325.

13. Woods, *Hamtramck, Then and Now*; Statistics for 1920 and 1921 from Polish Activities League, *Polish Women for Progress: The Polish Activities League, 1923–1973* (n.p.), copy at IHRC; Malvina Hauk-Abonyi and Mary Horvath-Morreal, "Touring Ethnic Delray" (Detroit: Southeast Michigan Regional Ethnic Heritage Studies Center, n.d., 1975?), 6–10, at IHRC; Wylie, *Poletown*.

14. Tentler, *Seasons of Grace*, 3, 423; *1926 Census of Religious Bodies*.

15. *St. Florian Parish, Hamtramck, Michigan, 1908–1983* (Hamtramck, Mich., s.n., 1985), 86, copy at Archives of the Archdiocese of Detroit (hereafter AAD).

16. Leslie Cahill and John Cornwell, eds., *The Life and Spirit of Our Lady Queen of Apostles Parish: Hamtramck, Michigan, 1917–1992* (n.p.); Polish Activities League, *Polish Women for Progress*.

17. JoEllen McNergney Vinyard, *For Faith and Fortune: The Education of Catholic Immigrants in Detroit, 1875–1925* (Urbana: University of Illinois Press, 1998), 149; "Golden Jubilee of St. Ladislaus Parish, 1920–1970" (n.p.).

18. John Dancy, "Unemployment," TMs (n.d., 1920?), in DUL, reel 1; National Industrial Conference Board, "The Cost of Living among Wage Earners," 3.

19. Hayden quoted in Melba Joyce Boyd, "Poetry from Detroit's Black Bottom: The Tension between Belief and Ideology in the Work of Robert Hayden," in *Robert Hayden: Essays on the Poetry*, ed. Laurence Goldstein and Robert Chrisman (Ann Arbor: University of Michigan Press, 2004), 209. On Hastings Street, see Paul Oliver, *Story of the Blues* (Boston: Northeastern University Press, 1969; reprint 1997), 87–89.

20. Forrester Washington to the City Editor of the Detroit News, February 20, 1918, in DUL, reel one; John Dancy, "History of the Negro Church in Michigan," in DUL, reel 5; Nicholson and Mays, *Negro's Church*, 213–225.

21. Thomas, *Life for Us*, 178–179; "Report," TL, August 3, 1926, DUL, reel 3; Dancy, "History of the Negro Church in Michigan," DUL, reel 5; Nicholson and Mays, *Negro's Church*, 219.

22. Nicholson and Mays, *Negro's Church*, 98; Arthur Huff Fauset, *Black Gods of the Metropolis: Negro Cults of the Urban North* (Philadelphia: University of Pennsylvania Press, 1944; reprint 2002) cites this source and places it in greater context, 79; Wallace D. Best, *Passionately Human, No Less Divine: Religion and Culture in Black Chicago, 1915–1952* (Princeton: Princeton University Press, 2005), 65. For useful context, see also Wolcott, *Remaking Respectability*, 113–126; Milton C. Sernett, *Bound for the Promised Land: African American Religion and the Great Migration* (Durham: Duke University Press, 1997), 162–165; Kimberly L. Phillips, "Making a Church Home: African-American Migrants, Religion, and Working-Class Activism," in *Labor Histories: Class, Politics, and the Working-Class Experience*, ed. Julie Greene, Eric Arnesen and Bruce Laurie (Urbana: University of Illinois Press, 1998).

23. On the development of urban "spirit conjuring," see Yvonne P. Chireau, *Black Magic: Religion and the African American Conjuring Tradition* (Berkeley: University of California Press, 2003); Marvin V. Arnett, *Pieces from Life's Crazy Quilt* (Lincoln: University of Nebraska Press, 2003), 25.

24. Michael Jackson, *Lifeworlds: Essays in Existential Anthropology* (Chicago: University of Chicago Press, 2013), 7.

25. Tentler, "Present at the Creation," 140.

26. Eduard Adam Skendzel, "A Centennial Parish: Sweetest Heart of Mary" (n.p.), 17, and Skendzel, *The Detroit St. Josaphat's Story: A History within a History* (Grand Rapids, Mich.: Littleshield Press, 1989), 303; Helen Hysko Dickerson, "Our Lady of Czestochowa," unpublished TMs, in Folklore Archive, ALUA.

27. Harriet Bauer Newberry to W. J. Norton, October 9, 1928, and John Dancy to Norton, October 17, 1928, both in DUL, reel 3; Arnett, *Pieces from Life's Crazy Quilt*, 79; Dickerson, "Our Lady of Czestochowa." For the racial ambiguities of Catholic religious rituals, see Robert Orsi, "The Religious Boundaries of an Inbetween People: Street *Feste* and the Problem of the Dark-Skinned 'Other' in Italian Harlem, 1920–1990," *American Quarterly* 44 (September 1992).

28. Dickerson, "Our Lady of Czestochowa."

29. Skendzel, *Detroit St. Josaphat's Story*, 367–368; Cahill and Cornwell, *Life and Spirit*, 53; "Clara Swieczkowska and Mrs. Tomaszewski Regarding Detroit Poles," in Eduard Adam Skendzel Collection (hereafter EASC), University of Notre Dame Archives, South Bend, Ind.

30. Ida M. Santini, "The Preservation of St. Joseph's Day and Something about the Sicilian Colony in Detroit," unpublished TMs, Folklore Archive, ALUA; David A. Badillo, "The Catholic Church and the Making of Mexican-American Parish Communities in the Midwest," in *Mexican Americans and the Catholic Church, 1900–1965*, ed. Jay P. Dolan and Gilberto M. Hinojosa (Notre Dame: University of Notre Dame Press, 1994), 276.

31. Skendzel, *Detroit St. Josaphat's Story*, 343–344; "Clara Swieczkowska and Mrs. Tomaszewski regarding Detroit Poles," in EASC; White quoted in Elaine Latzman Moon, *Untold Tales, Unsung Heroes: An Oral History of Detroit's African American Community, 1918–1967* (Detroit: Wayne State University Press, 1994), 60–61.

32. Manning Marable, *Malcolm X: A Life of Reinvention* (New York: Viking, 2011), 29; Randall K. Burkett, "Religious Ethos of the UNIA," in *African American Religious Thought: An Anthology*, ed. Cornel West and Eddie S. Glaude Jr. (Louisville: Westminster John Knox Press, 2003), 550–571; Wolcott, *Remaking Respectability*, 126–130.

33. Augustus Duncan, "Why the Negro Should Give Up the Shadow of His Political Rights" (Detroit, 1921), microfilm version; Anetta Louise Gomez-Jefferson, *In Darkness with God: The Life of Joseph Gomez, A Bishop in the African Methodist Episcopal Church* (Kent, Ohio: Kent State University Press), 69, 82–87, 96–97; "Minutes of the Detroit Council of Churches Social Service Department," November 16, 1921, in Metropolitan Detroit Council of Churches, Records, 1920–1971 (hereafter MDCC), Part II, Box 5, Folder 20, ALUA.

34. For Bratton's quote, see TL, February 21, 1921, Papers of the National Association for the Advancement of Colored People, Midwest Division, microfilm edition, reel 11; Announcement for St. Peter's service on TMs, January 3, 1927, DUL, reel 3. For context, see Allan Dwight Callahan, *The Talking Book: African Americans and the Bible* (New Haven: Yale University Press, 2006); Eddie S. Glaude, *Exodus! Religion, Race, and Nation in Early Nineteenth-Century Black America* (Chicago: University of Chicago Press, 2000).

35. *1926 Census of Religious Bodies*; Nicholson and Mays, *Negro's Church*, 100–101; for context, see Lynne Marks, "Challenging Binaries: Working-Class Women and Lived Religion in English Canada and the United States," *Labor: Studies in Working-Class History of the Americas* 6 (Spring 2009): 107–125; Evelyn Brooks Higginbotham, *Righteous Discontent: The Women's Movement in the Black Baptist Church, 1880–1920* (Cambridge: Harvard University Press, 1993); Robert A. Orsi, *Thank You, St. Jude: Women's Devotion to the Patron Saint of Hopeless Causes* (New Haven: Yale University Press, 1996).

36. "Report on Prostitution, the Police, the Law, and the Courts" (1926), in American Social Hygiene Association, Records, 1905–1975, Box 99, Folder 9, Social Welfare History Archive (hereafter SWHA), University of Minnesota, Minneapolis; Wolcott, *Remaking Respectability*, 120.

37. Rev. Louis G. Weitzman, S.J., "The Child and the Home—The Problem of Inadequate Religious Standards," in *Sixteenth Session of the National Conference of Catholic Charities* (Washington, D.C.: Catholic University of America Press, 1930), 232.

38. J. K. Robinson to Robert Bradby, TL, September 22, 1929, Records of Second Baptist Church of Detroit, Michigan (hereafter SBC), microfilm edition, reel 1; "Report of the Society of St. Vincent de Paul of Detroit and Its Child Caring Department" (1914), in Chancery Collection, Organizations, Box 4, Folder "St. Vincent de Paul," AAD.

39. George Edmund Haynes, *Negro New-Comers in Detroit: A Challenge to Christian Statesmanship, A Preliminary Report* (New York: Home Missions Council, 1918), 38; Tentler, *Seasons of Grace*, 429.

40. *St. Florian Parish, Hamtramck, Michigan*, 85. For context on the intersection of religion and sports, see Julie Byrne, *O God of Players: The Story of the Immaculata Mighty Macs* (New York: Columbia University Press, 2003).

41. Robert Bradby to Rev. Northcross, TL, January 18, 1926, SBC, reel 1.

42. Rankin, "Detroit Nationality Groups," 162; Norman Daymond Humphrey, "The Changing Structure of the Detroit Mexican Family: An Index of Acculturation," *American Sociological Review* 9 (December 1944): 624; Eva V. Huseby-Darvas, *Hungarians in Michigan* (East Lansing: Michigan State University Press, 2003), 66. On the lackadaisical attitude of Polish men prior to 1920, see *St. Florian Parish, Hamtramck, Michigan*, 68, AAD.

43. "Report on Prostitution, the Police, the Law, and the Courts," SWHA; Albert J. Mayer and Sue Marx, "Social Change, Religion, and Birth Rates," *American Journal of Sociology* 62 (January 1957): 384; Ralph Janis, *Church and City in Transition: The Social Composition of Religious Groups in Detroit, 1880–1940* (New York: Garland, 1990), 110–112; Peter A. Ostafin, "The Polish Peasant in Transition: A Study of Group Integration as a Function of Symbiosis and Common Definitions" (Dissertation, University of Michigan, 1948), 254–270.

44. "Report of the Michigan State Commission of Inquiry into Wages and the Conditions of Labor for Women and the Advisability of Establishing a Minimum Wage" (Lansing, Mich., 1915), 100–101.

45. George Deshon, "Advice for Catholic Working Girls" (1897), reprinted in *Gender Identities in American Catholicism*, ed. Paula Kane, James Kenneally, and Karen Kennelly (Maryknoll, N.Y.: Orbis Books, 2001), 149–150; Mrs. Edward A. Skae, in *Eleventh National Conference of Catholic Charities* (Washington, D.C.: Catholic University of America Press, 1925), 211–212; "Report of the Industrial Committee of the National Council of Catholic Women," 5–6.

46. On Mary Johnson, see Anthea D. Butler, "Church Mothers and Migration in the Church of God in Christ," in *Religion in the American South: Protestants and Others in History and Culture*, ed. Beth Barton Schweiger and Donald G. Mathews (Chapel Hill: University of North Carolina Press, 2004), 195–228; Arnett, *Pieces from Life's Crazy Quilt*, 29–30; Wolcott, *Remaking Respectability*, 124; "Souvenir Program, 2nd Anniversary, New Grace Baptist Church" (1942), in Georgia Washington Papers, Box 1, Folder "Miscellaneous Programs," BHL; Victor Woodward to John Dancy, TL, July 19, 1928, in DUL, reel 3.

47. Wolcott, *Remaking Respectability*, 176–183; "Greater Shiloh Informer," May 25, 1930, Greater Shiloh Missionary Baptist Church Records, ca. 1920–2008 (hereafter SMBC), BHL.

48. Chester Culver to "Gentlemen," TL, April 1925, and Chester Culver, TL, February 25, 1926, both in DUL, reel 16; "Minutes of the Detroit Council of Churches Social Service Department," TMs, April 20, 1926, DCC, Part II, Box 5, Folder 22, 103, ALUA; Klug, "Employers' Strategies in the Detroit Labor Market, 1900–1929," 65; John Dancy to PC Jones, TL, January 28, 1928, DUL, reel 3.

49. Paul Rajewski, Interview by Pat Pilling, and Nestor Dessy, Interview by Pat Pilling, both in Polish-American Autoworkers Oral History Collection, ALUA; Charles Denby, *Indignant Heart: A Black Worker's Journal* (Boston: South End Press, 1978), 29; Myron W. Watkins, "The Labor Situation in Detroit," *Journal of Political Economy* 28 (December 1920): 842, 851.

50. William L. Stidger, *The Pew Preaches* (Nashville: Cokesbury Press, 1930); Henry Ford, *My Life and Work* (Garden City: Garden City Publishing, 1922); Steven Meyer, "Adapting the Immigrant to the Line: Americanization at the Ford Factory, 1914–1921," *Journal of Social History* 14 (Fall 1980). For context on the broad appeal of the "work ethic," see Daniel T. Rodgers, *The Work Ethic in Industrial America, 1850–1920* (Chicago: University of Chicago Press, 1978).

51. *Messenger of St. Rose*, February 26, 1928, AAD; "Greater Shiloh Informer," August 18, 1929, SMBC.

52. Tentler, "Present at the Creation," 145–147.

53. *Messenger of St. Rose*, May 27, 1928, AAD; Goodman quoted in Moon, *Untold Tales, Unsung Heroes*, 60–61.

54. John Dancy to W. J. Norton, TL, October 17, 1928, and Dancy to F. M. McBroom, TL, October 4, 1929, both in DUL, reel 3.

55. Michael Zweig, *The Working Class Majority: America's Best Kept Secret* (Ithaca: Cornell University Press, 2000), 11; see the introduction for a discussion of theoretical debates about working-class religion.

56. Marx quoted in John H. Arnold, *History: A Very Brief Introduction* (New York: Oxford University Press, 2000), 85; Robert Anthony Orsi, *The Madonna of 115th Street: Faith and Community in Italian Harlem, 1880–1950*, 2nd ed. (New Haven: Yale University Press, 2002), xxii; for context, see Bruno, *Justified by Work*, 214–215; McCartin and McCartin, "Working-Class Catholicism," 104.

57. *Messenger of St. Rose*, May 27, 1928, AAD.

58. Lawrence D. Orton, *Polish Detroit and the Kolasinski Affair* (Detroit: Wayne State University Press, 1981); Leslie Woodcock Tentler, "Who Is the Church? Conflict in a Polish Immigrant Parish in Late Nineteenth-Century Detroit," *Comparative Studies in Society and History* 25 (April 1983).

59. Skendzel, "A Centennial Parish"; "Clara Swieczkowska and Mrs. Tomaszewski regarding Detroit Poles," EASC.

60. *Detroit Sunday News*, December 7, 1919, in EASC, Box 5, Folder 1; Cahill and Cornwell, *Life and Spirit*, 6–7.

61. Clement Kiraly, *Holy Cross Church, Detroit, Michigan, 1925–1975* (n.p., copy at IHRC).

62. John C. Dancy, *Sand against the Wind: The Memoirs of John C. Dancy* (Detroit: Wayne State University Press, 1966), 18; John Dancy to William Norton, TL, January 9, 1933, DUL, reel 4; Boykin, "Handbook of the Detroit Negro," 94; John Dancy to W. J. Norton, TL, October 17, 1928, DUL, reel 3.

63. See Jay P. Dolan, *The American Catholic Experience: A History from Colonial Times to the Present* (Notre Dame: University of Notre Dame Press, 1992), 237–240; Orsi, *Thank You, St. Jude*; *Michigan Catholic*, July 3, 1930; Tentler, *Seasons of Grace*, 411–413. For saint beliefs in Detroit, see also "Saint's Lore," unpublished TMs, in Folklore Archive, ALUA.

64. James M. O'Toole, "In the Court of Conscience: American Catholics and Confession, 1900–1975," in *Habits of Devotion: Catholic Religious Practice in Twentieth-Century America*, ed. James M. O'Toole (Ithaca: Cornell University Press, 2004), 136; *A Century of Conquest; The Story of St. Alphonsus Parish, Dearborn, MI* (Kingsport, Tenn.: Kingsport Press, 1952), in Parish History Collection, AUND, Box 62.

65. The quote "strong emotional bond" is from James M. Barrett, "The Blessed Virgin Made Me a Socialist: An Experiment in Catholic Autobiography and the Historical Understanding of Race and Class," in *Faith and the Historian: Catholic Perspectives*, ed. Nick Salvatore (Urbana: University of Illinois Press, 2007), 119. Barrett, an influential historian of working-class life, was reflecting on his childhood in a working-class Chicago parish much like the parishes of working-class Detroit; *Michigan Catholic*, January 30, 1930.

66. John Dancy to W. J. Norton, TL, October 17, 1928, and Dancy to F. M. McBroom, TL, October 4, 1929, both in DUL, reel 3; J. K. Robinson to Robert Bradby, TL, September 22, 1929, SBC, reel 1.

67. Santini, "The Preservation of St. Joseph's Day"; Wolcott, *Remaking Respectability*, 119–120.

68. Thaddeus C. Radzilowski, "Family, Women, and Gender: The Polish Experi-

ence," in *Polish Americans and Their History: Community, Culture, and Politics*, ed. John J. Bukowczyk (Pittsburgh: University of Pittsburgh Press, 1996), 65–66; Cummins cited in "Minutes of the Detroit Council of Churches Social Service Department," December 21, 1926, DCC, Part II, Box 5, Folder 22; "The Bureau of Catholic Welfare . . . Annual Report" (1930?), TMs, in UCS, Box 12, Folder 13.

69. Tentler, *Seasons of Grace*, 408; see also Orsi, *Thank You, St. Jude*, esp. 142–184; Sim Stovack, "A Collection of Folklore of Dearborn," unpublished TMs, Folklore Archive, ALUA.

70. Erdmann Doane Beynon, "Crime and Custom of the Hungarians of Detroit," *Journal of Criminal Law and Criminology* 25 (January-February 1935): 768; Mayer and Marx, "Social Change, Religion, and Birth Rates," 384. Philip F. Messana, "Supernaturalism in Sicilian Culture," unpublished TMs, Folklore Archive, ALUA.

71. "Negro Housing," April 26, 1924, TMs; "Detroit Negroes in Industry," March 1, 1926, TMs; untitled TMs, August 3, 1926, all in DUL, reel 3.

72. Boykin, "Handbook of the Detroit Negro."

73. Wolcott, *Remaking Respectability*, 113–126.

74. Cohen, *Making a New Deal*, has offered perhaps the most influential interpretation of the relationship between ethno-religious cultures and "mass" culture.

75. TMs, May 20, 1917, in DUL, reel 1; Rutledge in *Twelfth National Conference of Catholic Charities* (Washington, D.C.: Catholic University of America Press, 1926), 148; Haynes, *Negro New-Comers in Detroit*, 25; *Proletarian*, November 1918, copy at Minnesota Historical Society, St. Paul.

76. National Industrial Conference Board, "The Cost of Living among Wage Earners" (October 1921), 12; George B. Catlin, *The Story of Detroit* (Detroit: Detroit News, 1923), 703; R. D. McKenzie, *The Metropolitan Community* (New York: McGraw-Hill, 1933), 187–188; Rankin, "Detroit Nationality Groups," 179; Rev. Harold J. Markey, "The Delinquent Child," in *Proceedings of the Twenty-Third Annual Conference of Catholic Charities* (Washington, D.C.: Catholic University Press, 1937), 343–344. See also *Catholics in the Movies*, ed. Colleen McDannell (New York: Oxford University Press, 2007).

77. *Michigan Catholic*, May 3, 1934.

78. Leslie Woodcock Tentler offers the astute reading of St. Aloysius's architecture in *Seasons of Grace*, 309.

79. Duplessis and Leach quoted in Moon, *Untold Tales, Unsung Heros*, 90, 95; John Dancy, untitled TMs, April 8, 1931, DUL, reel 4; Haynes, *Negro New-Comers in Detroit*, 38; Jean Ernst Mayfield, Interview with Louis Jones, May 25, 2005, in Detroit WestSiders Oral History Project, ALUA.

80. Coleman A. Young and Lonnie Wheeler, *Hard Stuff: The Autobiography of Coleman Young* (New York: Viking, 1994), 143; Robert Bradby to William P. Rutledge, June 19, 1929, SBC, reel 1.

81. Rt. Rev. John M. Doyle, "Saint Aloysius Church: The Old and the New" (Detroit: Centennial Pub., 1930), in EASC, Box 17, Folder 7, 15, 30; Norman Daymond Humphrey, "The Housing and Household Practices of Detroit Mexicans," *Social Forces* 24,

no. 4 (May 1946). For a general reflection on the impact of radio, see Michele Hilmes and Jason Loviglio, eds. *Radio Reader: Essays in the Cultural History of Radio* (New York: Routledge, 2002).

82. Maryland Waller Wilson, "Broadcasting by the Newspaper-Owned Stations in Detroit, 1920–1927" (Dissertation, University of Michigan, 1952), 32–35, 50–52, 102–104.

Chapter 2. Power, Politics, and the Struggle over Working-Class Religion, 1910–1938

1. *Michigan Catholic*, June 9, 1937.

2. See, for instance, Mark A. Noll, *America's God: From Jonathan Edwards to Abraham Lincoln* (New York: Oxford University Press, 2002), esp. 53–93; Nathan O. Hatch, *The Democratization of American Christianity* (New Haven: Yale University Press, 1989).

3. Steve Fraser, "The 'Labor Question,'" in *The Rise and Fall of the New Deal Order, 1930–1980*, ed. Steve Fraser and Gary Gerstle (New York: Cambridge University Press, 1990), 55.

4. The classic "manifesto" of the social gospel is Walter Rauschenbusch, *Christianity and the Social Crisis* (New York: Macmillan, 1907); see also Henry F. May, *Protestant Churches and Industrial America* (New York: Harper and Row, 1949); Susan Curtis, *A Consuming Faith: The Social Gospel and Modern American Culture* (Baltimore: Johns Hopkins University Press, 1991); Paul T. Phillips, *A Kingdom on Earth: Anglo-American Social Christianity, 1880–1940* (Harrisburg: Pennsylvania State University Press, 1996); H. Paul Douglass, *The Church in the Changing City* (New York: Institute of Social and Religious Research, 1927), 151–159. For context, see Richard Wightman Fox, "The Culture of Liberal Protestant Progressivism, 1875–1925," *Journal of Interdisciplinary History* 23 (Winter 1993): 639–660.

5. Walter E. Kruesi, "Report upon Unemployment in the Winter of 1914–1915 in Detroit and the Institutions and Measures of Relief" (n.p. 1915), 5, 11–13.

6. This sentence plays with the elegant phrasing by Jane Addams, "The Subjective Necessity for Social Settlements," in *Philanthropy and Social Progress*, ed. Henry C. Adams (New York, 1893).

7. "Report of the Dodge Community House" (1930) in National Federation of Settlements and Neighborhood Centers, Records, 1891–1961 (hereafter NFSNC), Box 35, Folder 353, Social Welfare History Archive, University of Minnesota, Minneapolis; "The Franklin Scene: An Informal History of Detroit's Oldest Social Settlement" (1948), NFSNC, Box 35, Folder 351; H. Paul Douglass, *The Church in the Changing City* (New York: Institute of Social and Religious Research, 1927), 151–159; on the settlement movement, see Allen Davis, *Spearheads for Reform: The Social Settlements and the Progressive Movement, 1890–1914* rev. ed. (New Brunswick: Rutgers University Press, 1985).

8. "Detroit Is the City of Young Men," in United Community Services of Metropolitan Detroit, Records (hereafter UCS), Box 68, Folder 13, ALUA; "Minutes of

the Detroit Council of Churches, Social Service Department," January 15, 1924, and "Minutes," November 16, 1926, MDCC, Part II, Box 5, Folder 22; YWCA, 20th Annual Statement (1913), 14–15, in UCS, Box 68, Folder 17; "Minutes," TMs, April 20, 1926, DCC, Part II, Box 5, Folder 22, 103.

9. Florence B. Seymour, "Immigrant Welfare Work," in *Eighth National Conference of Catholic Charities* (Washington, D.C.: Catholic University of America Press, 1922), 300–301; Polish Activities League, *Polish Women for Progress*, IHRC, 91; Mrs. Edward A. Skae in *Eleventh National Conference of Catholic Charities* (Washington, D.C.: Catholic University of America Press, 1925), 208.

10. "Oral History Interview with I. Paul Taylor" (1961), TMs, ALUA, 1; I. Paul Taylor, *Prosperity in Detroit* (Detroit, 1919), 56, 58; "The Church League for Industrial Democracy: Containing the Major Portion of the Speeches Made at the Meeting in Arcadia Hall, Detroit, on Sunday Afternoon, October 19, 1919," Pamphlet Collection, Andover Theological Library, Harvard University, Cambridge.

11. Reinhold Niebuhr, *Leaves from the Notebook of a Tamed Cynic* (Chicago: Willett, Clark, and Colby, 1929), 94; Harlan Phillips, "Interview with Dr. Reinhold Niebuhr," Columbia University Oral History Project." On Niebuhr's time in Detroit, see Richard Wightman Fox, *Reinhold Niebuhr: A Biography* (San Francisco: Harper and Row, 1985), 88–110.

12. Niebuhr, *Leaves from the Notebook*, 96; Taylor, *Prosperity in Detroit*, 100.

13. Sean McCloud, *Divine Hierarchies: Class in American Religion and Religious Studies* (Chapel Hill: University of North Carolina Press, 2007), 77–97; consider also Ann Taves, *Fits, Trances, and Visions: Experiencing Religion and Explaining Experience from Wesley to James* (Princeton: Princeton University Press, 1999), 328–347.

14. Haynes, *Negro New-Comers in Detroit*, 31–35; "Report of the Mayor's Committee on Race Relations" (Detroit, 1926), Papers of the National Association for the Advancement of Colored People, Midwest Division, microfilm edition, reel 12.

15. Erdmann Doane Beynon, "Crime and Custom of the Hungarians," 772; Rankin, "Detroit Nationality Groups"; Santini, "The Preservation of St. Joseph's Day"; *Michigan Catholic*, July 3, 1930. On Catholic devotionalism, see Orsi, *Thank You, St. Jude*. D. K. Wilgus, "Country-Western Music and the Urban Hillbilly," *Journal of American Folklore* 83 (April–June 1970): 165.

16. Mayer and Sue Marx, "Social Change, Religion, and Birth Rates," 384; Wilgus, "Country-Western Music," 165; Elmer Akers, "Southern Whites in Detroit" (1937) in Milton Kemnitz Papers, Box 3, Folder "Southern Whites," 7, BHL; Wolcott, *Remaking Respectability*, 113–126; Phillips, "Interview with Dr. Reinhold Niebuhr."

17. John Dancy to F. Marion Woods, TL, September 28, 1928, and John Dancy to Julius Hadley, TL, February 25, 1930, DUL, reel 3. On the "sheep-like" analogy, see Beynon, "Crime and Custom of the Hungarians," 774; Woods, *Hamtramck, Then and Now*, 34.

18. Charles H. Brent, "A Clear Call to Industrial Improvement," in Lyman Pierson Powell, *The Social Unrest: Capital, Labor, and the Public in Turmoil* (Review of Reviews Co., 1919), 417; Lee S. McCollester, with Introduction by Mac H. Wallace, "A

New Emphasis on Some Old American Affirmations; An Address at the Thirteenth Interdenominational Citizens' Thanksgiving Service Detroit, November 1914" (Detroit 1914 [?]).

19. See especially Lazerow, *Religion and the Working Class*, and Fones-Wolf, *Trade Union Gospel*. For workers' traditions of anticlerical "true religion," see Clark D. Halker, *For Democracy, Workers, and God: Labor Song-Poems and Labor Protest, 1865–95* (Urbana: University of Illinois Press, 1991).

20. *American Federationist* 14 (1907); "The Church League for Industrial Democracy: Containing the Major Portion of the Speeches Made at the Meeting in Arcadia Hall, Detroit, on Sunday Afternoon, October 19, 1919"; Samuel Gompers, "An Open Letter to Ministers of the Gospel" (n.d.), in Chancery Collections, Organizations, Box 1, Folder "Association of Catholic Trade Unionists," AAD.

21. "Minutes of the Social Service Department of the Detroit Council of Church," TMs, October 16, 1922, in MDCC, Part II, Box 5, Folder 21, ALUA; "Report of the Detroit Council of Churches for 1922–1923," in UCS, Box 29, Folder 4; H. Paul Douglass, *Protestant Cooperation in American Cities* (New York: Institute of Social and Religious Research, 1930), 385.

22. *New York Times*, October 6, October 7, and October 9, 1926. Other accounts of this imbroglio are provided in Fox, *Reinhold Niebuhr*, 62–111; R. Laurence Moore, *Selling God: American Religion in the Marketplace of Culture* (New York: Oxford University Press, 1994), 219–220.

23. Bennett Stevens, *The Church and the Workers* (New York: International Pamphlets, 1932), 3–4.

24. Frank Marquart, *An Auto Worker's Journal: The UAW from Crusade to One-Party System* (University Park: Pennsylvania State University Press, 1975), 16; Annual Report of the Good Citizenship League, July 1920, and undated TMs (1922?), both in DUL, reel 2; *Michigan Catholic*, August 27, 1937.

25. David M. Kennedy, *Freedom from Fear: The American People in Depression and War, 1929–1945* (New York: Oxford University Press, 1999); Jeff Singleton, *The American Dole: Unemployment Relief and the Welfare State in the Great Depression* (Westport, Conn.: Greenwood Press, 2000); John Dancy to N. B. Allen, TL, March 25, 1933, and Irene Murphy to Arnold Hill, TL, October 27, 1931, and E. K. Jones, TL, March 2, 1933, all in DUL, reel 4.

26. Untitled TMs, July 31, 1934, and "Welfare," TMs, December 1934, both in DUL, reel 15.

27. James K. Pollock and Samuel J. Eldersveld, *Michigan Politics in Transition: An Areal Study of Voting Trends in the Last Decade* (Ann Arbor: University of Michigan Press, 1942), 4, 43–55.

28. Frank Murphy, "Christianity and World War I" (n.d.; 1920s) and Frank Murphy, "Spiritual Values" (n.d.; 1920s), both in Frank Murphy Papers, microfilm edition, BHL, Roll 141; Sidney Fine, *Frank Murphy: The Detroit Years* (Ann Arbor: University of Michigan Press, 1975), 226; Thurman A. Arnold, "Mr. Justice Murphy," *Harvard Law Review* 63 (December 1949): quote on 289.

29. Frank Murphy, "A Mayor's Interpretation of the Encyclical of Leo XIII, after Forty Years" (undated, 1931?), FMP, reel 141; see also Fine, *Frank Murphy*.

30. Dancy, *Sand against the Wind*, 105; "Mrs. John Garth" (Gibson) to Murphy, November 16 (1930?), DUL, reel 17; Edward H. Litchfield, "A Case Study of Negro Political Behavior in Detroit," *Public Opinion Quarterly* 5 (June 1941): 267–274.

31. Fine, *Frank Murphy*; Henry J. Pratt, *Churches and Urban Government in Detroit and New York, 1895–1994* (Detroit: Wayne State University Press, 2004); *Michigan Catholic*, July 5, 1934, September 6, 1934, April 1, 1937, and May 27, 1937; Earl Parker to Kurt Peiser, TL, November 23, 1935, UCS, Box 103, Folder 9; "Informal Committee Members' Suggested Points of Emphasis for Social Service Department," TMs (1942–3?), UCS, Box 29, Folder 13.

32. *Michigan Catholic*, February 8, 1934; *Messenger of St. Rose*, November 4, 1934, AAD.

33. Young and Wheeler, *Hard Stuff*, 38; Pratt, *Churches and Urban Government in Detroit and New York*; Judith Stephan-Norris and Caleb Southworth, "Churches as Organizational Resources: A Case Study of the Geography of Religion and Voting Behavior in Postwar Detroit," *Social Science History* 31 (Fall 2007).

34. "Oral History Interview with John Zaremba" (1961), UAW Oral History Project, ALUA; Dorosh and Roache quotes in Judith Stephan-Norris and Maurice Zeitlin, *Talking Union* (Urbana: University of Illinois Press, 1996), 53, 168; "Report on Mt. Olivet Community Methodist Church" (n.d.), and Owen Geer to William Wolfe, TL, November 26, 1945, in Liston Pope Social Ethics Pamphlets Collections (hereafter SEPC), RG 73, Box 97, Folder 3, Yale University, Divinity Library Special Collections, New Haven.

35. Peter Friedlander, *The Emergence of a UAW Local, 1936–1939: A Study in Class and Culture* (Pittsburgh: University of Pittsburgh Press, 1975), 131. On Friedlander, see Bernard Sternsher, "Great Depression Labor Historiography in the 1970s: Middle-Range Questions, Ethnocultures, and Levels of Generalization," *Reviews in American History* 11 (June 1983): 300–319.

36. *Michigan Catholic*, December 8, 1937; *United Automobile Worker*, January 1, February 5, 1938, and September 18, 1937. On Knox, see also Dillard, *Faith in the City*, 16, 88; *United Automobile Worker*, January 22, 1937; *West Side Conveyor*, September 21 and August 10, 1937. For background on James Myers, see Elizabeth Fones-Wolf and Ken Fones-Wolf, "Lending a Hand to Labor: James Myers and the Federal Council of Churches, 1926–1947," *Church History* 68 (March 1999). For background on Rice, see Heineman, *Catholic New Deal*.

37. *Michigan Catholic*, March 25, 1937; Frank Murphy, "Industrial Peace," *Christian Front* (November 1937); Murphy, "Christianity in Democracy," *Religious Digest* (May 1937), TMs in Frank Murphy Papers, Speech File, 1937; "Governor Frank Murphy's Commencement Address," University of Detroit, June 9, 1937, FMP.

38. *West Side Conveyor*, August 3, 1937; *United Automobile Worker*, April 30, 1938.

39. *West Side Conveyor*, September 7, 1937, October 26, 1937, and October 8, 1938.

40. *United Automobile Worker*, November 26, 1938.

41. *United Automobile Worker*, June 19, 1937.

42. *United Automobile Worker*, July 14, 1937; on the notion of a "culture of unity," see Cohen, *Making a New Deal*.

43. *United Automobile Worker*, May 26, 1936. For context, see Fones-Wolf, *Trade Union Gospel*.

44. "Oral History Interview with John Zaremba"; *United Automobile Worker*, October 22, 1938; Irving Howe and B. J. Widick, *The U.A.W. and Walter Reuther* (New York: Random House, 1949), 51.

Chapter 3. Making Worker Religion in the New Deal Era

1. Erwin A. Lefebvre, "The Encyclical Mass," *Christian Front* (July-August 1937); Labor Research Association, "How the Crisis Hit the Auto Workers" (February 1932), 2–3, DUL, reel 4; Erskine Caldwell, *Some American People* (New York: R. M. McBride and Company, 1935), 169. Quote from John Barnard, *American Vanguard: The United Auto Workers during the Reuther Years, 1935–1970* (Detroit: Wayne State University Press, 2004), 43. See also Steve Babson, *Building the Union: Skilled Workers and Anglo-Gaelic Immigrants in the Rise of U.A.W.* (New Brunswick: Rutgers University Press, 1991); Lichtenstein, *Most Dangerous Man in Detroit*; Robert H. Zieger, *The CIO, 1935–1955* (Chapel Hill: University of North Carolina Press, 1995).

2. Lefebvre, "The Encyclical Mass." See a number of Clancy's invocations, including "Invocation to Be Given at the War Emergency Conference," April 7, 1942, TMs, in Father Raymond S. Clancy Papers, 1896–1970 (hereafter RCP), Box 2, Folder 22, ALUA; quote in Edward Duff, S.J., "Activation in ACTU," *Queen's Work* (May 1946), copy in Norman C. McKenna Papers (hereafter NMP), American Catholic History Research Center, Catholic University of America, Washington, D.C. (hereafter ACHRS), Box 1, Folder 32.

3. Pastor of Our Lady of Help, quoted in Tentler, *Seasons of Grace*, 315; *St. Florian Parish, Hamtramck, Michigan*, 86, AAD; *Messenger of St. Rose*, January 28, February 4, and February 25, 1934, AAD.

4. Michael Denning, *The Cultural Front: The Laboring of American Culture in the Twentieth Century* (New York: Verso, 1996).

5. *Michigan Catholic*, April 15, 1937; see also "An American Workman's Creed," in *Michigan Catholic*, January 4, 1940.

6. On the banner, see *Michigan Catholic*, September 14, 1939; Eric Hobsbawm and Terence Rangers, eds., *The Invention of Tradition* (New York: Cambridge University Press, 1983). For intellectual background, see Thomas E. Woods, *The Church Confronts Modernity: Catholic Intellectuals and the Progressive Era* (New York: Columbia University Press, 2004). For an interesting assessment of Catholic architecture, see Paula M. Kane, *Separatism and Subculture: Boston Catholicism, 1900–1920* (Chapel Hill: University of North Carolina Press, 1994).

7. "I Worked for Ford," *Christian Front*, October 1938. On this ideology, see especially John T. McGreevy, *Catholicism and American Freedom: A History* (New York: W. W. Norton, 2003).

8. On Coughlin, see Alan Brinkley, *Voices of Protest: Huey Long, Father Coughlin, and the Great Depression* (New York: Knopf, 1982); Michael Kazin, *The Populist Persuasion: An American History* (New York: BasicBooks, 1995), 109–134.

9. See especially Barnard, *American Vanguard*, 53; Brinkley, *Voices of Protest*, 83.

10. Charles E. Coughlin, *Father Coughlin's Radio Discourses, 1930/31* (Royal Oak, Mich.: The Radio League of the Little Flower, 1931), 22, 86, 98. Charles E. Coughlin, *A Series of Lectures on Social Justice* (Royal Oak: Radio League of the Little Flower, 1935), 27, 53.

11. *United Automobile Worker*, May 1936; Steve Jeffrys, "'Matters of Mutual Interest': The Unionization Process at Dodge Main, 1933–1939," in Lichtenstein and Meyer, *On the Line*.

12. Brinkley, *Voices of Protest*, 269–283.

13. Mooney quoted in *Michigan Catholic*, September 16, 1937.

14. *Michigan Catholic*, August 3 and August 12, 1937, October 7, 1937, and December 8, 1937; *Catholic Worker*, June 1937; *United Automobile Worker*, January 1, 1938; Fr. Clare Murphy to members of Catholic Study Clubs, July 16, 1938, in F. J. Patrick McCarthy Papers, Box 17, Folder 6, Archives of the University of Notre Dame (hereafter AUND).

15. *Catholic Worker*, October 1937, and November 1937. On the Catholic Worker movement, see Mel Piehl, *Breaking Bread: The Catholic Worker and the Origin of Catholic Radicalism in America* (Philadelphia: Temple University Press, 1982) and James Terence Fisher, *The Catholic Counterculture in America, 1933–1962* (Chapel Hill: University of North Carolina Press, 1989).

16. *Catholic Worker*, May 1938.

17. For a profile of the Detroit group, and pronunciation of "Act Too!" see Duff, "Activation in ACTU"; on ACTU, see Douglas P. Seaton, *Catholics and Radicals: The Associated Catholic Trade Unionists and the American Labor Movement: From Depression to Cold War* (Lewisburg: Bucknell University Press, 1981); Steve Rosswurm, "The Catholic Church and the Left-Led Unions: Labor Priests, Labor Schools, and the A.C.T.U.," in *The C.I.O.'S Left-Led Unions*, ed. Steve Rosswurm (New Brunswick: Rutgers University Press, 1992).

18. Cort quoted in *Voices from the Catholic Worker*, ed. Rosalie Riegle Troester (Philadelphia: Temple University Press, 1993), 14; see also John C. Cort, *Dreadful Conversions: The Making of a Catholic Socialist* (New York: Fordham University Press, 2003).

19. "Constitution of the ACTU," July 15, 1938, in ACTU Detroit Chapter Records, 1938–1968 (hereafter ACTU), Box 1, Folder 1, ALUA; for quote see Duff, "Activation in ACTU."

20. "Minutes of the Meeting of January 26, 1939, to Plan Parish Labor Schools," in RCP, Box 1, Folder 15, LLUA; see also Raymond Clancy, "Detroit ALI," *Christian Social Action*, December 1939.

21. *Christian Social Action*, September 1939.

22. Philip Taft, "The Association of Catholic Trade Unionists," *Industrial and Labor Relations Review* 2, no. 2 (1949): 211, 215; Cort, *Dreadful Conversions*, 160; Denning,

Cultural Front; I borrow the phrase "spiritual front" from Fisher, *On the Irish Waterfront*.

23. Notices in ACTU, Box 1, Folders 4 and 5.

24. Newsletter in ACTU, Box 23, Folder "Chrysler Local 7."

25. "Minutes of St Gregory Unit" and "ACTU Bulletin" both in ACTU, Box 3, Folder "Parish Captain Minutes."

26. "ACTU Bulletin," in ACTU, Box 3, Folder "Parish Captain Minutes."

27. *United Automobile Worker*, April 16, 1938; *Catholic Worker*, January 1938; Fr. Clare Murphy to members of Catholic Study Clubs, TL, July 16, 1938, in F. J. Patrick McCarthy Papers, Box 17, Folder 6, AUND; "Interview with Msg. Clement Kern," TMs, April 7, 1979, in Non-Chancery Records, Personal Papers, Reverend Clement Kern, Box 24, AAD; Sebastian Erbacher to Norman McKenna, February 25, 1938, NMP, Box 1, Folder 6; Neil O'Connor, "Priests and Labor," *Christian Front*, October 1938.

28. *Michigan Catholic*, August 15, 1940; Raymond McGowan to Raymond Clancy, TL, July 26, 1940, Records of the Social Action Department, National Catholic Welfare Conference Collection (hereafter NCWC), ACHRC, Box 41, Folder 11. On the working-class origins of many Detroit priests after the 1910s, see Leslie Woodcock Tentler, "'God's Representative in Our Midst': Toward a History of the Catholic Diocesan Clergy in the United States," *Church History* 67 (June 1998): 326–349, esp. 330–331.

29. Clerical assessments of the labor schools in RCP, Box 1, Folder 18.

30. Ibid.

31. Student's assessments of the labor schools contained in RCP, Box 1, Folders 16 and 17.

32. On Pinkowicz, see Peter Friedlander, *Emergence of a UAW Local, 1936–1939: A Study in Class and Culture* (Pittsburgh: University of Pittsburgh Press, 1975), esp. 24–30; student's assessments of the labor schools contained in RCP, Box 1, Folders 16 and 17.

33. Richard J. Ward, "The Role of the Association of Catholic Trade Unionists in the Labor Movement," *Review of Social Economy* 16 (September 1956): 86, copy in George Gilmary Higgins Papers, 1932–2002, Subject Files: ACTU, 1949–1968 (partially processed; hereafter GHP), American Catholic History Research Center, Catholic University of America, Washington, D.C. (hereafter ACHRC); "Introductory Talk: 'Not by Bread Alone, Doth Man Live!'" TMs, ACTU, Box 3, Folder "ACTU Lectures." It is unclear who actually wrote this lecture.

34. *Messenger of Saint Rose*, November 18, 1934, AAD; prayer card in ACTU, Box 1, Folder 1.

35. For context, see Andrew Billingsley, *Mighty like a River: The Black Church and Social Reform* (New York: Oxford University Press, 1999); Ralph E. Luker, *The Social Gospel in Black and White: American Racial Reform, 1885–1912* (Chapel Hill: University of North Carolina Press, 1991); Lawrence H. Mamiva and C. Eric Lincoln, *The Black Church in the African-American Experience* (Durham: Duke University Press), 1990.

36. "Oral History Interview with Charles A. Hill," in UAW Oral History Collection, ALUA; Winter and Goodman quoted in Moon, *Untold Tales, Unsung Heroes*, 68, 261; "Conversation with Charles A. Hill," and "Conversation with Gloster Current," both in "Survey of Racial and Religious Conflict Forces in Detroit," Civil Rights Congress of Michigan, Box 71, Folder "Survey," ALUA; *Michigan Chronicle*, September 25, 1942.

37. Llody H. Bailer, "The Automobile Unions and Negro Labor," *Political Science Quarterly* 59 (December 1944): 548–577; August Meier and Elliott Rudwick, *Black Detroit and the Rise of the UAW* (New York: Oxford University Press, 1979), 9–10; "St. Matthew's Church," June 16, 1929, TMs, in St. Matthew's and St. Joseph's Episcopal Church, Records, Box 2, Folder "Newsletters," BHL.

38. John Dancy to Robert Weaver, April 23, 1934, and "Survey" by Michigan State Employment Service (May 1934?), in DUL, reel 5; John Dancy to Forrester Washington, January 26, 1933, in DUL, reel 5; "March Report" of Department of Public Welfare (1934), in DUL, reel 15; Department of Public Welfare to John Dancy, September 6, 1933, in DUL, reel 15; "Minutes of the Social Service Department," May 11, 1937, in MDCC, Part II, Box 5, Folder 32.

39. John Dancy to Walter White, March 9, 1932, DUL, reel 5; McKinney quoted in Moon, *Untold Tales*, 123; Robert Bradby to Dr. Stewart Hamilton, July 31, 1929, and Robert Bradby to Robert Oakman, December 30, 1930, both in SBC, reel 1.

40. Wright and Ross quoted in Moon, *Untold Tales, Unsung Heroes*, 94. Department of Public Welfare to John Dancy, September 6, 1933, in DUL, reel 15; Solomon Ross in "Greater Shiloh Informer," May 25, 1930, in Greater Shiloh Missionary Baptist Church Records, ca. 1920–2008, BHL.

41. Erdmann Doane Beynon, "The Voodoo Cult among Negro Migrants in Detroit," *American Journal of Sociology* 43 (May 1938). See also Marable, *Malcolm X*, 86–90.

42. Beynon, "Voodoo Cult," 905; Fauset, *Black Gods of the Metropolis*, 42–43; A. N. Henniger to Milwaukee Urban League, February 11, 1935, and John Dancy to Milwaukee Urban League, February 18, 1935, DUL, reel 5; "Oral History Interview with Shelton Tappes, Interview #1, Part #1," UAW Oral History Project (1961) TMs, ALUA, 25.

43. Untitled TMs, October 6, 1931, DUL, reel 3; John Dancy to Andrew Sneed, March 8, 1937, reel 6.

44. *United Automobile Worker*, July 24 and July 31, 1937; John Dancy to William Peck, July 9, 1937, DUL, reel 6.

45. Robert Bradby to Rev. R. Moody, TL, April 23, 1931, and Bradby to Walter White, April 24, 1931, both in SBC, reel 1.

46. *United Automobile Worker*, March 5, 1938; Wolcott, *Remaking Respectability*, 213; "What Are You Going to Do about It?" January 1934, DUL, reel 4; Dillard also discusses Grigsby in *Faith in the City*.

47. Meier and Rudwick, *Black Detroit and the Rise of the UAW*, 16; "Oral History Interview with Malcolm Dade," TMs (1969), UAW Oral History Project, ALUA, 4–5.

48. John Dancy to Samuel Allen, TL, March 20, 1935, DUL, reel 5; Meier and Rudwick, *Black Detroit and the Rise of the UAW*, 33.

49. Horace A. White, "Who Owns the Black Church?" *Christian Century*, February 9, 1938; *United Automobile Worker*, June 23, 1937.

50. "Oral History Interview with Malcolm Dade"; for an interesting self-assessment of his religious work, see Malcolm D. Dade, "Recollections of Missionary Work among Blacks in the Episcopal Diocese of Michigan, 1936–1972," in Episcopal Church, Diocese of Michigan Records, Box 1, BHL.

51. "Oral History Interview with Malcolm Dade," 16.

52. Dillard, *Faith in the City*, esp. 27–40. Unfortunately, Hill's papers at the BHL do not provide much biographical background.

53. Ibid.

54. "Oral History Interview with Charles A. Hill."

55. On Bowman, see Meier and Rudwick, *Black Detroit and the Rise of the UAW*, 43; *United Automobile Worker*, June 30, 1937.

56. "Oral History Interview with Shelton Tappes," UAW Oral History Project (1961), ALUA, 37; Boggs quoted in Moon, *Untold Tales, Unsung Heroes*.

57. "Oral history Interview with Charles A. Hill"; Winter and Goodman quoted in Moon, *Untold Tales, Unsung Heroes*, 68, 261.

58. See the many notices of social groups in Records of Hartford Ave. Baptist Church, BHL; Margaret McCall, *The History of Plymouth Congregational Church, 1919–1969* (Detroit: Historical Committee, 1969).

59. Louis Adamic, "The Hill-Billies Come to Detroit," *The Nation*, February 13, 1935; Erdmann Doane Beynon, "The Southern White Laborer Migrates to Michigan," *American Sociological Review* 3 (June 1938).

60. Margaret Terry Buchanan, "The Migration of Workers from Tennessee to Michigan" (Nashville: Vanderbilt University, 1940); "Interview with Andrew Cotham," and Akers, "Southern Whites in Detroit" (1937), 19–21, in Milton Kemnitz Papers, Box 3, Folder "Southern Whites," BHL.

61. Akers, "Southern Whites in Detroit"; Erskine Caldwell, *Some American People* (New York: R. M. McBride and Company, 1935), 180–182; Margaret Collingwood Nowak, *Two Who Were There: A Biography of Stanley Nowak* (Detroit: Wayne State University Press, 1990).

62. Akers, "Southern Whites in Detroit," 2; Wilgus, "Country-Western Music,"165.

63. Liston Pope, *Millhands & Preachers* (New Haven: Yale University Press, 1942), 91; Wilgus, "Country-Western Music," 158–159; Beynon, "Southern White Laborer Migrates to Detroit."

64. See Jacquelyn Dowd Hall, *Like a Family: The Making of a Southern Cotton Mill World* (Chapel Hill: University of North Carolina Press, 1987); Randall J. Stephens, *The Fire Spreads: Holiness and Pentecostalism in the American South* (Cambridge: Harvard University Press, 2010); Paul Harvey, *Freedom's Coming: Religious Culture and the Shaping of the South from the Civil War through the Civil Rights Era* (Chapel Hill: University of North Carolina Press, 2005); Deborah Vansau McCauley, *Appalachian Mountain Religion: A History* (Urbana: University of Illinois Press, 1995).

65. For context, see Christine Leigh Heyrman, *Southern Cross: The Beginnings*

of the Bible Belt (Chapel Hill: University of North Carolina Press, 1998); Thomas S. Kidd, *The Great Awakening: The Roots of Evangelical Christianity in Colonial America* (New Haven: Yale University Press, 2009), 234–267.

66. Elizabeth R. Hooker, "Religion in the Highlands: Native Churches and Missionary Enterprises in the Southern Appalachian Area" (New York: Home Missions Council, 1933), 153.

67. Akers, "Southern Whites in Detroit," 56.

68. Wayne Flynt, "Religion for the Blues: Evangelicalism, Poor Whites, and the Great Depression," *Journal of Southern History* 71 (February 2005): 3–38; Callahan Jr., *Work and Faith in the Kentucky Coal Fields*; Hooker, "Religion in the Highlands," 152.

69. James M. Gregory, *The Southern Diaspora: How the Great Migrations of Black and White Southerners Transformed America* (Chapel Hill: University of North Carolina Press, 2005), 202–209; Barry Hankins, *God's Rascal: J. Frank Norris and the Beginnings of Southern Fundamentalism* (Lexington: University Press of Kentucky, 1996), 90–91.

70. Carpenter, *Revive Us Again*, 49–51.

71. Hankins, *God's Rascal*, quote on 108; *Fundamentalist*, June 5, 1936 (copy at Minnesota Historical Society, St. Paul).

72. See Matthew Avery Sutton, "Was FDR the Antichrist? The Birth of Fundamentalist Antiliberalism in a Global Age," *Journal of American History* 98, no. 4 (2012): 1052–1074.

73. Lloyd Langworthy and Iva Langworthy to Detroit Community Fund, May 24, 1937, and R. Jenkins to Percival Dodge, June 19, 1937, both in United Community Services of Metropolitan Detroit, Records, Box 68, Folder 7, ALUA.

74. "Interview with Eva Anderson," in Milton Kemnitz Papers, BHL; Akers, "Southern Whites in Detroit," 55; Flynt, "Religion for the Blues," 27–28.

75. Beynon, "Southern White Laborer Migrates to Michigan," 335; Akers, "Southern Whites in Detroit," 24 and 58; for Strong, see Nancy Felice Gabin, *Feminism in the Labor Movement: Women and the United Auto Workers, 1935–1975* (Ithaca: Cornell University Press, 1990), 79; the intermingling of religion and labor protest was far from unusual for poor white southerners during the Great Depression; see Flynt, "Religion for the Blues," 20–21; Jarod Roll, *Spirit of Rebellion: Labor and Religion in the New Cotton South* (Urbana: University of Illinois Press, 2010).

76. "I Was a Ford Preacher," *United Automobile Worker*, November 15, 1940.

77. Ibid.

Chapter 4. Race, Politics, and Worker Religion in Wartime Detroit, 1941–1946

1. *United Automobile Worker*, June 11, 1938; Hankins, *God's Rascal*, esp. 90–117.

2. *United Automobile Worker*, November 29, 1939; *United Automobile Worker*, May 1, 1940. On Coughlin, see Brinkley, *Voices of Protest*; Kazin, *Populist Persuasion*. On Smith, see Glen Jeansonne, *Gerald L. K. Smith: Minister of Hate* (New Haven: Yale University Press, 1988); Leo P. Ribuffo, *The Old Christian Right: The Protestant Far*

Right from the Great Depression to the Cold War (Philadelphia: Temple University Press, 1983).

3. On Williams, see Gellman and Roll, *Gospel of the Working Class*, and Dillard, *Faith in the City*.

4. Beth T. Bates, "'Double V for Victory' Galvanizes Black Detroit," in *Freedom North: Black Freedom Struggles outside the South, 1940–1980*, ed. Jeanne Theoharis and Komozi Woodard (New York: Palgrave Macmillan, 2003), 17–39; Nelson Lichtenstein and Robert Korstad, "Opportunities Found and Lost: Labor, Radicals, and the Early Civil Rights Movement," *Journal of American History* 75 (December 1988): 786–811.

5. *Cross and the Flag*, August 1943 and September 1943. For context, see Joel A. Carpenter, *Revive Us Again: The Reawakening of American Fundamentalism* (New York: Oxford University Press, 1997); Daniel K. Williams, *God's Own Party: The Making of the Christian Right* (New York: Oxford University Press, 2010).

6. See Jenny Franchot, *Roads to Rome: The Antebellum Protestant Encounter with Catholicism* (Berkeley: University of California Press, 1994); McGreevy, *Catholicism and American Freedom*.

7. McGreevy, *Catholicism and American Freedom*, 170–172; Peter D'Agostino, *Rome in America: Transnational Catholic Ideology from Risorgimento to Fascism* (Chapel Hill: University of North Carolina Press, 2004), esp. 197–281.

8. "Interview with Joseph Ferris," *UAW Oral History Project*, ALUA, 8; "Interview with John Zaremba," *UAW Oral History Project*, ALUA; *Wyndham Mortimer, Organize! My Life as a Union Man*, ed. Leo Fenster (Boston: Beacon Press, 1971), 96–97; *United Automobile Worker*, November 26, 1938; on Coughlin and fascism, see Brinkley, *Voices of Protest*, 261–283.

9. Raymond Clancy, "Talk on the Industrial Dispute," November 15, 1939, RCP, Box 4, Folder 2; *Michigan Catholic*, November 16, 1939; see also Cort, *Dreadful Conversions*, 103–104.

10. George Addes to Raymond Clancy, November 20, 1939, and Frank Boucher to Raymond Clancy, November 16, 1939, both in RCP, Box 4, Folder 2.

11. Clancy, "Talk on the Industrial Dispute."

12. "Resolution," August 5, 1938, ACTU, Box 34, Folder "UAW, 1938–1940," ALUA. The ACTU paper, *Wage Earner*, published its economic platform in nearly every issue from the early 1940s. For context, see Rosswurm, "The Catholic Church and the Left-Led Unions."

13. Sebastian Erbacher to Norman McKenna, February 25, 1938, NMP, Box 1, Folder 6, ACHRS; *Wage Earner*, October 14, 1940; Richard Deverall to George Seldes, April 6, 1942, in NMP, Box 1, Folder 14; "Industrial Conference Reports, Season 1939: The Detroit Meeting," NCWC, ACHRC, Box 36, Folder 13.

14. Unattributed TL, February 16, 1946, in NMP, Box 1, Folder 32; Horace Sheffield quoted in Stephan-Norris and Zeitlin, *Talking Union*, 173.

15. ALI student surveys in RCP, Box 1, Folders 16 and 17; statement of support for Reuther in ACTU, Box 3, Folder "UAW"; see also Edward Duff, S.J., "Activation in ACTU," *Queen's Work* (May 1946), copy in NMP, Box 1, Folder 32.

16. *Michigan Catholic*, November 16, 1939; "Conversations with Father J. L. Cavanaugh and Father John Coogan, S.J.," in "Survey of Racial and Religious Conflict Forces in Detroit" (September 1943), Civil Rights Congress of Michigan, Box 71, Folder "Survey," ALUA; "Oral History Interview with Frank Marquart," UAW Oral History Project, ALUA; Sheffield quoted in Stephan-Norris and Zeitlin, *Talking Union*, 173.

17. "Coughlin Family Activities at the Shrine of the Little Flower," in "Survey of Racial and Religious Conflict Forces in Detroit."

18. Edgar DeWitt Jones, "Strange Churches Rise in Detroit," *Christian Century*, December 9, 1942; War Emergency Commission of the Detroit Council of Churches, "Mobilization for War-Time Services and Reconstruction" (1943?), MDCC, Part II, Box 5, Folder 1, ALUA; "Report for the Summer, 1945," in MDCC, Part II, Box 5, Folder 2; "The Religious Ferment in Detroit" and "The Hill-Billies as Strikebreakers," both in "Survey of Racial and Religious Conflict Forces in Detroit."

19. Charles Allen to the Detroit Council of Churches, TL, April 30, 1943, in Claude Williams Papers (hereafter CWP), Box 2, Folder 20, ALUA; Claude Williams, "The Hell-Brewers of Detroit," and Claude Williams, "The Scriptural Heritage of the People," in Liston Pope Social Ethics Pamphlet Collection (hereafter LPSEPC), RG 73, Box 111, Folder "People's Institute of Applied Religion," Special Collections, Yale University Divinity Library, New Haven; Thomas's comments in "First Report of Peoples' Congress of Applied Religion (July 22–24, 1944)" in CWP, Box 19, Folder 5.

20. Wilbur Larremore Caswell, "Educating the 'Bible Christian,'" *Churchman*, February 15, 1944; *Cross and the Flag*, April 1942 and July 1942; "Survey of Racial and Religious Conflict Forces in Detroit."

21. *Cross and the Flag*, July 1943 and September 1945; "Harvey Springer to Invade the East," in "Survey of Racial and Religious Conflict Forces in Detroit."

22. Henry Jones, and the ministers of Central Methodist and Bethel Evangelical, to William Ostrander, February 1941, CWP, Box 18, Folder 10. See also Jones's commissioned biography, Cedric Belfrage, *A Faith to Free the People* (New York: Dryden Press, 1944).

23. Claude Williams, "From Personal Notes to a Friend" (n.d.), TMs, CWP, Box 18, Folder 10; see also Belfrage, *Faith to Free the People*.

24. Sourlock (first name unknown), "The People's Institute of Applied Religion" (July 1945) in LPSEPC, RG 73, Box 111, Folder "People's Institute"; Claude Williams to Benjamin Bush, et al., May 11, 1944, in CWP, Box 19, Folder 12.

25. Henry Jones, et al., to Jacob Long, Board of National Missions, April 30, 1943, CWP, Box 2, Folder 20; Claude Williams to Herbert Hudnut, March 9, 1944, CWP, Box 19, Folder 12; Williams, "Report on Work under War Emergency Program," August 31, 1944, CWP, Box 19, Folder 12.

26. Williams, "Scriptural Heritage of the People."

27. Belfrage, *Faith to Free the People*, 260; Studs Terkel, *Hard Times: An Oral History of the Great Depression* (New York: Pantheon Books, 1970), 380.

28. Claude Williams, "The Galilean and the Common People," CWP, Box 18, Folder

15; see, for example, *Michigan Chronicle*, May 29 and October 30, 1943; Belfrage, *Faith to Free the People*, 260–261; *United Automobile Worker*, November 15, 1940.

29. Terkel, *Hard Times*, 379; Williams, "Scriptural Heritage of the People"; *Songs in CWP*, Box 19, Folder 6.

30. Claude Williams, "Creative Churchmanship among Urban Industrial Workers" (February 1945) and Claude Williams, "One God, One People, One Goal: Theistic Collectivism," in LPSEPC, RG 73, Box 111, Folder "People's Institute," TMs (n.d., May 1944?), CWP, Box 18, Folder 22; Claude Williams to Benjamin Bush, et al., TL, May 11, 1944, CWP, Box 19, Folder 12.

31. "Gospel Preachers' Council" announced on TMs (1944), CWP, Box 18, Folder 10; "The Man Who Has an Answer" in LPSEPC, RG 73, Box 111, Folder "People's Institute"; Claude Williams to "Sponsors and Friends" (1943) in United Presbyterian Church in the U.S.A., Records (hereafter UPC), Box 8, BHL.

32. Claude Williams to Herbert Hudnut, TL, March 9, 1944, CWP, Box 19, Folder 12; undated TMs (May 1944?), CWP, Box 18, Folder 22.

33. "First Report of Peoples' Congress of Applied Religion" (July 22–24, 1944) CWP, Box 19, Folder 5; CWP, Box 19, Folder 5; Williams, "Report on Work," August 31, 1944, CWP, Box 19, Folder 12. The Peoples' Institute would later be named as a Communist front in the sensationalist exposé by J. B. Matthews, "Reds and Our Churches," *American Mercury* 77 (July 1953): 3–13.

34. Williams, "Creative Churchmanship."

35. Williams, "Report on Work."

36. Belfrage, *Faith to Free the People*, 283–288; Norris is quoted in "The Man Who Has an Answer"; National Laymen's Council, "Special Report—Involving the Rev. H. P. Marley," TMs (1944?) UPC, Box 8.

37. *Cross and the Flag*, November 1944, February 1945, September 1945, and March 1946.

38. *Cross and the Flag*, June 1943 and October 1944; Minutes of St. Gregory Chapter, September 25, 1939, in ACTU, Box 3, Folder, "Parish Captain Minutes."

39. Bates, "'Double V for Victory'"; Dillard, *Faith in the City*.

40. Dade, "Recollections of Missionary Work"; *Michigan Chronicle*, April 8, 1944, and March 2, 1946.

41. "TO: The Committee on Race Relations of the Michigan Council of Churches" (June 1943), UCS, Box 107, Folder 15; "Oral History Interview with Charles A. Hill," *UAW Oral History Project*, ALUA, 7, 41. For the broader context of "Brotherhood," see David W. Wills, "An Enduring Distance: Black Americans and the Establishment," in *Between the Times: The Travail of the Protestant Establishment in America, 1900–1960*, ed. William R. Hutchison (New York: Cambridge University Press, 1989).

42. See *Michigan Chronicle*, May 15, 1943, February 8, 1947, February 15, 1947, and May 3, 1952.

43. *Wage Earner*, June 11 and June 25, 1943.

44. *Michigan Catholic*, July 15 and October 28, 1943; Catholic Interracial Council, "Bulletin" (September 1946), in ACTU, Box 11, Folder "Catholic Interracial Group."

45. Claude Williams, "Anti-Semitism, Racism, and Democracy," in LPSEPC, RG 73, Box 111, Folder "People's Institute."

46. "'Of One Blood All Nations': An Interracial Code for Protestant Churches," February 17, 1944, in UCS, Box 29, Folder 14; "Summary of the Interracial Workshop Conference Sponsored by City of Detroit Interracial Committee," June 1, 1945, in UCS, Box 101, Folder 14.

47. Louis E. Martin, "Profiles: Detroit," *Journal of Educational Sociology* 17 (January 1944): 285; Dade, "Recollections of Missionary Work," 12; *Michigan Chronicle*, April 8, 1944, and February 22, 1947.

48. "Interview with the Rev. Claude Williams," in "Survey of Racial and Religious Conflict Forces in Detroit"; Williams to Herbert Hudnut, March 9, 1944, in CWP, Box 19, Folder 12.

49. Meier and Rudwick, *Black Detroit and the Rise of the UAW*, 125–136; Zieger, *CIO*, 155; Wood in "Race Conflicts in Detroit Riots," in "Survey of Racial and Religious Conflict Forces in Detroit."

50. "Talk with Leroy Spradley," in "Survey of Racial and Religious Conflict Forces in Detroit."

51. "Visit to Bishop Stephen Woznicki" and "Relations between Poles and Jews," in "Survey of Racial and Religious Conflict Forces in Detroit"; see also John T. McGreevy, *Parish Boundaries: The Catholic Encounter with Race in the Twentieth-Century Urban North* (Chicago: University of Chicago Press, 1996), 74–77.

52. Dominic J. Capeci, *Race Relations in Wartime Detroit: The Sojourner Truth Housing Controversy of 1942* (Philadelphia: Temple University Press, Date?); Sugrue, *Origins of the Urban Crisis*, 33–57.

53. Charles Livermore to Robert MacRae, December 5, 1941, in UCS, Box 110, Folder 9; "Conversation with Father Constantine Djuik [*sic*]," in "Survey of Racial and Religious Conflict Forces in Detroit"; "Detroit: A Survey and a Program of Action," TMs (n.d., but probably around 1944), in UCS, Box 101, Folder 13.

54. *Catholic Worker*, March 1942.

55. Capeci, *Race Relations*, 93, 98–99. On Jeffries's hard swing to the right on racial issues, see Carl O. Smith and Stephen B. Sarasohn, "Hate Propaganda in Detroit," *Public Opinion Quarterly* 10 (Spring 1946): 24–52.

56. "To Loyal and Patriotic Polish-Americans Living near Sojourner Truth Homes" (1942), UCS, Box 110, Folder 10; "A Statement of a Point of View Regarding the Sojourner Truth Homes Controversy" (1942) in UCS, Box 110, Folder 11; "Oral History Interview with Charles A. Hill," LLUA, 14.

57. "Michigan Governor's Committee to Investigate the Detroit Race Riots" (1943), Box 1, Folder 2, University of Chicago, Special Collections, 12–13.

58. *Cross and the Flag*, July 1943.

59. *Michigan Chronicle*, August 21, 1943.

Chapter 5. The Decline of Worker Religion, 1946–1963

1. See correspondence from William Ryan to ACTU members and area priests, August 1955, ACTU, Box 4, Folder "Labor Day 1955," ALUA; "Labor Day Missal, Mass of Saint Joseph, the Workman," ACTU, Box 4, Folder "Labor Day Mass, 1956."

2. *Wage Earner*, July 1959.

3. Jason W. Stevens, *God-Fearing and Free: A Spiritual History of America's Cold War* (Cambridge: Harvard University Press, 2010), esp. 87–141. For context, see also Stephen J. Whitfield, *The Culture of the Cold War* (Baltimore: Johns Hopkins University Press, 1996), 77–100.

4. "Assumption Grotto Parish, 1832–1982," EASC, Box 16, Folder 12, AUND. For context, see Colleen Doody, *Detroit's Cold War: The Origins of Postwar Conservatism* (Urbana: University of Illinois Press, 2013), and Paula M. Kane, "Marian Devotions since 1940: Continuity or Casualty?" in *Habits of Devotion: Catholic Religious Practice in Twentieth Century America*, ed. James M. O'Toole (Ithaca: Cornell University Press, 2004), 131–186.

5. *Michigan Catholic*, May 4, May 27, and April 27, 1954; "Golden Jubilee of St. Ladislaus Parish, 1920–1970: The Growth of a Community" (n.p.); *Michigan Catholic*, August 3, 1950; Susan Parkanzky, "A Study of Folklore in Catholic School," unpublished TMs, Folklore Archive, ALUA.

6. George Higgins to Edward Mooney, January 3, 1956, and John Coogan to George Higgins, December 9, 1956, both in GHP, Subject Files: "Correspondence: Archdiocese of Detroit," ACHRC.

7. *Michigan Catholic*, July 22, 1954; Fr. Karl Hubble, Untitled TMs, ACTU, Box 4, Folder "Fr. Hubble's Report"; *Work* (August 1956), in GHP, Subject files: ACTU, 1949–1968.

8. Michael H. Rawlins to Archbishop Mooney, August 28, 1948, Chancery Collections, Organizations, Box 1, Folder "Catholic Workers," AAD.

9. Sourlock, "The People's Institute of Applied Religion," and Royal Wilbur France, "The Case of Claude Williams" (1953?), both in LPSEPC, RG 73, Box 111, Folder "People's Institute of Applied Religion," Special Collections, Yale University Divinity Library, New Haven; Claude Williams to Henry Jones, February 3, 1945, and Claude Williams to Benjamin Bush, et al., May 11, 1944, both in CWP, Box 19, Folder 12, ALUA.

10. Henry Jones and John Forsyth to the Board of Church Extension, February 7, 1945, UPC, Box 8, BHL.

11. "Minutes of Presbytery Committee to Sponsor the Program of our Minister to Labor," December 1, 1944; Shelton Tappes to Leslie Bechtel, February 21, 1945, and Cecil Galey to Bechtel (n.d.), all in UPC, Box 8.

12. Sourlock, "The People's Institute of Applied Religion," and Royal Wilbur France, "The Case of Claude Williams" (1953?), in LPSEPC, RG 73, Box 111, Folder "People's Institute"; "PIAR Bulletin," August 1946, and "PIAR Bulletin," May 1947, both in CWP, Box 18, Folder 2.

13. *Michigan Chronicle*, April 5, 1947; "Oral History Interview with Charles A. Hill," UAW Oral History Archive, ALUA; Young and Wheeler, *Hard Stuff*, 44.

14. Many news clippings from the late 1940s, collected in the Charles A. Hill Papers, BHL, document Hill's associations; see also Dillard, *Faith in the City*.

15. Horace White's testimony in "Communism in the Detroit Area: Hearings before the House Committee on Un-American Activities," 82nd Congress, Second Session (February 1952); *Michigan Chronicle*, April 12, 1947.

16. Documents in ACTU, Box 18, Folder "FEPC-Council Ordinance, 1951"; see also documents in UCS, Box 101, Folder 21, ALUA; Sugrue, *Origins of the Urban Crisis*, 170–177.

17. Marie Oresti, to members, July 17, 1951; DCCEEO Press Release, June 29, 1951; Michigan State Committee of the Communist Party, Press release, July 20, 1951, all in ACTU, Box 18, Folder "FEPC-Council Ordinance, 1951."

18. *Michigan Chronicle*, February 15, 1947.

19. Sugrue, *Origins of the Urban Crisis*, 143–144; Jacqueline Jones, *American Work: Four Centuries of Black and White Labor* (New York: W. W. Norton, 1998), 359.

20. Bryan Thompson and Carol Agocs, "Mapping the Distribution of Ethnic Groups in Metropolitan Detroit: A Preliminary Report," n.p. (April 1972), IHRC, 30–31; Sugrue, *Origins of the Urban Crisis*, 130–135; Mel Ravitz, "Problems and Possibilities of the City Church" (1959), MDCC, Box 12, Folder "Problems," ALUA; Mary West Jorgensen, "F.O.B. Detroit" (n.d., probably 1950) and "Franklin Neighborhood" (1951), both in NFSNC, Box 35, Folder 351, University of Minnesota, Minneapolis.

21. Sugrue, *Origins of the Urban Crisis*, 23; Gerhard Lenski, *The Religious Factor: A Sociological Study of Religion's Impact on Politics, Economics, and Family Life* (Garden City, N.Y.: Doubleday, 1961), 66–67; Detroit Urban League, "A Profile of the Detroit Negro, 1959–1967" (n.p., 1967), 49.

22. McGreevy, *Parish Boundaries*; J. David Greenstone, "A Report on the Politics of Detroit" (Cambridge: Joint Center for Urban Studies of the Massachusetts Institute of Technology and Harvard University, 1961), 1–5; Lenski, *Religious Factor*, 34–44; John O'Grady, "The Changing Parish" (n.d.), in Records of the National Conference of Catholic Charities, Reference folder 3 (partially processed), ACHRC.

23. *Michigan Catholic*, February 9, 1956; Sophie Wright Settlement, Annual Report (1956), in NFSNC, Box 74, Folder 7; Thompson and Agocs, "Mapping the Distribution of Ethnic Groups," 31; Paul Clemens, *Made in Detroit: A South-of-8-Mile Memoir* (New York: Doubleday, 2005), 52.

24. Skendzel, *Detroit St. Josaphat Story*; *St. Florian Parish, Hamtramck, Michigan*, 68, AAD; Cahill and Cornwell, *Life and Spirit*.

25. Genevieve M. Casey, *Father Clem Kern, Conscience of Detroit* (Detroit: Marygrove College, 1989).

26. In 1962, Michigan Congressman Charles Diggs read a profile of Kern, written for the *Detroit Free Press*, into the *Congressional Record* to commemorate Kern's service; for a copy, see GHP, "Correspondence: Clement Kern." See also *Wage Earner*, February 1959.

27. *Wage Earner*, June 1959; *Time*, January 1, 1973.

28. Daniel M. Cantwell to George G. Higgins, August 10, 1971, and "NC News Service: Cardinal Dearden Named Detroit 'Big Wheel,'" GHP, "Correspondence: Clement Kern"; Abraham Citron to Gene Wesley Marshall, November 27, 1962, MDCC, Box 8, Folder "Open Occupancy"; *Michigan Chronicle*, February 6, 1965.

29. "Interview with Msg. Clement Kern," April 7, 1979, in Non-Chancery Records, Personal Papers, Reverend Clement Kern, Box 24, AAD; Casey, *Father Clem Kern*.

30. See, for instance, correspondence between Kern and George Higgins regarding Kern's labor surveys in Latin America; GHP, "Correspondence, Clement Kern." See also *Wage Earner*, August 1958, September 1958, and May 1959.

31. *Wage Earner*, November 1958; "Franklin Settlement Progress Report" (December 1965), in NFSNC, Box 73, Folder 20.

32. F. H. Luebke and John Fraser Hart, "Migration from a Southern Appalachian Community," *Land Economics* 34 (February 1958): 44–53.

33. Cleo Boyd, "Detroit's Southern Whites and the Store-Front Church," in MDCC, Series II, Box 12, Folder "Dept of Research and Planning Reports: Detroit's Southern Whites and the Storefront Churches, 1958."

34. Ibid.; Mayor's Commission for Community Action, Working Papers, "Religion and the Store Front Church" (September 1963), microfilm edition.

35. Sidney Fine, *Violence in the Model City: The Cavanaugh Administration, Race Relations, and the Detroit Riot of 1967* (Ann Arbor: University of Michigan Press, 1989), 62–63; Thompson and Agocs, "Mapping the Distribution of Ethnic Groups," 26; James H. Boyce, *Community Research Needs: From the Perspectives of Community Residents* (Detroit Area Inter-Ethnic Studies Assoc., Monograph 2), 26, IHRC.

36. *Michigan Chronicle*, April 20 and May 18, 1963, and February 20, 1965; on the relocation of New Bethel Baptist, see Salvatore, *Singing in a Strange Land*.

37. *Michigan Chronicle*, February 20, 1965; Marian Hibbard and Phyllis Santo, "The Negro, His Church, and Urban Renewal: A Study of the Impact of Urban Redevelopment on the Church Participation of a Sample of Detroit Negroes, Two Years after Relocation," Master of Social Work, Wayne State University, 1964.

38. *Michigan Chronicle*, January 9, 1960.

39. "Plant Phase Report of: The Ecorse Project," April 1958, and "PIP-D Report to Presbytery," Fall 1960, both in Detroit Industrial Mission Records (hereafter DIM), Box 3, Folder PIP-D, ALUA; Scott Paradise, *Detroit Industrial Mission: A Personal Narrative* (New York: Harper and Row, 1968). See also the DIM newsletter *Life and Work* (Summer 1965) for background on Doster, Parishfield Records, 1948–1971, Box 2, Folder "Detroit Industrial Mission, 1958–1967," BHL.

40. "Report to Presbytery, Fall 1960" and "Life, Death and Destiny in the Minds of Workers" (n.d.), both in DIM, Box 3, Folder PIP-D, Phase Reports; Paradise, *Detroit Industrial Mission*, 46.

41. Williams, "The Galilean and the Common People," and other "lessons," CWP, Box 18, Folder 15.

42. Coughlin, *Father Coughlin's Radio Discourses*, 86, 98, 176.

43. *Michigan Catholic*, May 2, 1940; Fr. Clare Murphy to members of Catholic Study Clubs, July 16, 1938, in F. J. Patrick McCarthy Papers, Box 17, Folder 6, AUND; "May Day" (n.a.), in ACTU, Box 4, Folder "May Day 1940."

44. "May Day" (n.a.), in ACTU, Box 4, Folder "May Day 1940."

45. *Michigan Catholic*, March 14, 1940.

46. Nowak, *Two Who Were There*, 28–42, 103–119; on cigar workers, see *St. Florian Parish, Hamtramck, Michigan*, 87–100, AAD; on Ternstedt, see also Lichtenstein, *Most Dangerous Man*, 52–55.

47. *Michigan Catholic*, August 5 and 19, 1954; *Wage Earner*, July 1959; "Facing the Issues," February 1961, UCS, Box 101, Folder 7, ALUA.

48. Detroit Metropolitan Area Regional Planning Commission, "Employment of Women in the Detroit Region" (Detroit, 1959), 15–20; Arthur William Kornhauser, *Detroit as the People See It; a Survey of Attitudes in an Industrial City* (Detroit: Wayne University Press, 1952), 91. Arthur William Kornhauser, *When Labor Votes: A Study of Auto Workers* (New York: University Books, 1956), 176–812. For context, see Kevin Boyle, "The Kiss: Racial and Gender Conflict in a 1950s Automobile Factory," *Journal of American History* 84 (September 1997).

49. Throughout the 1950s, the *Michigan Chronicle* featured a "Church Woman of the Week" column as well as hosting "most popular Church Woman" contests; the fact that the paper continued to highlight different women week after week over the course of years indicates the depth of female leadership in Detroit's black churches; for citations, see March 22, 1952, April 26, 1952, and May 24, 1952. For context, see Allison Calhoun-Brown, "No Respect of Persons? Religion, Churches, and Gender Issues in the African-American Community," in *New Day Begun: African American Churches and Civic Culture in Post-Civil Rights America*, ed. R. Drew Smith (Durham: Duke University Press, 2003).

50. *Michigan Chronicle*, February 9, 1946, September 7, 1946, and February 15, 1947.

51. *Michigan Chronicle*, February 9, 1952, January 12, 1952, and April 5, 1947; Dade, "Recollections of Missionary Work," 20; see also Dillard, *Faith in the City*.

52. *Michigan Chronicle*, May 4, 1946, February 16, 1952, and May 10, 1952; Dade, "Recollections of Missionary Work," 18.

53. *Michigan Chronicle*, May 31, 1952.

54. "Interview with Charleszetta Waddles" (1980) in *The Black Women Oral History Project, Vol 10*, ed. Ruth Edmonds Hill (Westport, Conn.: Meckler, 1991), 93.

55. Ibid., 73.

56. Ibid., 76.

57. "Report to Presbytery, Fall 1960," in DIM, Box 3, Folder PIP-D.

58. Pat Hamilton, "Factory 'Hand' Finds Meaning, Worth in Labor," *Michigan Catholic*, April 4, 1957.

59. Ibid.

60. *Dodge Main News*, January 28, 1956.

61. Isaac Jones, "Sermons I Shall Remember," *Michigan Chronicle*, January 19, 1952, February 15, 1947, and January 4, 1947.

62. *Michigan Chronicle*, April 12, 1952, and March 22, 1947; Bruno Nettl, "Preliminary Remarks on Urban Folk Music in Detroit," *Western Folklore* 16 (January 1957): 38–39; Frances E. Carter, "The Function of Folk-Songs in the A.M.E. Zion Church Service," unpublished, Folklore Archive, ALUA; Joseph R. Washington, *Black Cults and Sects* (Garden City, N.Y.: Doubleday, 1972), 77.

63. Ellen J. Stekert, "Southern Mountain Medical Beliefs," unpublished TMs, Folklore Archive, ALUA.

64. *Michigan Catholic*, August 5, 1954; Parkanzky, "Study of Folklore," 15.

65. *Michigan Catholic*, March 18, 1954, March 7, 1957, and July 11, 1957.

66. Washington, *Black Sects and Cults*, 116–117; John Kobler, "Prophet Jones: Messiah in Mink," *Saturday Evening Post* (March 5, 1955): 72–78.

67. *Michigan Chronicle*, January 12, March 29, and May 10, 1952. See also the comments of Washington in *Black Cults and Sects*: "The floundering black underclass was deceived at the moment of her highest hope" by religious charlatans, such as Jones, in the urban North (108).

68. *Michigan Chronicle*, September 25, 1943, and January 5, 1952; these ads were common. On the transformation of black folk religion in the urban North, see Chireau, *Black Magic*.

69. Richard M. Dorson, *Negro Folktales in Michigan* (Cambridge: Harvard University Press, 1956), 114.

70. G. F. Wojcik, "A Study of the Folk Material in the Quinn Road Community Clinton Township," unpublished TMs, Folklore Archive, ALUA.

71. Ralph Pezda, "Biblical Legends," unpublished TMs, Folklore Archive, ALUA.

72. Paradise, *Detroit Industrial Mission*, 12–13; "Christman-Plant Phase Report 1-10-59" and "Comments of Men at Cadillac Relative to Class Structure," in DIM, Box 3, Folder "Ecorse-study Papers."

73. Arnett, *Pieces from Life's Crazy Quilt*, 37; Shirley Coleman, "The Traditional Concepts of the Black Minister as Collected from Black People," unpublished TMs, Folklore Archive, ALUA; Isaac Jones, "Rascals in the Church," *Michigan Chronicle*, January 5, 1952.

74. *Michigan Chronicle*, July 27, 1946.

75. Ibid.

76. This conclusion broadly corresponds with Jefferson Cowie and Nick Salvatore, "The Long Exception: Rethinking the Place of the New Deal in American History," *International Labor and Working-Class History* 74 (Fall 2008): 3–32.

Chapter 6. Race and the Remaking of Religious Consciousness

1. Sugrue, *Origins of the Urban Crisis*, 237; Fine, *Violence in the Model City*.

2. *Michigan Catholic*, July 27, 1967, and May 9, 1968. On the "black Jesus," see also McGreevy, *Parish Boundaries*, and Thompson, *Whose Detroit?* 259.

3. See Dillard, "Religion and Radicalism," 153–176.

4. See especially Pratt, *Churches and Urban Government*.

5. "FEPC: A Catholic View," ACTU, Box 18, Folder "FEPC Pamphlets," ALUA.

6. "Joint Statement" by Mooney, Lenox, and Adler, March 8, 1957, MDCC, Box 8, Folder "Civil Rights Press Releases"; "A Challenge to Conscience: Report of the Metropolitan Conference on Open Occupancy" (Detroit: Detroit Metropolitan Conference on Religion and Race, 1963), 8, 1; Abraham Citron to Gene Wesley Marshall, November 27, 1962, in MDCC, Box 8, Folder "Open Occupancy."

7. Citron to Marshall, November 27, 1962, MDCC, Box 8, Folder "Open Occupancy."

8. "Challenge to Conscience," 6, 8, 21.

9. Wells, "Youth in the Inner City," 16, and Wagner, "Children and Youth in the Inner City; Insight from Church Studies," 24, 26, both in National Council of Churches of Christ in the United States of America, Department of Social Welfare records, microfilm edition (hereafter NCC), reel 5, Folder 45.

10. *Michigan Chronicle*, February 9 and February 16, 1963; *Wage Earner*, September 1963; "Remarks before Holy Name Men, Church of the Madonna," February 13, 1966, in Jerome P. Cavanaugh Papers, 1960–1979 (hereafter JCP), Box 313, Folder 4, ALUA.

11. "Challenge to Conscious," 6, 8, 21. For context, see Thomas J. Sugrue, *Sweet Land of Liberty: The Forgotten Struggle for Civil Rights in the North* (New York: Random House, 2009).

12. Dillard, *Faith in the City*, 239–251; Fine, *Violence in the Model City*, 24–27.

13. *Michigan Chronicle*, March 30 and April 6, 1963.

14. *Michigan Chronicle*, May 18, 1963; Chappell, *Stone of Hope*, 45.

15. Salvatore, *Singing in a Strange Land*, 244–254; *Michigan Chronicle*, June 8 and 22, 1963; "The Negro Revolution" June 3 and June 24, 1963, in Parishfield Records, 1948–1971 (hereafter PR), Box 2, Folder "Staff—James Guinan," BHL.

16. Boggs and Marks quoted in Moon, *Untold Tales, Unsung Heroes*, 155, 264–265.

17. "Parishfield-Detroit," February 10, 1966, in PR, Box 2, Folder "Background—Parishfield Histories"; "Parishfield 1964," TMs in PR, Box 2, Folder "Staff—Roger Barney."

18. "The Negro Revolt, Summer 1963," June 23, 1963, PR, Box 2, Folder "Staff—James Guinan."

19. Ibid.

20. "Parishfield 1964" TMs, February 10, 1966, in PR, Box 2, Folder "Staff—Roger Barney"; *Sword and the Shield*, November–December 1964, July–August 1965, PR.

21. "Roger W. Barney Journal," September–November 1965, and November 13, 1965, in PR, Box 2, Folder "Staff—Roger Barney."

22. Detroit Urban League, "A Profile of the Detroit Negro, 1959–1967," 49; *Wage Earner*, September 1958; "An Historic Church Serves a Changing Community" (1955?), UCS, Box 75, Folder 10, ALUA; "Franklin Settlement Progress Report," December 1965, NFSNC, Box 73, Folder 20, SWHA.

23. Fine, *Violence in the Model City*, 70–75; *Wage Earner*, June 1959.

24. Jones, *American Work*, 365; G. Merrill Lenox to Jerome Cavanaugh, January 25, 1966, JCP, Box 281, Folder 1. The National Council of Churches was particularly enthusiastic about the War on Poverty, and produced literature almost certainly read

by Detroit mainliners; see the booklet series, "Action Guides for the Churches toward the Elimination of Poverty in the U.S.A.," which were developed in January 1966.

25. For the WCO and Venus quotes, see Fine, *Violence in the Model City*, 30; Memo to Jerome Cavanaugh, May 15, 1967, re "Activities of Reverend David Eberhardt, Pastor, Riverside Lutheran Church," JCP, Box 363, Folder 4; see also Rev. David Eberhard to Cavanaugh, JCP, TL, October 17, 1966, Box 295, Folder 1; Arlie Porter to Jerome Cavanaugh, September 1, 1966, and October 1, 1966, and "Resolution Concerning Housing Needs in Detroit," all in JCP, Box 295, Folder 1.

26. *Detroit News*, February 24, 1965, in MDCC, Box 9, Folder "War on Poverty"; "The Church and the City," October 23, 1966, JCP, Box 314, Folder 8; *Michigan Chronicle*, January 23, 1965; "Press Release," February 11, 1966, MDCC, Box 8, Folder "Civil Rights Press Releases, 64–68"; *New York Times*, April 30, 1967.

27. "Franklin Settlement Progress Report," NFSNC, Box 73, Folder 20.

28. *Michigan Catholic*, May 13, 1965.

29. *Michigan Catholic*, January 28, 1965; "'Special Newsletter' of Protestant Community Services: Anti-Poverty Program Developments in Detroit Area," MDCC, Box 10, Folder "War on Poverty"; Pratt, *Churches and Urban Government*, 86–88.

30. Prof. Charles Quick to Jerome Cavanaugh, November 30, 1968, and "Committee Report on the AOP," in JCP, Box 434, Folder 1.

31. Ibid.; *Michigan Catholic*, September 26, 1968.

32. "Open Letter" from "Hourglass," October 14, 1968, JCP, Box 434, Folder 1.

33. *Michigan Chronicle*, February 6, 1965; *Michigan Catholic,* May 27, 1965.

34. *Michigan Catholic*, May 16, 1968.

35. Ibid.

36. Douglas B. Koller, "Belief in the Right to Question Church Teachings, 1958–1971," *Social Forces* 58 (September 1979): 290–304; "Insight: Our Faith Today," in John F. Dearden Papers, 1960–1987 (hereafter JDP), Published Matter, Box 1, Folder 75, AUND.

37. Sermons in MDCC, Box 13, Folder "Labor Sunday."

38. "Limbo," NFSNC, Box 74, Folder 1.

39. Phyllis Kernsten and Joel Nickel, "R Is for Religion," ed. Paul Malto (Medford, Ore.: Morse Press, 1964).

40. *Michigan Catholic*, March 11, 1965; *Michigan Catholic*, April 1, 1965.

41. *Detroit News*, April 15, 1964, copy in Charles A. Hill Papers, BHL; "Oral History Interview with Charles A. Hill," UAW Oral History Collection, ALUA, 41.

42. *Michigan Chronicle*, January 23, 1965.

43. Sarah H. Schuman, "The Polish Priest in Metropolitan Detroit" (1970), in JDP, Box 32, Folder 16; *Michigan Catholic*, May 16, 1968. For an anthropological perspective on these changes, see Paul Wrobel, *Our Way: Family, Parish, and Neighborhood in a Polish-American Community* (Notre Dame, Ind.: University of Notre Dame Press, 1979).

44. "Irate Residents" to Charles Hill, March 29, 1964, in Hartford Avenue Baptist Church, Records, BHL.

45. Gibson Winter, "Man and Freedom in a Technological Society" (Detroit: Detroit Industrial Mission, 1967).

46. Fine, *Violence in the Model City*, 316–317; Interfaith Emergency Council, "Does God Use the 'Riot' to Speak to Us? A Call to Self-Examination, Repentance, and Response," in Riot Packet: Collection of Pamphlets and Reprints Relative to Church and Riots (1966–1968).

47. Cameron Wells Byrd, "Black Power, Black Youth, the City's Rebellion: Implications for Youth Ministry," in Riot Packet; Cavanaugh quoted in Pratt, *Churches and Urban Government*, 68.

48. *Michigan Catholic*, July 27, 1967; "Interested Citizens of Cathedral, Community Affairs Council" to Jerome Cavanaugh, November 17, 1967, in JCP, Box 363, Folder 5.

49. *Michigan Catholic*, August 3, 1967, and May 9, 1968.

50. Dillard, *Faith in the City*; Young and Wheeler, *Hard Stuff*, 172.

51. Dan Georgakas and Marvin Surkin, *Detroit I Do Mind Dying* (Cambridge, Mass.: South End Press, 1998), 111–112.

52. Reprinted in Edwin S. Gaustad and Mark A. Noll, eds., *A Documentary History of Religion in America Since 1877* (3rd ed.; Grand Rapids, Mich.: William B. Eerdmans, 2003), 494–496. See also Georgakas and Surkin, *Detroit I Do Mind Dying*.

53. Dillard, *Faith in the City*, 295–296.

Index

Second Baptist Church, 23–24, 32–33, 48, 52, 67, 96–97, 99, 103, 173
Second Vatican Council, 8, 156, 197, 199
Sheffield, Horace, 102, 124–25, 158
Siedenburg, Rev. Frederic, 70
Smith, Gerald L. K., 7, 10, 85, 119–21, 127–28, 132–34, 142–43
Social Gospel, 5, 7–9, 56–66, 69, 72, 76, 79, 96, 101–2, 112, 118, 137, 159, 170
Society of St. Vincent de Paul, 32, 58
southern whites, 5, 9, 16–18, 62–63, 79, 106–14, 119, 128, 130, 150, 159, 161, 174, 193
spiritualism, 32, 36, 44, 47, 49, 98, 169
St. Albertus Catholic Church, 21, 28–29, 42
St. Cyprian's Episcopal Church, 101–3, 106, 138, 188
St. Florian Catholic Church, 21–22, 33, 79–80, 90, 156, 166
St. John Episcopal Church, 56, 191
St. Ladislaus Catholic Church, 22, 147, 202
St. Louis the King Catholic Church, 140–41
storefront churches, 15, 24–25, 32, 35–36, 40, 46, 62, 79, 102, 132, 159–62, 169–70
St. Paul AMEZ Church, 27, 40
St. Rose of Lima Catholic Church, 39–40, 42, 70, 80, 94
Sugrue, Thomas, 7, 154
Sweetest Heart of Mary Catholic Church, 27, 29, 34, 42–43, 79, 156
Swieczkowska, Clara, 28, 42

Tappes, Shelton, 98–99, 104, 150
Taylor, I. Paul, 60–61
Temple Baptist Church, 110–11, 113, 138

Tentler, Leslie Woodcock, 3, 26
Thomas, R. J., 88, 127
Thompson, E. P., 3, 6

United Automobile Workers (UAW), 7, 9, 11, 55, 57, 81–82, 87–90, 92–93, 99–101, 107, 118, 120, 124–25, 127, 129, 133–36, 138–39, 148, 150, 152, 154, 157–59, 166–67, 172, 176, 180, 184–85, 195–96; attitudes of southern-born whites toward, 113; conflicts with churches/religion, 71, 75, 132; recruitment of Catholic workers, 86; relationship with Charles Coughlin, 83–85, 119, 121–22; relationship with religious African American workers, 96, 99, 102–5, 141, 151; use of the social gospel, 72–74, 76, 79

Waddles, Charleszetta, 170–71
Weber, Paul, 88, 124–25, 136–37. *See also* Association of Catholic Trade Unionists
West Central Organization, 194
White, Horace, 8–9, 101–6, 131, 135–36, 138, 143, 152, 176–77, 180–81, 188
Williams, Claude, 7, 9, 120, 128–34, 137–39, 143, 149–51, 160, 164, 168, 199
Winter, Gibson, 7, 203
Woodcock, Leonard, 84, 158

Young, Coleman, 52, 71, 151, 206
Young Men's Christian Association (YMCA), 33, 59, 66, 112, 180, 187
Young Women's Christian Association (YWCA), 59, 128, 132, 169

MATTHEW PEHL is an associate professor
of history at Augustana University.

The Working Class in American History

The University of Illinois Press
is a founding member of the
Association of American University Presses.

University of Illinois Press
1325 South Oak Street
Champaign, IL 61820-6903
www.press.uillinois.edu